ALSO BY MARILYNNE ROBINSON

FICTION

Jack

Lila

Home

Gilead

Housekeeping

NONFICTION

What Are We Doing Here?

The Givenness of Things

Absence of Mind: The Dispelling of Inwardness from the Modern Myth of the Self

When I Was a Child I Read Books

The Death of Adam: Essays on Modern Thought

Mother Country: Britain, the Welfare State and Nuclear Pollution

READING GENESIS

READING GENESIS

MARILYNNE ROBINSON

FARRAR, STRAUS AND GIROUX
NEW YORK

Farrar, Straus and Giroux
120 Broadway, New York 10271

Library of Congress Cataloging-in-Publication Data
Names: Robinson, Marilynne, author.
Title: Reading Genesis / Marilynne Robinson.
Description: New York : Farrar, Straus and Giroux, [2024]
Identifiers: LCCN 2023038966 | ISBN 9780374299408 (hardback)
Subjects: LCSH: Bible. Genesis—Criticism, interpretation, etc.
Classification: LCC BS1235.52 .R59 2024 | DDC 222/.1106—
    dc23/eng/20231115
LC record available at https://lccn.loc.gov/2023038966

Designed by Gretchen Achilles

Our books may be purchased in bulk for promotional,
educational, or business use. Please contact your local bookseller
or the Macmillan Corporate and Premium Sales Department at
1-800-221-7945, extension 5442, or by email at
MacmillanSpecialMarkets@macmillan.com.

www.fsgbooks.com
Follow us on social media at @fsgbooks

1   3   5   7   9   10   8   6   4   2

CONTENTS

———————

READING GENESIS

The Bible is a theodicy, a meditation on the problem of evil. This being true, it must take account of things as they are. It must acknowledge in a meaningful way the darkest aspects of the reality we experience, and it must reconcile them with the goodness of God and of Being itself against which this darkness stands out so sharply. This is to say that the Bible is a work of theology, not simply a primary text upon which theology is based. I will suggest that in the early chapters of Genesis God's perfect Creation passes through a series of changes, declensions that permit the anomaly of a flawed and alienated creature at the center of it all, ourselves, still sacred, still beloved of God. To say that the narrative takes us through these declensions—the Fall and the loss of Eden, then the Flood and the laws that allow the killing of animals and of homicides, then the disruption of human unity at Babel—is not to say that they happened or that they didn't happen, but that their sequence is an articulation of a complex statement about reality. The magnificent account of the onset of Being and the creation by God of His image in humankind is undiminished in all that follows despite the movement away from the world of God's first intention—modified as this statement must be by the faith that He has a greater, embracing intention that cannot fail. Within the final mystery of God's purpose there are the parables of prophets and sages. History and experience are themselves parables awaiting their prophets.

However it came about, this narrative sequence establishes a profound and essential assertion of the sacred good, making pangs and toil a secondary reality, likewise the punitive taking of life. This construction of reality, absolute good overlaid but never diminished or changed by temporal accommodations to human nature, allows for faithfulness to this higher good. Grace modifies law. Law cannot limit grace.

I will speak of "the writers" of the books of Moses because these texts appear to me to have been the product of reflection and refinement that took place over the course of generations or centuries. This is not a version of the so-called documentary hypothesis, which claims to find in them separate, identifiable sources, documents that can be attributed to writers of particular regions or factions and which are so little reconciled or assimilated to one another that there are, in effect, sutures in the text, inconsistencies in such non-trivial matters as the nature of God. I know that the suggestion of human authorship can seem to some like a denial of the unique sacredness of the Bible. But the Bible itself names human authors for most of its books, meaning no more perhaps than that a collection of writings shared an affinity for the thought of a particular teacher or school. In other words, whether or not these attributions reflect authorship as we understand it, the Bible itself indicates no anxiety about association with human minds, words, lives, and passions. This is a notable instance of our having a lower opinion of ourselves than the Bible justifies.

I take it that in the course of their development the Scriptures were pondered very deeply by those who composed and emended them, and that this created a profound coherency, stabilizing difficult concepts or teachings to the point that earlier and later passages can be seen as elucidating one another. I imagine a circle of the pious learned, rabbis before the word, remembering together what their grandmothers had told them, finding the loveliness of old memory in an odd turn of phrase, realizing together that these strange tales sustained a sense of the presence of God that was richly renewed for them in their reverent deliberations. This is how religions live in the world. I take it that, in a wholly exceptional degree, their deliberations found their way to truth.

For us moderns there is a kind of safety in finding a taint of factionalism or self-interest in anything human beings have done. The hermeneutics of suspicion arose early in nineteenth-century readings of these very texts. If they were in fact patched together from various "documents" whose writers can be deduced from their language and emphasis, and whose purposes were not theological after all but instead political or factional, then thousands of years of credulity have been embarrassed by a flood of journal articles.

No one wants to be found among the credulous. Belief itself exists in disturbing proximity to credulity, a fact that has afflicted the church with a species of tepid anguish for generations. I am proposing here that there is a hermeneutics of self-protectiveness that has disabled interpretation and that has generalized into an abandonment of metaphysics as a legitimate mode of thought. Does it make any sense that if the supposititious band of document writers known to scholars as E, J, P, and D with all their supernumeraries were not thinking theologically, therefore metaphysics itself is foreclosed? This is like saying that if the moon landing was actually filmed in Arizona there is no universe. It is striking how the scale of thought has contracted with the loss of serious theology. A contemporary Kant or Hegel would find little purchase in the vocabulary of thought allowed to us now. In any case, biblical texts in general may seem to exist under the shadow of a demystification that happens not to have touched them yet. But they are really far too tough-minded to be the products of ordinary this-worldly calculation. This quality of mind is carried forward through the whole of the Bible.

Collective decisions having to do with the language of creeds, the accuracy of translations, and so on have been accepted as highly authoritative from the early history of Christianity. The canons of the Hebrew and the Christian Bibles were determined by councils. The writings of major theologians can be virtually deuterocanonical, even or especially when it is forgotten that a doctrine has a history and an origin. I assume that the reflection on Scripture by its compositors was theological in nature, governed by beliefs of overriding importance, first of all that God is one. Crucially, the literature could only have been dependent on deep faith that the community that created, studied, and revered it did so in service to an extraordinary calling, to embed in language a knowledge of God. I assume that the text as a whole developed with a full awareness of the text as it existed to that point and of the traditions, thoughts, and events that might be assimilable to it. Scripture grew from this basis for centuries, continuously reflecting on itself, seeing ongoing history as meaningful or revelatory just as the lives of the patriarchs and the great exodus had been.

According to Scripture, a pastoralist clan with a shared ancestor, Abraham, were enslaved for centuries in Egypt, then migrated under the leadership of a figure named Moses to the land of Canaan. There, over time, they became a society, a nation. The unifying belief that made one people of this federation of tribes was that they were a special case in God's dealings with humankind, first of all in their having a knowledge of God that arose from a relationship with Him, initiated by Him. He had made a covenant that assured His loyalty to them through His bond with their ancestors. When God identifies Himself to Moses as "the God of Abraham, the God of Isaac, and the God of Jacob," He is invoking a very remote past, four hundred years distant from the generation of the exodus. There seems to have been no continuity of covenant patriarchy to be invoked in the intervening period, no way of life of the people within Egypt to be preserved after their migration, though there were elements of social order among them, tribes and elders. A memory of the God of Abraham must survive among them, since Moses asks God for a name the people will recognize and he is given YHWH, a name which modern scholars spell and pronounce Yahweh. (In Genesis 4:26, during the time of Cain, it is said that men began to call on this name.) It is noted in the text that the mother and father of Moses and his brother Aaron are of the priestly tribe of the Levites. Their mother has a theophoric name, Jochebed. And Moses carries the bones of Joseph to Canaan, faithful to his last wish. Only these details suggest a continuity with the faith and culture of the patriarchs.

Then where do the stories of the patriarchs come from? I take the narratives of Genesis to have been collected at the time of the exodus and after, when the fact that this liberated multitude was participating in a history and an identity associated with these names would have prompted a great interest in old stories about them. If Moses was adopted by an Egyptian princess, he would probably have remained with his wet-nurse mother for a number of years, until he was a sturdy child, at least. So his mother could have filled his mind with Hebrew lore, visions of the old freedom, before his acculturation as an Egyptian had begun. On the other hand, he is taken to be an Egyptian, even by other Hebrews. Moses and Aaron are both Egyptian names, and no Hebrew names are remembered for them. Moses only began to identify with his people as a grown man, and then in a sudden impulse that alienated him from them. After he realized that their God had spoken to him, invoking these ancient names, Abraham, Isaac, and Jacob, he might have listened with great interest to every story about the tribes of Israel in the generations before their descent into Egypt. It should be noted that, by comparison with the hero stories that are taken to anchor the identities of other ancient cultures, these tales of the patriarchs are notably human in scale, gentle, even domestic. In any case, these stories are the nucleus of a powerful literature and a powerful identity.

All this assumes that Moses himself is a historical figure. There are so many great lawgivers in antiquity, so many creators and heroes of nations, that doubt in his case seems tendentious. Dido, Queen of Carthage, was an actual woman, the outcast sister of an actual Pygmalion. Because the historical consequences of Moses's life have been and continue to be immeasurably great, it is easy to forget that, measured by the standards of a Cyrus or a Tamerlane or an Alexander, he is a very minor figure. In terms of lives taken, countries subjugated, or wealth amassed, his impact was extremely modest and entirely credible. I will assume that Moses, he to whom the Lord spoke face-to-face, and his tradition are primary influences on the composition of Genesis.

• • •

It has been usual for a century and a half for writers on the Old Testament to compare the biblical narratives of Creation with the myths of the surrounding cultures. Similarities among them are generally taken to indicate borrowing, and the borrowing to be proof that the biblical texts are derivative, the early chapters of Genesis, as the younger literature, being derived from these pagan tales. I will look at the ways in which the texts are comparable, and the ways in which these points of comparison establish profound differences in the conceptions of the very systems of Being articulated by these narratives.

The fact that Western thought has been deeply influenced by concepts like creation ex nihilo and the Fall of Man makes clear that the Genesis narratives serve very ably as troves of conceptual language. Large assertions are made in the text, for example, that the reality we experience had a beginning, an idea disputed by major scientists into the twentieth century. An emergent universe brings innumerable mysteries, scientific as well as theological— Why did it happen? How will it end?—which the ancients both anticipated and variously addressed in language that is figurative and therefore charged with meaning.

Babylonia was a great cultural influence in its region and period. Because they are most often discussed by

scholars in relation to Genesis, and because, in the literatures of the ancient Near East, they are most comparable
with it, I will restrict my comparison of biblical and pagan literature to these two great Babylonian narratives, the
Epic of Gilgamesh and the *Enuma Elish*, variants of which
appear throughout the region. Other cities adopted them
as their own, changing little more than the names of the
heroes and gods involved. The Genesis stories, rather
than adopting or appropriating them, instead engage the
literatures to which they are often compared, accepting
an image or a term but transforming its meaning within a
shared language of thought. Of course we have no knowledge of the preliterate life of these narratives or of their
ultimate origins.

The *Enuma Elish* is actually a theogony, a tale of the
emergence of the gods and the rise of one god, Marduk,
as dominant among them. An attempt is made to describe
Marduk:

> His limbs were ingeniously made, beyond
>   comprehension,
> Impossible to understand, too difficult to perceive.
> Four were his eyes, four were his ears;
> When his lips moved, fire blazed forth.
> The four ears were enormous
> And likewise the eyes; they perceived everything.

The gods of the *Enuma Elish* suffer hunger, terror, and loss
of sleep. There are generations of them, born of one an-

other, the great mother of them all being Tiamat, a serpent monster, who, provoked by the noise the younger gods make, determines to kill them. She is so terrifying that the young god Marduk alone is able to defeat her. He splits her corpse like a fish, uses half to make the sky, the other half the earth, makes her two weeping eyes into the Tigris and the Euphrates, and so on. This could hardly be more remote from the infinite serenity of "let there be . . . and there was."

Against this background of ambient myth, to say that God is the good creator of a good creation is not a trivial statement. The insistence of Genesis on this point, even the mention of goodness as an attribute of the Creation, is unique to Genesis. A Babylonian, drawing on the account of things made in the narratives of his or her religion and, for that matter, on his or her experience as a human being, might beg to differ. Their gods are fickle, engrossed in conflicts and resentments, indifferent or hostile to humankind. To the degree that the epic of a culture influences its people's experience of the world, a cup of water might taste of the tears of a vast serpent forever alive in death. It is not difficult to imagine how the rigors of ancient life might have yielded this alarming view of things. It can smack of realism down to the present day. Yet Babylonia was also like ancient Greece in that it was civil and humane by the standards of the time. Its laws were literally exemplary, quite probably a direct influence on the law of Moses.

Where did the relative benignity of the Hebrew cosmos come from? It certainly does not depend on a denial of the reality of evil, understanding the word to embrace such things as loss or harm as well as transgression or malice. Indeed, it seems to come with the recognition of evil. The Fall and its consequences, Cain's killing of his brother, the Flood—these events are the *foreground* of biblical history. If Genesis should be attributed to the influence of Moses, it was written after the centuries of slavery in Egypt and then the desert wandering, two periods of extreme suffering, which were followed by the barbarous turmoil described in the books of Joshua and Judges. In any case, to assert the existence of evil in the broad sense, as it is understood in the primordial stories, Genesis 2:4 to 11:32, is essential to the whole narrative of Scripture. The Babylonian epic describes wars between rival armies of gods. For them "good" seems to be the order that comes with the triumph of Marduk. In Genesis, from the first, good is intrinsic to the whole of Creation. So in this very important respect the literatures are conceptually unlike. The Hebrew writers were not simply appropriating prevailing myths. They had weighty, human-centered concerns of their own, concerns entirely unique to them.

There is no reason to suppose that, over the medium term, any ancient people would have been exempt from the afflictions brought on by the vagaries of nature, not to mention by human greed or violence. Given the importance of evil in experience, the Hebrews were set a remarkable problem by their monotheism, their one just and loving God. Evil could not be understood as an aspect of God's nature or laid to a consort or a rival god. There was no serpent monster Tiamat to unleash a deluge for reasons of her own. In this essential regard, to assign causes to events is clearly not the method or intention of biblical narrative. We don't know why Abel's offering was acceptable and Cain's was not, why Jacob was favored over Esau or Israel over the nations. Events have their origins and meaning within God's truly inscrutable intention. The suffering of the people is foreseen when childless Abraham, faultless and favored, is given a vision of futurity in the form of a terrible dream. Causality is changed, more or less disabled, when events are predestined.

This reticence can be considered a positive statement about emergent history within the emergence of reality itself. Humankind has seized upon unnumbered accounts of the character of classes, genders, and ethnicities, their probable actions, gifts, and pathologies, many of these biases having the status and the consequences of plain certainty. Behind every prejudice there is an assumption about the behavior that might or might not be expected of an individual or a population. These assumptions are frequently codified as restrictions that preclude challenges to their predictive force. This is only one instance of an obdurate confidence that afflicts us generally, the idea that we know the causes of things. It is the basis from which we reason backward to arrive at explanation. Why do human beings exist? To make offerings to Marduk and the gods. Why *do* human beings exist? The God of Genesis is unique in His having not a use but instead a mysterious, benign intention for them.

. . .

Abraham was, at the time of "an horror of great darkness" and a terrible dream, a wanderer with no heir and no country and no certain place to bury his dead. He did have the singular attention of God, who confronted him again and again with promises, blessings with the force of demands. There is nothing conditional about them, though Abraham's "belief" makes him suitable to receive them. He leaves his father's house and, with his family, goes to a distant country the Lord has promised him and his descendants, and where he cannot stay because there is famine. To an observer his life might look like the life of any pastoralist, this stranger drifting through the countryside, looking for grazing for his herds. By epic standards there is a very great quiet around the dealings of God with Abraham. Though Abraham is engrossed inwardly in an awareness of God that will indeed make him the father of nations, and though God's intense awareness of Abraham is essential to all that follows, the surface of the commonplace is broken only a few times in the course of this very immediate and radically asymmetrical companionship— as good a word as any, since the Lord, as a stranger, has

accepted, no doubt enjoyed, Abraham's hospitality. They
have broken bread together. It might be true that Abraham's
conception of God is limited by his having lived in a world
of multitudes of gods with special and limited powers—
nature, tribal, and household gods. But the conception of
God in the text, in the telling, understands Him as the God
of history. By means of landless and childless Abram, his
name until God renames him Abraham, "a father of many
nations," He will bless all the families of the earth. It should
be noted that this is a very sweet promise, a credit to Him
Who makes it and him who is moved by it. I know of nothing in any way comparable. The very great tact with which
God enters the human world through Abraham, respecting
its expectations, is entirely consistent with the centrality He
has given humankind in His Creation.

As an interpretation of his people's history cast back on
patriarchal times, Abram's dream vision makes authoritative an understanding of the slavery and wandering of the
Hebrew tribes as divinely intended and providential. The
darkness of the dream and the weirdness of its occasion
make clear that grief and cruelty are foretold in it. No reason for them is given. On its face the bondage in Egypt is
neither a reward nor a punishment. It is a long moment in
providential history, not to be explained in other terms.
In any case, the blackness of darkness is never minimized.
Over time, the biblical narrative inverts the apparent
meaning of the suffering of many generations, no slight
thing. Grueling misfortune prepares for singular favor, difficult favor, whose main product and proof might be the

narratives that record and interpret this history. The narrative introduces the idea of divine purpose, relative to humankind, its intention to be realized over vast stretches of time. This is an understanding of God and humanity that has no equivalent in other literatures, God both above and within time, His providence reaching across unnumbered generations. The character of everything, good fortune and bad, is changed when its ultimate meaning awaits the great unfolding of His intention. So the problem of evil is not solved but is instead infinitely complicated. When Jesus says of his executioners "They know not what they do," we can appreciate how very radically his words understate the case. If the same were said of the mythic progenitors of human history, Adam and Eve, or of the splitters of the atom, the creators of antibiotics, and all the rest of us, the truth of these words would overwhelm our power to conceive.

. . .

Skeptical interpretations of religion tend to treat it as a primitive attempt to explain things that reason and science would in the course of time make a true and sufficient account of. Say Babylonia believed that the world had suffered a great inundation meant to destroy the human race because the gods found human beings irksome. Who knows what belief is, even when it is culturally and ritually instilled through ages and when there is no competing vision available? But these epics might have taken authority from the fact that they describe a melancholy form of dynamic equilibrium. The gods, faint with hunger, once decided it was more practical to limit human population by assigning a spirit to steal infants from their mothers' laps than to destroy them wholesale. (This according to a variant of the epic called Atra-Hasis.) They would have "explained" infant mortality. How many infants died when Pharaoh, like a god of Babylon, set about reducing the number of Hebrews in Egypt by destroying their infants? We know only that the infant Moses lived. Babylonian myth rationalized the deaths of children by supposing the gods to be indifferent to human sorrow and hostile to human life, insofar as it exceeded the numbers the gods found useful to themselves. In stark contrast, the Hebrew myth explains nothing. Or it offers two explanations that seem incompatible on their face. One is the wickedness of Pharaoh. The other, simultaneous with it, is the will and intent of God. This crime, this sorrow, is simply among the first things that must happen in order for the darkest part of Abram's dream to be fulfilled and the extraordinary promise made to his descendants to be realized.

There are in effect two forms of fatalism in play. A Babylonian might console herself with the thought that the gods must do as they must do. On these terms a kind of stability has been reached between gods and humankind. A Hebrew could say that her God had a great purpose unfolding in time, far too vast in its workings to be readily described as providential, except in faith. The very remarkable belief of these ancient Hebrews that God loved the world and valued humankind persisted among them through every difficulty. It gave them the conception of time as open-ended from a mortal point of view but utterly purposive, shaped by a divine intention for which a thousand years are like a day when it is past. Time is implicated in the idea of covenant or promise. Destiny will be fulfilled, loyalty will be maintained, into a future unlike all the misery and happiness that must intervene between now and then. Within this great certainty little can be assumed.

Genesis acknowledges a crucial variable that is not present in the Babylonian epics—human culpability. To have been too noisy is more anodyne, even, than to have tasted an apple. But Adam and Eve disobeyed, doubted, tried to deceive. These are all complex acts of will. The old Christian theologies spoke of felix culpa, the fortunate fall. This is in effect another name for human agency, responsibility, even freedom. If we could do only those things God wills, we would not be truly free, though to discern the will of God and act on it is freedom. Our human nature as fallen and our human nature as divine have a dynamic, asymptotic relation with each other, meeting at infinity, perhaps. In any case, the centrality of humankind in the creation myth of Genesis is from the beginning an immeasurable elevation of status, made meaningful in the fact of our interacting with God even at the level of sacred history. This is unique to the Bible and central to both Testaments. Could Moses really have refused to return to Egypt? Might Judas have refused to betray Jesus, who knew he must be betrayed? All this is related to the fact that the Bible does not exist to explain away mysteries and complexities but to reveal and explore them with a respect and restraint that resists conclusion.

This irresolvable question regarding the origin and meaning of human actions persists in crucial contexts throughout both Testaments. Yes, Moses could have refused to return to Egypt because he was a wanted man there and he did not yet know this God who was laying claim to him; but no, in that Moses was crucial to the unfolding of history. Could Pilate have spared Jesus his death on a cross? Yes, in that we recognize his experience of reluctant choice, and in that the drama of the moment is palpable in the accounts made of it; no, because the event of Jesus's death would be, again, epochal. It is the centrality of humankind, exceptional among the myths of neighboring cultures, that draws down this order of attention to the great mystery of the origins and meaning of individual actions, and the meaning of individual lives. If questions arise about my illustrating points about the Hebrew Bible with instances from the New Testament, I think it is relevant to interpretation that this aspect of the older text is sustained in the newer one despite all the time and cultural change that stands between them, and that it is in both cases unique among comparable literatures. For my purposes here, the recurrence of the question in moments of greatest significance demonstrates the loyalty of both traditions to the setting of human experience against and within cosmic history, one unfathomable, the other qualitatively unlike anything we know. When they are seen to occur together, much may be apprehended, but nothing is explained. Ecclesiastes makes the point elegantly: "I have seen the travail, which God hath given to the sons of men to be exercised in it. He hath made every thing beautiful in his time: also he hath set the world in their heart, so that no man can find out the work that God maketh from the beginning to the end." The engrossing beauty of the vanishing present exists within the knowledge that "whatsoever God doeth, it shall be for ever: nothing can be put to it, nor any thing taken from it."

. . .

The matter of the universality of the meaning of Abraham's life is touched on after a surprisingly untypical tale of his rescuing and restoring the wealth of some kings, and his nephew Lot, as well, who have been raided and abducted by other kings. On his return he is met by Melchizedek, king of Salem, who is priest of El Elyon, God Most High, "possessor of heaven and earth." This mysterious figure brings out bread and wine and blesses Abram in the name of his god—or of God. Abram gives this priest a tenth of what he has recovered and says he has sworn to "the LORD, the most high God, the possessor of heaven and earth," that he will keep nothing for himself. The word *Lord* replaces the name YHWH in translation, so it could be that Abram is claiming for God the attributes Melchizedek has claimed for El Elyon, the highest god in the Canaanite pantheon.

But Abram seems to have accepted the priest's blessing, his bread and wine. And he has given him a tithe.

The implication is that Melchizedek, who can only be thought of as pagan, is indeed a priest of God. The recurrence of this figure in Scripture supports this reading. Melchizedek appears again, strange as ever, in Psalm 110, which is a messianic psalm of David, quoted by Jesus as such. That is, it is taken in Jewish, then Christian tradition to anticipate the Messiah, who will be, in the words of the psalm, "a priest for ever after the order of Melchizedek." So tradition affirms the special, though mysterious, importance of this encounter between Abram, whose relationship with God would seem to make him the one non-pagan in the world at the time, and this priest of El Elyon, a god who, in Canaanite texts, is not more godlike than the other figures in the Babylonian pantheon. Abram responds to Melchizedek in a way that grants him the kind of respect priesthood implicitly claims.

It is interesting that the matter of the worship of false gods does not arise in the story of Abraham, where it might seem to have come up almost inevitably. I will once more scandalize scholarly norms by looking to the New Testament for help in understanding this. In his Letter to the Romans, Paul offers an account of the origins of paganism. He says of the Lord, "For the invisible things of him from the creation of the world are clearly seen, being understood by the things that are made, even his eternal power and Godhead." But of idolators: "Professing themselves to be wise, they became fools, and changed the glory of the incorruptible God into an image made like to corruptible man, and to birds, and fourfooted beasts, and creeping things." Paul goes on to denounce sexual practices he, as a Jew, associates with paganism. Historical Christianity has tended to seize upon prohibitions and condemnations to the neglect of matters of greater importance. In seeing paganism as a declined form of an original and potentially universal knowledge of God, Paul is granting it a degree of truth. In the same way, he speaks to the Athenians about an altar, among the many objects of their worship, inscribed "TO THE UNKNOWN GOD." He tells them, "Whom therefore ye ignorantly worship, him declare I unto you." The apostle is seizing on one possible, slight departure from the city's robust expressions of polytheism to make an account of a God unknowable in pagan terms. "God that made the world and all things therein, seeing that he is Lord of heaven and earth, dwelleth not in temples made with hands; neither is worshipped with men's hands, as though he needed any thing, seeing he giveth to all life, and breath, and all things." Men should seek after God,

> Though he be not far from every one of us:
> > For in him we live, and move, and have our
> > being;
> As certain also of our own poets have said,
> > "For we are also his offspring."

A fundamental universalism is clearly a consequence of the conception of God as one. The question is whether and how Genesis acknowledges this.

• • •

"In the beginning God created the heaven and the earth." One might expect that the writer or writers of this grandest poem would have declared YHWH, Yahweh, the Lord, the God of Abraham, Isaac, and Jacob, to be the Creator of all that is. But the word that appears is Elohim, a plural form of El, a common word meaning god, which is also the name of the highest Canaanite god, El Elyon.

When I think there was a day when a human hand first wrote those words, I am filled with awe. This sentence is a masterpiece of compression. It approximates as closely as words allow the instantaneous realization of an intent, the bringing into being of the diversity of things that make up the world of fundamental human experience. The *Enuma Elish* begins with an account of the gods in their generations emerging into a preexisting state of unbeing. Hesiod's *Theogony*, a much later work that had authority as an inspired text among the ancient Greeks, also begins with the begetting of gods, though without the interesting Babylonian pause over the question of what preceded them. In the Hebrew narrative, Creation is unified by the recurrent phrase "and it was so," evoking again the sense of the instantaneous efficacy of God's will, a sense of the marvelous particularity of each enrichment of the living world, and also a kind of reverent amazement on the part of the unimaginable knower, in effect observer, of this emergence of being out of a formless void. It is the world we know— the sun giving light to the earth, sea creatures swarming, birds in flight across the heavens—all seen in their wondrous singularity, yet made one in the seven iterations of the word *good*. The poem at the end of the book of Job tells us that, at Creation, "the morning stars sang together, and all the sons of God shouted for joy." If this seems not strictly monotheistic, the poem sets itself the problem of evoking Creation, new and replete with divine intention, the highest, most perfect consciousness and awareness filling everything, dealt with here by letting the stars sing. To isolate the mind of God, to think of Him as limited by even the loftiest of His attributes, is surely an error, an anthropomorphism. At the same time, by the grace of God, we know something of this joy.

. . .

We may consider that *good*-ness was created together with everything that is called *good*, since the narrative allows us nothing but the world as it emerges, nothing to which comparison can be made, no antecedents and no context. Contemporary cosmology is comparable in its reticence. Something happened, once, so far as we can tell, that eventuated and continues to eventuate in Being as we know it and do not know it, as we will and will not know it, all its consequences borne along in time, which may be, as

Einstein said, our most persistent illusion. The vast cosmos was infinitesimal at its origins, presumably a particle, but this might be supposition, an aid to the imagination, which finds true Nothing inconceivable.

The history of the relationship of science and religion teaches that the two are best kept apart, even when points of comparison between them are not trivial. Religion is ancient, and science, presented as one side in a controversy with religion, is antique. It is one of the mysteries of human experience that *ancient* has and deserves a positive valence while *antique* is distinctly invidious. Since the middle of the nineteenth century Darwin has anchored what has been offered, typically by nonscientists, as the position of science in opposition to religion. Their version of evolutionary theory is antique, a fossil rationalism. The very great complexity and mutability of the gene and all that pertains to it is somehow discounted by them in defense of a simple model of causality, an explanation of everything so forthright as to displace all mystifications.

To propose a divine actor in any account of things is widely assumed to be ignorant, childish, primitive. This might be fair, the judgment true and deserved, if the theist view that divine origins have implanted a sacredness in existence could be disproved, and if theism were barren of great thought, high aesthetic achievement, humane influence. Atheism is a relatively minor element in world culture, so its contributions are harder to assess. History offers a very mixed testimony, for example, on whether religion promotes civilization or impedes and distorts its advance. Having the bleak advantage of living in a period when the natural order and the social order are fraying together, and the metaphysical side of religion, the very conception of the sacred, has vanished like the atmosphere of a lifeless planet, it is fair to wonder what depended on what and urgent to discover how the fracturing of reality as we have known it can be stopped or slowed.

In the first Creation narrative in Genesis 1:1 to 2:4 nothing is causally related to anything else. The reserve of the first Creation narrative in maintaining a perfect silence about what might have happened or existed before "the beginning" sets it apart from myth and invites comparison to scientific cosmology. In ancient Near Eastern myth there is an elsewhere, a habitation of the gods where they feast and sleep and make war on one another. Foolish, vulnerable, self-centered, these were the gods of sophisticated and influential civilizations. They were well suited to accounting by their vast power and their utter fecklessness for the disasters that plague human life.

In the myths of surrounding cultures we are told that the gods have houses, that there is a non-earthly theater for the acting out of their desires and jealousies and quarrels, triumphs and defeats. Scripture returns repeatedly to insist that God is not like this, that is, that this conception of the divine is in error. When Solomon dedicates the famous temple in Jerusalem, when he has "built the house for the name of the LORD God," he prays, "O LORD God of Israel, there is no God like thee in the heaven, nor in the earth; which keepest covenant, and shewest mercy unto thy servants . . . But will God in very deed dwell with man on the earth? Behold, heaven and the heaven of heavens cannot contain thee; how much less this house which I have built." In 2 Corinthians, Paul speaks of one "caught up to the third heaven." This image of utter transcendence is sustained throughout the Scriptures, just at the limit of what can be apprehended and uttered, granting the astonishing human privilege of knowing about these things at all.

Humankind are very marginal in the *Enuma Elish*, servants of the gods in the sense that they perform the labor involved in building their temples and feeding them. The second narrative in Genesis with its anthropomorphisms seems meant to invite comparison with such myths. It says no, in fact it is the Lord who has created a habitation for humankind, and it is *He* who provides food for *them*. Humankind are the center of creation. They have no competitors for God's attention. He is present with them in what must be a desire to share the pleasures that are intrinsic to Creation, for example, the evening and the morning. Their disobedience is a failure of trust in His benevolence toward them.

The Genesis narrative as a whole can be thought of as a counterstatement of this kind, retelling the Creation in terms that reject in essential points the ancient Near Eastern characterization of the divine, of humankind, and of Creation itself. We know that Babylon was a sophisticated culture, and we also know that in the modern period its myths have been understood as tending to support a project of demystification of the biblical texts that is invested in seeing them all, pagan and Hebrew, as primitive. So their myths deserve to be looked at again. For our purposes it is sufficient to say that these myths swept the civilizations of the ancient Near East and engaged the attention of Hebrew mythopoesis.

The biblical way of telling the story of Creation differs from ambient narratives precisely at the points of their likeness. Similar terms are adopted for the purposes of argument, God or gods, El or Elohim being important instances of this. Imagine proponents of different forms of government all using the terms *justice* or *legitimacy*. At these points the most important disagreement would occur. It seems appropriate to find a pattern of controversy focused on shared themes or images. This would allow for the possibility that the narratives of Babylonian myth were also philosophic, in Josephus's sense of the word, existing somewhere between truth and parable, containing assertions about the nature of things that also render felt reality. The great rivers, Tigris and Euphrates, are lively and violent, humankind can be swept away as if by malice or whim. The world was created by gods who depend on it, sometimes overwhelm it on slight pretexts but otherwise care little about it. The first and second Creation narratives in Genesis, and the Flood, are the three passages most frequently seen as sharing in the mythic landscape of Canaanite or Babylonian culture.

The biblical narratives establish their unlikeness most powerfully in their reticence. What came before that first moment? If we imagine that time itself arose from that first event, which is perfectly possible by scientific standards of possibility, then we must also imagine that cause and effect, as we have understood them, would not exist in time's absence. Time is the medium of change, the medium of the transactions among things and conditions. God is active in time and is beyond time, aloof from it. The biblical vision of Creation is structured around there being no preexisting reality of any kind, an absolute difference from other myth. The Bible ponders the anomaly of time, for example in Psalm 90, which is called "a prayer of Moses."

> Before the mountains were brought forth, or ever
>   thou hadst formed the earth and the world, even
>   from everlasting to everlasting thou art God.
> . . .
> For a thousand years in thy sight
>   are but as yesterday when it is past,
>   and as a watch in the night.

God inhabits and *is* an eternal present, while the temporal world changes and the generations emerge and perish in their turn. Time is duration, say, the number of hours or years a hope lingers until it is fulfilled or abandoned. Such an interval can seem endless, though it occurs entirely as present experience, as the *now* that is gone as the word *now* is said. However inescapably a moment might come burdened with shock or grief or illumination, it is itself vanishingly, indefinably slight. Duration, which cannot be escaped, is the sum of unquantifiable, boundaryless moments that cannot be grasped. It is brilliant to compare time in the view of eternity with "yesterday when it is past." The immediacy that is our experience is dispelled from it as present becomes past, becomes both irrecoverable and determining, another thing entirely. Moses's one hundred twenty years of life and forty years of desert wandering end with a prayer or a plea: "Establish thou the work of our hands upon us; yea, the work of our hands establish thou it." His work has had profound consequence for hundreds of generations. This great fact is another instruction in the complexity and mystery of time.

In the second Creation narrative, Genesis 2:4 to 3:24, the story uses mythic elements very selectively. God "appears," but only to create and to enjoy His creation—the primordial orchard, the evening air, the beautiful moment. What is behind or beyond Creation is as exempt from fantasy or speculation in the second narrative as in the first. The second narrative is usually treated as if it were a borrowing from the ambient lore about the origins of things, especially from the Babylonian epic, *Enuma Elish*. God's "presence" here is evoked in human-seeming terms, so the fact that He is not actually "seen" can be overlooked. He is anthropomorphic in the sense that He enjoys a pleasure He has prepared for His man and woman and all their descendants to enjoy as well, an evening breeze, a walk in a garden. This can be read as His

unique identification with His creatures rather than as being mythic in any usual sense. His presence changes nothing and implies nothing in the way of a more primary or
glorious reality or mode of being. Creation in its integrity
is the whole ground of the narrative.

. . .

The fact that there is a Babylonian account of the origins of
things, a "Babylonian Genesis," has been oddly important
to Old Testament scholarship. In theory, I suppose, these
narratives could be more dissimilar, though in fact this is
hard to imagine. When the existence of this epic broke
upon the world—very dramatically, considering that it
had been known of since antiquity—the tablets on which
it was written were often fragmented and translation was
difficult, sometimes speculative. This may have allowed
early interpreters to supplement their reading with the expectation of influence, borrowing.

It is true that there is a deluge with human survivors in
the *Epic of Gilgamesh*. There is also a mythic Greek flood,
survived by Deucalion and Pyrrha. An all-overwhelming
deluge is a powerful image. If the near obliteration of humankind brought on by the gods was a subject of interest
to the ancients, then its recurrence indicates something
deeper than borrowing.

There are details the Noah story has taken from the
Babylonian tale of the Flood. In the *Epic of Gilgamesh*,
a man named Utnapishtim finds favor with the god Ea,

who warns him to build a boat and stock it with all living things. Then a flood overwhelms the earth. Like Noah, in order to know when he can leave the boat, Utnapishtim releases birds. If they return to him the waters have not begun to recede. There is no sign of embarrassment in the appropriation by Hebrew Scripture of these story elements, which would have been widely known throughout the ancient Near Eastern world. The pretty business of the bird looking for a place to rest its foot, returning to Noah's hand with a sprig in its beak in the more expansive biblical version, must have been too pleasing to omit, even while it made its literary indebtedness entirely obvious. This being true, the transformation in the meaning of the story from one telling to the next, Babylonian to Hebrew, is a study in how biblical thought can suffuse material originally foreign to it.

The Flood narrative in the *Epic of Gilgamesh* is framed by the story of a young king to whom Marduk gives an ideal friend, Enkidu, a wild man, his equal in strength. The two share adventures, struggle together with mythic beasts. Then Enkidu dies. Gilgamesh is heartbroken, and he is terrified of death despite somewhat consoling mentions in the text of a netherworld where something like life goes on. He hears that there is one man who has not died, Utnapishtim the Far Distant. Gilgamesh finds him and asks him how he became immortal. Though immortality seems to have little to recommend it, Utnapishtim tells him how he received it, having survived a great flood.

Utnapishtim's patron god, Ea, knows that the other

gods have all decided to exterminate humankind. He reveals the plan to his favorite, Utnapishtim—not directly but by speaking to a wall, so as not to have violated his pact with the other gods. On his overheard instructions, the man builds an ark, takes his wife, the creatures, and artisans as well, and waits out the flood. Afterward, when he is found to have survived, the gods are furious.

In Genesis there are no artisans on board the ark, only Noah and his family. The biblical Flood is a second Creation, a restoring of the world on somewhat altered terms. It is like the first Creation in that there is only one human family. Noah is a second Adam. The accounts that follow of Noah's descendants spreading into the regions of the world as they knew it make the point again, and so does the story of Babel, in which differences of language scatter one people. The familial unity of humankind could not have been an issue for the Babylonians in the same way because in their epics people can be created simply as needed, for example, Enkidu, as well as the Fish-man, the Scorpion-man, and other half-human entities made to be weapons in the war of the gods. The Hebrews surely had as strong a consciousness of themselves as a group as any other ancient people. Their striking collective history and their belief in a privileged knowledge of God would have made this inevitable. But the implied genealogies that structure the primordial tales in Genesis preclude the idea that differences between groups could ever be of a qualitative kind, deeper than differences within a family. This is extraordinarily important to their ethics and law, and also to the meaningfulness of their exploration of the nature of humankind. Paul tells the Athenians that God "made of one blood all nations of men for to dwell on all the face of the earth, and hath determined the times before appointed, and the bounds of their habitation."

Utnapishtim and his wife have no descendants, and yet the world of Gilgamesh has cities. Where do the people come from? The same question arises in the biblical story of Cain and Abel. Cain is afraid someone will kill him because he is a murderer—when he, with his father and mother, would have been the only people on earth. My theory about the composition of Genesis allows me to say that the story is about something important enough to justify a departure from a standard of realism that is impressive over against comparable Babylonian or Egyptian or Greek stories. For them, of course, the fabulous is at the center of the telling. In its literary context, the this-worldliness of Genesis feels like rigor. One God, and Adam's children. These are its whole subject.

The question in the *Epic of Gilgamesh* is whether death is truly universal and inevitable, even for a hero king who is only one-third human. The ending is slightly equivocal—Utnapishtim tells him to find a particular water plant that will make him immortal, but a serpent steals it away from him. So the question is not really answered. It is a little disappointing that the resolution, such as it is, is not offered at the same level of seriousness as the problem. In any case, the single-minded intention of the gods to destroy all of humanity and their anger at finding that there were these few survivors is starkly different from the biblical version. The gods are reminded by the destruction they have brought down on humanity that they themselves can starve, that they are actually dependent on people to feed them. On these terms they accept a human presence.

God solicitously preserves a human family. In Genesis there is a reconciliation between God and humanity after the Flood, or an accommodation of God's expectations to the reality of human nature. God makes a covenant with Creation never again to destroy it by flood, and He gives the survivors a few essential laws. This is the second "beginning," this time setting the terms on which the human race will continue and will exist in relation to God, by His grace. This is an entire departure from the Babylonian narrative.

In Genesis, the Flood is a judgment brought on by human evil. Here divine expectation has nothing to do with dependency and everything to do with human moral behavior, notably our propensity to violence. The Flood is a great instance of an "event" in narrative functioning as a term in a controversy. Flooding was a factor in Mesopotamian life but not in Canaan or Israel. Granting the occasional fact of catastrophe in one form or another and assuming the reality of deities that would unleash it, what would their motives be? For the Babylonians they might have been a tetchy indifference coupled with a lack of foresight. The gods would have learned restraint from their own terror, their own potential mortality. The God of Genesis is moved by human evil. The text, as usual, does not draw particular attention to the nature of the sin, though violence is mentioned several times. Human beings are making earth a hell so He acts to put an end to it all, saving only Noah, "a just man and perfect in his generations," with his family and the male and female of all the creatures.

These two stories differ crucially at their points of similarity. The Deluge might well arise as an instance of the problem of evil among people who experienced catastrophic flooding. The tale was popular and influential, and philosophically minded Hebrews might have said: Granted such things do happen. Famine, pestilence, and invasion destroy great cities indiscriminately. The Deluge is a good metaphor for the world returned all at once to a primal state. So, granting the Deluge for purposes of argument, why would such a thing happen? Modern readers struggle with this narrative, asking, as if it were a real event, whether a good God would wipe away almost His whole creation, when surely the idea of divine goodness could not include such an act. If the ancients had been writing fiction, they might well have omitted the episode entirely and many more like it. But in fact they were trying to conceptualize something true, that disasters which obliterate life as if it had no value are a factor in human experience. In the myths of Babylon, the gods were volatile, impulsive, but also needy, therefore constrained and able to be placated. Evil in the large sense is always an aspect of their nature. This is to read back from experience, to attribute disaster to the great forces that had created reality, and that animated all its properties, both wonderful and terrible, in order to form some conception of these makers.

In adapting the narrative of the Deluge for its purposes, the biblical tradition compounded every difficulty with its loyalty to the conception of God as one, as wholly good, and as engaged by and committed to humankind. At the same time, the evil that, according to Genesis, brought on the Deluge was found in "the thoughts of his [man's] heart." Humankind is a moral actor in this drama, not simply a victim. It is in the nature of these primordial stories that they never really end. They define the terms of everything that follows. It is not just anyone who disgraces himself when the world is first being restored, but righteous Noah, a second Adam, the progenitor of us all, human like us all.

After the Flood come the earliest laws, a distinctively Hebrew response to the problem of evil and to the possibility of human righteousness in a reality that clearly does not enforce virtuous or even rational behavior. Utnapishtim the Far Distant cannot share immortality with Gilgamesh. This is to say, we all die. Noah brings transgression into the restored world. This is to say, we all sin. But God has made a covenant with Noah and with the whole Creation, which He will honor despite all. This is the climax in the Hebrew telling of the tale. The goodness of God is affirmed in His forbearance and loyalty. The value of humankind is affirmed by them as well. "What is man, that thou art mindful of him?" This great question, from a psalm of David, is a profound reversal on the problem seemingly posed by the Deluge. It reverberates through the whole great narrative. Turbulence is introduced into the Genesis Creation by human beings, and it is utterly meaningful.

. . .

This world is suited to human enjoyment—"out of the ground made the LORD God to grow every tree that is pleasant to the sight"—in anticipation of human pleasure, which the Lord presumably shares. This is an extremely elegant detail. The beauty of the trees is noted before the fact that they yield food. It is a rich goodness that the Lord intended and created for our experience. Two things are signified, that God as the creator of beauty intends it for us to see and enjoy, and that He gives us the gifts of apprehension this pleasure requires, which is nothing less than a sharing of His mind with us in this important particular. That God Himself in some celestial sense has and enjoys this kind of perception gives us an insight into the meaning of our being made in His image. The world is imbued with these reminders that there is a beautiful intention and assurance expressed in every perception we have of loveliness in the natural world.

I enlarge on this detail about the trees because it contains statements about the nature of God and humankind and Creation that are radically unlike those offered in

Babylonian myth. Those gods can be disturbingly human in their emotions, which cluster around self-aggrandizement, but they are not of a kind to let us know that our pleasure has been anticipated in the art of Creation. In this deep sense we are made to be companions with God.

If the actual forming of humankind out of dust alludes to it, it also departs from the making of human beings in the *Enuma Elish*. First, the creation of a single man and a single woman in Genesis is full of consequence, against the fourteen men and women without names or attributes to be fashioned out of clay in the Babylonian narrative. A goddess makes these people for the purpose of relieving a defeated army of rebel gods of the penal servitude to which they have been sentenced. There is nothing exalted in this, no thought of enchanting these nameless drudges with the beauty of the world. An intriguing detail—the clay from which these humans are to be made is mixed with the blood of a god, who has been killed for the purpose, the leader of the failed insurrection. So, nameless as they are, they have in their nature something both of the divine and of the profoundly rebellious.

Rebellion of a vastly milder kind figures in Genesis, of course. Adam, Dust, is given life by God's breath. And he is sentenced to toil. But he himself, humanity itself, committed the trespass for which the punishment was due. Responsibility and attendant guilt might seem a dubious gift, except by comparison with the absolute determinism implied in having evil as an essential component of human nature. Granting that the Fall of Adam and Original

Sin are ideas that skirt very near this view of things, the difference is crucial. The manifestations of fallenness in any individual person are a matter of what we experience as choice or character. The predisposition can be called rebellion against God, like the taint in the flesh of humankind as the Babylonian myth represents the matter. But there is a complication of the conception of human evil in the fact that, male and female, Adam and Eve, they were exalted in their creation as images of God. When they fell, the ground was cursed, but they were not. They and we were made subject not to God but to difficulty and necessity. And reality was changed with reference to our transgressions, which would be ongoing. That human beings were so central to the Creation that it would be changed by them, albeit for the worse, is, whatever else, a kind of tribute to what we are.

This likeness to God or participation in a divine nature of course has the meaning the narrative gives it—in the Babylonian mythos gods can act in defiance of other gods, which may mean in the moment or the context that they can be evil, that they can be defeated and subjugated. The God of the Hebrew mythos is creative, provident, attentive to his human creatures even to the point of demanding righteousness of them—demanding that they identify with Him, that is, obey Him, by choice. Famously, they do not. And they are put to work, like the defeated gods of the *Enuma Elish* and then the human beings who exist in order to toil in the place of these gods. Even here, in the matter of toil, which in both cases is, whatever else, a response to the fact that human life is full of endless difficulty, it is notable that Adam toils for bread, for his, their, own subsistence, while in the Babylonian view humans work for the gods' subsistence and build ziggurats and temples to please them and make them approachable. The God of the Old Testament scorns the idea that He needs sacrifices, that is, that He hungers. He does not sleep. He does not dwell in a house. It seems bizarre to anyone with a Judeo-Christian conception of God, however secular, however merely cultural, even to say such things. But in the surrounding polytheisms it is important that the gods experience fear—their terror at the flood they unleash signifies that there is a limit to their extremes of destruction. They sleep—it is the disruptive noisiness of the lesser gods, then humankind, which keeps the serpent mother Tiamat from sleeping and moves her to wipe them out. The gods faint with hunger when the human population is too reduced to keep them fed.

So these simple statements, God does not hunger or sleep, are explicit and necessary distinctions with profound theological meaning having to do with the nature of God and His relationship to His Creation. Words like *omniscience*, *omnipotence*, *transcendence*, and *immanence* can enter theology, language about God, because the Old Testament makes and maintains these distinctions, even though the Hebrews, Israelites, first-century Jews engage in ritual sacrifice, as all the Mediterranean cultures seem to have done. The laws of the Torah make it clear that, at least at the appointed festivals, the sacrifices were feasts shared among communities with special reference to widows, orphans, and strangers. As a method of contributing to every kind of communal well-being this is a wonderful adaptation of a seemingly universal impulse and custom. The Homeric gods wanted their white thighbones. The Carthaginians were said to have sacrificed male children to Baal-Peor and his consort, Anat. In these cases some value was thought to have been transmitted to a god or gods by the human act of sacrifice. In the Torah the festivals are memorials of the origins and history of the community, that is, of the self-revelation of God in the events that formed them as a people. Like many provisions of the law of Moses, they also distribute nourishment in the course of asserting bonds that always include the needy. On these grounds they might well be pleasing to God and a contribution to the achievement of His purpose in the creation of a priestly people.

The narrative of the Flood in its Hebrew version explains how law becomes intrinsic to Creation. We now can imagine all too readily that the human world might become hellish enough that God could repent having made it: "The earth also was corrupt before God, and the earth was filled with violence." We can be so contemptuous and abusive of one another, we images of God who are so prone to desecrating other images of God, individually and collectively. Law is not so much limitation as instruction, because it is finally up to us to keep it or break it.

Law crystallizes or precipitates moral decision. Any one of us is as free as Adam to set it aside. Presumably God could have repopulated the world with a humanity capable only of righteousness. But His intention toward us, which is also His loyalty to us, has valued our autonomy. That our autonomy is still intact after the Flood is made clear in the fallibility of Noah.

The fact that certain Westerners have believed that Scripture should bear no relation to other ancient literatures has made its having borrowed a famous tale, though adapted to its own uses, a scandal of the kind that electrifies both fundamentalists and religion's cultured despisers. One side in the controversy is rebuilding the ark to demonstrate its seaworthiness, or tramping up Ararat looking for its wreckage. The other sees the story as cribbed and fraudulent. If it is a trope, a fable or parable used to constellate essential terms so that they can be seen and characterized together and in relation to one another, then a literal interpretation is clearly not appropriate. The text, so obviously borrowed, does not tell us that God once subjected the world to an all-obliterating flood. It gives us a parable.

In a fable of our own we might propose a good god, maker of a good creation, who peopled it with creatures of a special brilliance and dignity and with a broad latitude that allowed them to act humanely and well, and to act against the god's wishes and against their own well-being. Let us say they committed terrible violence, active and passive, against themselves, humankind, at every cost to nature and civilization. Say they used peace to study war, investing their brilliance in the devising of weapons whose destructive power could hardly be imagined. Say they permitted and created poverty so profound that it unleashed plague and destroyed them by the millions. Say these crimes were persisted in, and that they accelerated over thousands of years. Might not the good god repent of having made humankind, even decide to put them out of their misery?

This is not the story the Babylonians tell, because for them human beings are not central to Being itself. In the myth they are not moral actors. Forces that destroy them, whether wars or wild beasts, simply keep their relationship with the gods in balance.

This is not the story the Hebrews tell, either. The first thing we know about Noah is that he is righteous "in his generations," which might mean righteous by the standards of the time. Nevertheless, we can conclude that Noah is rewarded for his good character, or we can conclude that Noah is saved, with pairs of all the species, because his righteousness is of a kind to make him able to have a part in the re-creation of the world. Species are saved on the boat of Utnapishtim, too, but the flood that has left the land as flat as a roof and returned humankind to clay falls out of the tale; the Flood and its effects simply end. In the Hebrew version the destruction prepares for a new creation. The animals are released from the ark. The *Epic of Gilgamesh* is silent on this point, as it is in the matter of the preference shown to Utnapishtim, the quality that endeared him to the god Ea.

· · ·

In a long dialogue with Abram, God tells him that He will not destroy Sodom if ten righteous men are to be found in it. The fate of Sodom indicates that there were not ten righteous men, nor even one. In Noah we see the whole earth being saved by one righteous man, in his case before there are laws to instruct him. *Righteousness* is a very important word in Scripture, too little considered by interpreters, perhaps. The book of Job ponders righteousness, what it is and how it is rewarded. That God is righteous is preeminently true of Him, and it can also be true of men, and women, too, notably those Old Testament heroines who are named in the Gospel according to Matthew's genealogy of Jesus. The book of Proverbs meditates on the righteous, often associating them with life. Psalm 92 says, "The righteous shall flourish like the palm tree: he shall grow like a cedar in Lebanon." It says also "the wicked spring as the grass, and . . . all the workers of iniquity do flourish" but "they shall be destroyed for ever." Righteousness is associated with life that is not doomed to destruction. It can save a city. It can save Creation. If one could imagine righteousness breaking out in earth's saddest places, and among the exploiters of violence and poverty, one could anticipate the stable, long-term flourishing of something that deserved to be called life.

These old tales look directly at the possible de-creation of the living world. Fragile as its cities and settlements were at the time, its crops and herds, they know how this might happen. The variant of the Gilgamesh epic called Atra-Hasis has a graphic description of people experiencing starvation. The Christian belief in life after death—I share and treasure this belief—can distract attention from life itself, which is, after all, an ultimate good in the next world as in this one. Minus life, this planet is a grain of sand, a tiny captive of gravity, one of endless quadrillions, no doubt. We have no evidence that there is anything like earth, any other bearer of life. We create life and we destroy it, but we don't know what it is. If it is the essence of everything, a breath of the very Spirit of God, it is fit and right that, first, as the basis of all understanding, of all righteousness, life itself should be properly felt and valued. Though this is by no means possible.

As I have said elsewhere, God makes a moral judgment of the behavior of human beings. What they do to one another matters to Him. "God saw that the wickedness of man was great in the earth, and that every imagination of the thoughts of his heart was only evil continually. And it repented the LORD that he had made man on the earth, and it grieved him at his heart." This verse from Genesis 6:5–6 is very important to the story because it is the first part of an *inclusio*, a literary device often used in Scripture to frame a section of text so that section will be considered as a self-referential whole. The second part of the *inclusio* comes at Genesis 8:21. "The LORD said in his heart, 'I will not again curse the ground any more for man's sake; for the imagination of man's heart is evil from his youth; neither will I again smite, any more every thing living, as I have done.'" What has happened between the first and the second of these thoughts in the heart of God? Noah and his family have waited out the Flood, left the ark when they could, and, like Utnapishtim, offered fragrant sacrifices. The Lord "smelled a sweet savour," as the pagan gods do. The sacrifice might mollify Him in some way, because Noah has hoped to restore a bond of experience between God and man. But something much deeper has happened. The Lord, in the thoughts of His heart, has yielded to His love for the incorrigible—in Old Testament terms, His Absalom; in New Testament terms, the Prodigal; in theological terms, the lot of us. The story has been made to express God's passionate expectation of righteousness and also His loving faithfulness, two divine attributes that might seem to be at odds, though righteousness is a quality that supports the well-being of others. In this the story departs utterly from its Babylonian model.

Tales that are told again and again tend to be structured around suspense. Here the startling reversal, from utter condemnation to unconditional pardon, is not forgiveness for any single offense but grace without reference to offenses. The listener shares the secret with the teller of the tale. Instead of destruction there comes a great assurance of ongoing life: "While the earth remaineth, seedtime and harvest, and cold and heat, and summer and winter, and day and night shall not cease." This is the love and grace that lie behind a covenant, in this case a great unearned gift to the earth itself. A brilliant adaptation of a borrowed story is made to unfold a very Hebrew concept that is central to the whole of Scripture.

Language of Creation prepares for this reversal. When the Flood is at its height "God made a wind to pass over the earth, and the waters asswaged." The Hebrew word translated here as "wind" can also mean spirit or breath. So, while *wind* is no doubt correct here, since the wind is *made* to blow by God, the echo of Genesis 1:2, "the Spirit of God moved upon the face of the waters," conditions everything that follows. On the third day of Creation, "God said, 'Let the waters under the heaven be gathered together unto one place, and let the dry land appear.'" As the Flood is ending "the waters returned from off the earth continually."

When Noah is told to leave the ark he also releases "every beast, every creeping thing, and every fowl, and whatsoever creepeth upon the earth." They are to "be fruitful, and multiply upon the earth." God blesses Noah and his sons also with these words from the first Creation: be fruitful and multiply. Read against the Babylonian tales, which turn on the idea that people can be intolerably numerous, infuriating the gods with the noise they make, this call for more life, more humankind, expresses a wholly different conception of God and of humanity as well. The Hebrew Flood narrative is an ingenious intertwining of the biblical Creation with the *Enuma Elish* and the *Epic of Gilgamesh*. Most of us encounter it first in a coloring book and next as a proof that Genesis is a mere pastiche. It is, however, a complex and distinctive theological statement or vision or claim or midrash. Its context and allusiveness make apparent that it is a work of literature.

The real climax of the narrative is still to come, the giving of the so-called Noachide Laws. Humankind in the person of Noah is helped to be less offensive to God, first of all—and this is notable and surprising—by God's relaxing limits that were imposed on humankind in the person of the newly created Adam. He/they are to have dominion "over every living thing that moveth upon the earth," but apparently it is a mild form of dominion. He/they and every creature that has the breath of life are "given every green herb for meat." Having said it is good, God then blesses the sixth day.

In the first of the "laws" given to Noah, dominion is a much darker thing. The Lord blesses Noah, and then he says, "The fear of you and the dread of you shall be upon every beast of the earth, and upon every fowl of the air, upon all that moveth upon the earth, and upon all the fishes of the sea; into your hand are they delivered. Every moving thing that liveth shall be meat for you; even as the green herb have I given you all things. But flesh with the life thereof, which is the blood thereof, shall ye not eat." The Lord has made an important concession to the human violence He deplored. The creatures so lovingly enumerated in every telling of Creation, appearing in beautiful succession like evening and morning, can now be killed and eaten, with an acknowledgment of their life in the scruple regarding their blood.

Putting aside brief and cryptic mentions of Nimrod, the only hunter in the Bible is Esau. This is striking, considering the magnificent bas-reliefs of hunting scenes made by Babylonians and Assyrians, celebrating their gods and kings as well as the beauty of their prey. There are many wild creatures in the Bible, named in Psalms and the book of Job especially. Here is Psalm 104:

> . . . As for the stork, the fir trees are her house.
> The high hills are a refuge for the wild goats: and the
> rocks for the conies . . .
> Thou makest darkness, and it is night: wherein all the
> beasts of the forest do creep forth.

But wild creatures seem to be left unmolested. When God boasts to Job, invoking the wonders of Creation, many of these wonders are strange and powerful animals. The prophet Isaiah, and then a later poet who wrote in his tradition, envision a holy peace. Among all the creatures, a great pact of harmlessness will prevail when "the lion shall eat straw like the bullock" and "the sucking child shall play on the hole of the asp." The later Isaiah foresees a new Creation, "the new heavens and the new earth," reconciliation between God and humanity so profound that "before they call I will answer; and while they are yet speaking, I will hear." And "the wolf and the lamb shall feed together, and the lion shall eat straw like the bullock." He quotes First Isaiah: "They shall not hurt nor destroy in all my holy mountain, saith the LORD."

When God has decided to accept humanity as it is, after Noah has offered his sacrifice, "the LORD said in his heart, I will not again curse the ground any more for man's sake." The text is alluding here to the Fall narrative in Genesis, the first change of Creation away from its original, and presumably intended, state. Because Adam and Eve have sinned, food, good in itself, must be gotten from the earth by toil. Childbirth, a blessing in itself, must involve great pain. Creation might be said to have suffered a decline as a consequence of human sin. So the principle that such a thing can happen is established, though the pattern is not repeated. After the Flood, beautiful living things are to be sacrificed, so to speak, to human appetites. This must mean that people had already been eating flesh, that this was a part of the violence God despised. A practice that is not good is made lawful, which is not at all the same thing.

Then a sadder concession is made. God requires a human life for a human life, lawful vengeance. Again, what is lawful is not therefore good. The Lord says, "Of every man's brother will I require the life of man. Whoso sheddeth man's blood, by man shall his blood be shed: for in the image of God made he man." Hebrew has several words that are translated as "man." In these three verses, the word translated as "man" is *Adam*, which also means "humankind." Whoever sheds the blood of Adam, by Adam shall his blood be shed. Law notwithstanding,

homicide is self-destruction. The application of this principle is potentially very broad. In any case, the fact of destroying an image of God, language of Creation reiterated
by God, should be terrible enough to lift homicide out of
the ordinary calculus of justice or desert. Yet in every situation in Genesis where revenge seems just and inevitable,
no revenge is taken. The first instance of this restraint occurs very early, in the matter of Cain and Abel.

The idea that God would make concessions to these
most regrettable human propensities might seem at odds
with the righteousness and the compassion that are His
preeminent attributes. It is consistent, however, with there
being a series of covenants, and the promise of new covenants, to establish terms on which God and humankind
can reach some kind of peace and mutual enjoyment.
Many centuries later in biblical history, the prophet Jeremiah, speaking for the Lord, says Israel and Judah have
broken the covenant He made with their ancestors when
He brought them out of Egypt. With a new covenant,
"I will put my law in their inward parts, and write it in
their hearts; and will be their God, and they shall be my
people." God's great constancy lies not in any one covenant but in the unshakable will to be in covenant with
willful, small-minded, homicidal humankind. Jeremiah's
vision of this state of things would not involve any ratch-
eting down of divine hopes, except in the important particular that it would diminish human choice, the loving
acceptance that should be the response of human beings
to their loving Creator. We must assume, on the basis of

history, the present, and the foreseeable future, that God still honors our freedom to choose against Him, and for Him. As Psalm 103 has it:

> He hath not dealt with us after our sins,
> nor rewarded us according to our iniquities.
> For as the heaven is high above the earth,
> so great is his mercy toward them that
> fear him.

Revenge arises as an issue early in Genesis, when Cain, having killed his brother, is told by the Lord that "a fugitive and a vagabond shalt thou be in the earth." Cain fears that "every one that findeth me shall slay me." Vengeance against fugitives and murderers was approved practice throughout the ancient world, and still a matter of honor in early modern Europe for the "avenger of blood"; Hamlet and Laertes, for example. Revenge is dealt with repeatedly in the law of Moses, to impose limits on it. In those laws a number of cities are designated as cities of refuge, to which anyone accused of a capital crime can flee and where he can live in safety until some resolution is found. A very humane response to the problem.

There is a passage from the New Testament, Romans 12:18–21, that is widely taken to characterize God as vengeful. Context does not support this reading. Paul says, "If it be possible, as much as lieth in you, live peaceably with all men. Dearly beloved, avenge not yourselves, but rather give place unto wrath: for it is written, 'Vengeance is mine; I will repay, saith the Lord.' Therefore, if thine enemy hunger, feed him . . . Be not overcome of evil, but overcome evil with good." Clearly Paul is telling the Roman Christians not to avenge themselves, instead to deal kindly with enemies. He cites two Old Testament passages in making his case. In other words, this view of revenge takes its restraint from the older literature.

The problem with this potent phrase goes deeper than the absence of context. *Vengeance* is one of those fierce old words like *abomination* that is rare outside Scripture. It has a history in Europe that has shaped its meaning. It came into English through French from the Latin *vindicare*, a word that can mean to vindicate, to justify or find innocent, as well as to find at fault. It implies judgment in the scriptural sense, the establishing of justice. There are always those who thrill at the thought of divine vengeance, imagining themselves to be exempt, even to be its agents, and perhaps this is one reason vengeance in the ferocious European Middle Ages shed any suggestion of vindication. As for the Hebrew sense of the word translated as "vengeance," Genesis deals again and again with the scant resemblance between divine purpose and human notions of justice. *Wrath* has a part in all this, being the anticipated impulse behind divine vengeance. It comes from Old English and seems to have meant anger and no more. But again, in the special environment of scriptural language, words take on exceptional qualities. Wrath is singularly terrifying. Extraneous to the text as these words are, they characterize God in the minds of serious, even reverent readers. It seems we may, so to speak, impute to the Lord words that are not in His lexicon. The thought should give us pause.

Revenge is the concern that is important enough to be allowed to disrupt the story of the first fratricide, the story of Cain and Abel. I was teaching a class on Genesis in my church. Two women recently arrived from a non-Western country to study at the university sat in on the class. They became indignant. One of them asked, "What kind of God would *not* kill a man who killed his brother?" An excellent question. This episode indeed characterizes God and is relevant to the whole of Scripture for this reason. The mark that God gives Cain to protect him from possible avengers is often read as something meant to stigmatize him as a killer, though the text very clearly says otherwise. When he says he fears he will be killed, the Lord says, " 'Therefore whosoever slayeth Cain, vengeance shall be taken on him sevenfold.' And the LORD set a mark upon Cain, lest any finding him should kill him." For all we know, it could have made him disarmingly beautiful.

Predictably, the notion has sometimes flourished that this supposedly stigmatizing mark is hereditary. But Cain goes on to have a wife and son and found a city. He seems to have had the full satisfactions of the patriarchal life. His descendants are credited with "fathering" many of the arts and skills of civilization. It might suggest another instance of fatherly devotion that he names the city for his son Enoch. In stories so economically told as these are, no detail should be dismissed, and this detail is unique in

Scripture. If there is any thought that the arts of civilization are corrupt in their origins, having arisen in Cain's city and among his descendants, his son Enoch has an exceptional place in the tradition, having "walked with God" through a long life, until "he was not; for God took him." The tradition that he did not die is cited in the New Testament book of Hebrews, which says, "By faith Enoch was translated that he should not see death." This is true of one other figure only, the great prophet Elijah. God gave Cain particularly estimable descendants, which would seem to discourage the notion of a hereditary curse. But this famous tale is a study in the fact that people see what they want to see, even in Holy Scripture, whose presumed authority should encourage careful reading. And these interpretations escape the study or the pulpit and merge with wild strains of feeling on the subject, giving the appearance of biblical authority to the primitive urge to avenge, in the course of imputing primitivity to "the God of the Old Testament."

In fact, God's great leniency toward Cain does seem to ask for some kind of explanation, or sense of circumstance. The story raises the question of revenge, first in God's awareness of the crime, which He might be expected to give an equivalent punishment, and then in His defense of Cain against vengeance from any source. It surprises, perhaps disappoints, expectations. The Hebrew word for punishment here also means "sin" or "crime"—my crime is heavier than I can bear. So perhaps Cain's crying out is weightier and more moving to God than English can render.

And context is always relevant. This crucial passage, His treatment of Cain, is a characterization of God in His righteousness and compassion, two attributes that are not always easily reconciled. Scripture will return to them again and again. In the Bible, great men, for example Eli and David, are very indulgent fathers. Their sons are no better for the fact. God, in His dealings with Cain, is as indulgent as any of them. He comforts Cain in his grief at not having made an acceptable sacrifice. Interestingly, He is not reported to have said anything to Abel, toward whom, with his sacrifice, He is said to have "had respect." The name Abel means "emptiness" or "vanity" or "something transitory." The story was always about Cain. The sacrifices were of no real importance.

Like a good father who notices his son's disappointment at failing to please him, a loving disappointment, God tells him that he can still "doest well," at the same time being aware that he might go wrong because of his resentment of his brother. Sin, like the serpent in Eden, takes on some part of the blame for the potential transgression. It is represented as a crouching beast with designs on Cain. This could be a naïve lapse into pagan thinking, or it could be a gentle way of speaking of potential wrongdoing without ascribing it directly to this man who is so desperately sensitive to His disapproval. It would be hard to argue that

Cain's worship was not offered in good faith, given the potency of his reaction to its inadequacy. Of course this does nothing to mitigate the crime of premeditated murder, of spilling his brother's blood. But it gives Cain complexity. It might also suggest a condition, Cain's piousness, for God's extraordinary faithfulness to him. Or the long genealogical view of the family of Cain reflects God's knowledge of the lives that would be spared with his life. Murderous Lamech is one, and Noah, son of Lamech, is another. And, after Noah, the whole fruitful and multiplying world. But rationalizing what God does involves the risk of losing its difficulty and otherness to human expectations. His great forgiveness of the first criminal offends people's sense of justice, unless they can find a way to read vengefulness into the tale. We are instead to learn that mercy is nearer than justice to Godliness, and that mercy can release an abundance far exceeding whatever might come of attempting to impose justice as we mortals understand that word.

The narrative includes an instance of the perversion of divine will by a man who knows something about it—a familiar type. Clearly Lamech, Cain's descendant a few generations on, has heard about the assurance God has given his ancestor. Rather than finding in it the protection of a murderer from revenge, he takes it as permission or incitement to be unrestrainedly vengeful. "Lamech said unto his wives, Adah and Zillah, 'Hear my voice; ye wives of Lamech, hearken unto my speech: for I have slain a man to my wounding, and a young man to my hurt. If Cain shall be avenged sevenfold, truly Lamech seventy and sevenfold,'" overlooking the fact that divine protection on one hand and brutal self-aggrandizement on the other are very different things. The vengeance permitted in the law given after the Flood, since it allows the taking of one life for one life, would be a deterrent to violence or a containment of it. Lamech boasts of lethal violence in reaction to relatively minor injury. He vastly multiplies the pretexts for homicide and exults in this before his wives, poor things. We have here the turn of mind that would change *vindicatio* to *vengeance*.

Lamech is not among the prophets. About his son, Noah, he says, "This same shall comfort us concerning our work and toil of our hands, because of the ground which the LORD hath cursed." This does not happen. But in his own person Lamech does allow us to see some part of the future that God sees.

The boast of Lamech, together with the Noachide Law permitting the taking of a life for a life, frames the Hebrew version of the Flood narrative, which is much longer and more fully imagined and elaborated than the Babylonian versions. This suggests an enjoyment in the telling. Remembering always that God did not really send an all-destroying Flood, the story could be enjoyed without discomfort. Whatever drastic experiences the Mesopotamians may have had with their great rivers, they no more than the Hebrews were ever brought near extermination, let alone the extinction of all life. This story in both its versions, Hebrew and Babylonian, is not about an actual disaster but about the fact of disaster and how to understand gods or God in the face of this fact.

Utnapishtim is told by the god Ea to dismantle his house to build a boat. Utnapishtim asks the god what he should tell the townspeople about what he is doing. Ea says Utnapishtim should tell his doomed neighbors that he is out of favor with a god and must leave that place, and when he is gone they will be showered with great abundance. The omitting of this detail in the Hebrew version is consistent with Noah's righteousness. Utnapishtim's neighbors are understandably eager to help with his leave-taking. Both he and Noah are given fairly elaborate instructions for the construction of these boats, different because Mesopotamians used reeds for building and Noah used something called gopher wood, different also because Utnapishtim has the help of the neighbors, whom he has deceived, in carrying out a hard task—the carpenter, the reed-worker, children to carry bitumen. With difficulty, launching rollers set it afloat.

"Thus did Noah; according to all that God commanded him, so did he." Then the ark was ready to receive that procession of animals, including "every creeping thing of the earth," the humblest category of creature, which almost always has a place in these catalogues. The loving recitation of the varieties of animals here recalls the Hebrew account of Creation and the spirit in which they were made. Utnapishtim is told to "put aboard the seed of all living things," including cattle and wild beasts. He is told to close up his boat, while Noah is shut in by the Lord. The rains come.

The Babylonian Flood begins to recede after seven days. The biblical ark is afloat for ten months. The Hebrew version follows the older story, departing in fairly minor ways until the great Babylonian tempest arises and the narrative of Utnapishtim becomes a pagan theophany, the works of the gods and their presence revealed in a terrifying storm. Profound darkness descends, in a black cloud the storm god Adad rages. The "flood-weapon" passes over "like a battle force." The gods themselves are afraid of the flood they have unleashed:

> The gods cowered, like dogs crouched by an outside
>   wall.
> Ishtar screamed like a woman giving birth.
> They repent of what they have done.
> The gods, humbled, sat there weeping.

This is very remote from the biblical conception of God, of course. There is a crucial detail on which all the difference rests. God tells Noah that "every thing that is in the earth shall die. But with thee will I establish my covenant." Noah is for these purposes the human race. Again, *that* everything will die is a given in the debate between Hebrew and Babylonian. The Babylonians may have been unaware of such a debate or indifferent to it. But the Hebrews were dealing with the influence of Babylonia, a great, brilliant civilization that may well have invented the literary epic. Polytheism is always a temptation for the ancient world's only monotheists. And stories are highly communicable, carrying with them assumed beliefs in memorable, even spectacular passages. The images of raging and cowering gods are the most vivid part of Utnapishtim's tale. The Bible gives the Hebrews their own story, a truer tale, which serves important theological purposes as it raises Hebrew questions and incorporates Hebrew beliefs into this Babylonian querying of the nature of things.

God will establish a covenant with Noah, and He tells him this. He has an intention for him. This assurance, in advance of the Flood, means that events are under God's control. He is not in the tempest. He will not frighten Himself with His own excesses. In fact, there is no tempest. The flood waters come from rain and from "all the fountains of the great deep," natural, God-made sources that are not divinized, as the sun and moon, the whole of nature, are not divinized in the Creation. While the Babylonian flood is a great storm that lasts a matter of days, the biblical flood is an amassing of water on a scale that could cover the mountains and truly destroy all life. It imagines the world taken back to its beginnings, Noah and his wife, their sons and their wives like the family of Adam. From them all human life will proceed. Utnapishtim and his wife, though they are made immortal, are also isolated and alone.

The intention of the biblical God is fulfilled. The world is prepared for something like a new beginning.

The Babylonian gods are shocked and threatened by the consequences of their own decisions and actions, and they regret them and at least scale back their homicidal intentions for the future. As freely as God wills the world and all it contains into being in the first Creation, and as freely as He could presumably create it all again, He preserves a human family, and He preserves the long list of animals, a synecdoche for the whole world of them. The creeping things crept into the ark, and they creep out again. Utnapishtim is told to take the seed of living things on board his boat. This is a story element the biblical version adapts to important purposes. Nothing is made of this saving remnant of life in the Babylonian tale. In the Bible the care to record its presence after the Deluge reveals a loyalty to Creation as it first emerged. There is a great constancy embracing all change. Humankind may have become or showed themselves to be violent, corrupt in their imaginations, but they are as they were created, images of God. This is asserted in the context where it seems most open to doubt, in the law that permits homicide in response to homicide, and does so because "God created man in His own image." This law anticipates a humankind not different from or other than those swept away in this hypothetical Flood. The arc of narrative from Cain's crime to this acknowledgment of the human necessity of limited revenge, a violation of the sacred in answer to a violation of the sacred, is important because it acknowledges that the very high sacredness that is the distinguishing human trait is unchanged despite anything. We are disastrously erring and rebellious, and irreducibly sacred. And God is mindful of us.

Ishtar displays her lapis necklace, God sets His bow in the heavens. There's genius, even delight, in the fact that the Hebrew writers can borrow a familiar story, follow it closely, and transform it profoundly.

The covenant given to the earth blesses it all over again. Blessing itself in this context is a transformative change in the story, having to do with a central question in both versions, the nature of God or the gods, especially in relation to the created world. There is a long tradition in theology of divine "impassibility," which teaches that God has no emotions, since if He were capable of anger or pleasure that would mean He was capable of change, including change caused by something outside Himself. The Hebrew Flood narrative is interesting as a meditation on this question. It tells us that God can be grieved and angered, and at the same time that God is and will be faithful, to earth and to Adam. He can change and not change. Immutability is not an inevitable consequence of His nature, as if options were denied Him by philosophical consistency. Rather, as the psalmist says, His steadfast love endures forever. Who is speaking when the God of the Bible makes this unsought, unmerited vow? Point of view is an interesting question in any sacred text. I am content to believe that certain early Hebrews, under the influence of Moses and still pondering the faithfulness of God that they saw in their liberation from bondage, were inspired with a true insight into His nature. Putting impassibility aside, there is a great, and complex, consistency in the divine nature evoked by them. If God does not love kindness and hate bloodshed, He has no stable character as the Father of us all. It would mean nothing that the rain falls on the just and the unjust because grace would be no necessary part of His abundant providence. Impassivity could account for it all. Since the terms of His being within His Creation are wholly of His choosing and are strongly centered on His human creatures, to have a stable character relative to them would require that He be responsive to them. In other words, immutability as an attribute of "the living God" makes Him inconstant, neither righteous nor compassionate. It makes Him inconceivable as the image in which all of us are made because it places Him wholly outside our experience. It is not impassibility but God's covenanted faithfulness that allows humankind to be what we are, with all that this will entail. What kind of God would bear with us? From this point in Scripture we begin to enter history.

God has set His bow in the heavens and made His covenant with "all flesh that is upon the earth." The three sons of Noah—Shem, Ham, and Japheth—leave the ark for the renewed world, blessed by God, told to be fruitful and multiply and fill the earth, just as Adam and Eve had been told, "and of them was the whole earth overspread." The tale of the Flood in its Hebrew iteration arrives at the statement of a central truth, that humankind are a family. Ultimately they share a common descent, a common nature, a common enjoyment of God's grace in His covenant with all flesh. These insistences, not only that God is one but that humankind is also one, the Adam who is killed, the Adam who kills, and the Adam who avenges the killing, should not be overlooked. However it was that these stories were preserved and interpreted, they reflect a generous awareness of the known world not to be found in comparable literatures. True, the Hebrews had their time in brilliant Egypt, but much of it was a time of bitter slavery. They were surrounded by tribes and nations with whom they struggled and whose pagan influence was a constant problem. Yet they too are blessed in the person of Adam, whose name means humankind, and Eve, "the mother of all living." When God makes His covenant with Abraham, He says, "In thee shall all families of the earth be blessed." Such breadth of view is never to be assumed of any group. In many readings of the Five Books of Moses and the Old Testament in general, just the opposite is assumed.

The issue arises in the stories of the origins of peoples that complicate this great unity. The fact of familial relationship never guarantees peace or mutual sympathy—Cain killed Abel—but shared descent is as real in these stories as the denials of it and transgressions against it. The story of Noah's drunkenness introduces a complex conflict involving status among brothers. On several grounds the story is not pleasing. People can be surprised even to find it in the Bible. Noah "drank of the wine, and was drunken;

and he was uncovered within his tent." His son Ham saw him naked and warned his brothers so that they would not be guilty of the same unintended offense against their father. Noah woke, somehow "knew what his younger son had done to him," and cursed not Ham but Ham's son Canaan, making him a slave to Ham's brothers, Shem and Japheth. This is very puzzling. Some interpretations take there to have been some kind of gross depravity committed by Canaan in the traditional story that was lost or edited out in the biblical version. The sad fact is that these verses were used for a very long time to prove that slavery that was racial and hereditary had a basis in Scripture.

Perhaps its importance for this purpose has biased reading, and interpreters have found ways to overlook its peculiarities. For example, Ham seems to have been considerate of his father and brothers. If Noah realizes why this would have been necessary and is shamed and therefore angry on waking from a drunken sleep, and if he curses whoever happens to be in sight in an attempt to recover his dignity and authority, then the fact that there is no fault here, only his humiliation, is consistent with common human behavior. It means that the curse was an error and an injustice, and, to the extent that it affected relations within the human family, a calamity. Noah at this point can be compared to his father, Lamech. Both of them exact revenge, Lamech by killing anyone who injures him, Noah by making "a servant of servants" of a boy who has done him no harm. In both cases they are attempt-

ing to imitate God and getting it wrong, Lamech because
before the Flood God does not avenge or countenance
vengeance, Noah because God does not curse Adam or
Cain but instead tells Adam "cursed is the ground for thy
sake," and Cain "now art thou cursed from the earth."
After the Flood, the Lord says, "I will not again curse the
ground any more for man's sake," His language recalling
the two instances in which He responded to transgression without cursing the perpetrators or diminishing their
human standing. Noah does what God will not do. He
curses a human being.

Noah is a patriarch, so the issue is again the relationship of father and son. God as father is compassionate
and forgiving. Noah is arbitrary and cruel. Whatever a
curse might have meant to Hebrew culture at the writing of this passage, there is no reason to assume that the
writers meant to affirm this meaning. The Bible tells us in
the Fall that the earth we know, with toil and birth pangs
and Eden behind us, is not quite as it was meant to be.
It tells us again in the Flood and the law that requires a
life for a life that it is a long step further from what it was
meant to be. This staged progression, in which lesser degrees of reality modify an original state of things that fully
expressed God's will, means that what is actual or customary is always open to criticism, over against the purer
standards of a less declined world. We have the example
of the restraint, forgiveness, providence, and faithfulness
of God, and we have the drunken rage of Noah. Whatever

became of Canaan, to suffer the hostility of a powerful man or of society can look and feel very like a curse. To honor a curse, whatever potency it was thought to have, more highly than the blessing God gives through Noah to all people can only be a very grave error.

There is a tendency in biblical scholarship to treat these stories as if they are too primitive to arise from or to sustain a context in light of which they can be interpreted. It seems fair to me to say that the stories of Noah and his father, Lamech, comment on each other in a way that has important interpretive consequences. There are little poems, boasts, attributed to them both. Lamech celebrates his own vengefulness and Noah enacts revenge, cursing the unoffending Canaan three times over. Poetry has a mnemonic function. It preserves itself and its associations. So these little taunts might have been called up from deep collective memory and given authority by the fact that they were old and shared. Or they are framed in the narrative by details that undercut them. God almost despairs of the world on account of violence, which Lamech exults in. Noah's shame and rage are not inconsistent with his waking from a drunken sleep. Both father and son err drastically in their brutal use of power. For the purposes of understanding these texts it seems very worth remembering that we are Lamech and we are Noah. Unlimited or misplaced vengeance pervades our societies under the name of justice and always has.

Vengefulness has long been taken as a primary trait of "the God of the Old Testament," and to be sanctified for human purposes by this association. The endless disaster of the enslavement of Africans was said to be aligned with divine will, as revealed in Noah's impulse of drunken shame. The Epistle of James says, "The tongue is a little member, and boasteth great things. Behold, how great a matter a little fire kindleth! And the tongue is a fire." These small instances show how great crimes are committed among us, by opportunistic misuse of Scripture where relevant and available, and in any case where power overrides all respect for the sanctity of human beings. As James says also, "the wrath of man worketh not the righteousness of God." These little episodes can be associated with great and ongoing consequences because human nature and history do aggregate numberless little episodes of anger, cruelty, presumption, and the rest. The Hebrew writers knew how history happens. Theologically speaking, the possibility that, however obscure we think we are, we can be or refuse to be the agents of great harm, seems brilliantly designed to make anyone at all a significant moral actor. The law of Moses will make explicit the fact that life is invested with the kind of meaning expressed in the word *righteousness* and also the word *sin*, both having everything to do with our sacredness in a sacred world.

Shem, Ham, and Japheth were the sons of Noah, "and of them was the whole earth overspread." The genealogies of nations are laid out, seventy of them. The logic behind the groupings is not wholly clear, but the larger meaning, that humankind are one family, is served by the effort to include the far-flung world in this enumeration and by using the number seventy, which means a totality. The descendants of Shem, the Semites, receive more attention than the others, no doubt because much more would have been known about them by the Semitic writers, but also because the great narrative that is about to unfold is centered on them. What this history will mean, that it is the work of the one God and will bless all the families of the earth, is affirmed in this remarkable catalogue. It is a counterweight to the intensity of focus that will fall on Abraham, his family and descendants. It is commendable of the writers and the tradition that they correct against this centripetal movement. The God of Creation is mindful of it all.

If humankind are one family, we might reasonably be expected to have one language. But in fact the great multiplicity of tongues divides us. How has this come to be? The Bible says, after the Flood, that "the whole earth was of one language, and of one speech." People migrated to a plain in the region of Babylon and set about building a city and a tower in the Babylonian style, "brick for stone, and slime had they for morter." Presumably burned brick would be far lighter than stone. Slime, bitumen, is viscous, stickier than mortar. With luck and skill, using these materials it would have been possible to make structures that were very tall by the standards of the time, ziggurats, towers with their tops in the heavens. But their height and the materials used in building them would also have made them fragile and have made a collapse spectacular, the stuff of regional lore.

An unstable tower serves very well as a symbol for human overreaching. In the fable that forms around the tower of Babel, the Lord descends to see what the humans are up to and He demolishes the tower. This is a predictable interpretation of such an event. Hubris has its comeuppance. But more than hubris is at issue here. The Lord reacts not to what people have tried and failed to do but to what they might do if nothing deters them—"this they begin to do: and now nothing will be restrained from them, which they have imagined to do." The Lord sees neither failure nor frustrated intention nor a chastening of presumption in the tower and its destruction but potential for human success in doing the impossible. This is an astonishingly high estimate of human capability. Now that we have split the atom and spliced the gene and sent a kind of emissary into interstellar space we may have some idea of the possibilities the Lord saw adumbrated in the aspirations of early humankind. The story turns on wordplay, appropriately. The word *babel* meant "gate of God" in Babylonian and sounded like the Hebrew word that meant "nonsense" or "confusion." The tale is an etiology of the diversity of languages, and a demonstration of the reality of its effect. No doubt it is also an admiring joke at the expense of the Babylonians and their wonderful constructions.

The story is also, and primarily, a statement about God's relationship with His too-brilliant creatures. The first thing to be noted is that He does not disable them. He scatters them and He disrupts communication among them, impeding the expression of their plans and aspirations as harmlessly as might be, without any intrusion on their human nature.

The story is an etiology of the phenomenon of tribes and nations, as well. The extreme compression and efficiency of a fragment of narrative like this one makes it feel as though it has been turned and turned, considered in every light, but first of all in light of the belief that God is one and that He is loyal to the whole of Creation. The writers, certainly among the first to practice the art of writing in their language, might have made Hebrew the original or the favored language, perhaps the one spoken by God Himself. But in fact they are completely evenhanded. They might have said that humankind spread out and away from Canaan, but they place the tower and city in Babylonia, which is made to embody the whole of humanity, and whose culturally specific practice is made a synecdoche for the flawed cleverness of the species. It is not usual for the phenomena of tribe and nation to be acknowledged without judgment as to greater and lesser, better and worse, whether directly or by implication, but here again there is perfect evenhandedness. We are all one family, every one of us with a genealogy going back to Adam, like the genealogy of Jesus in the book of Luke. The distinctions among us that encouraged separate myths of origin, as among the Greek cities, or a shared origin but without familial relations, as in the Babylonian epic of Creation, are, says this dense little fable, difference for the sake of difference itself, all intended by God in order to tamp us down, to discourage collaboration. Again, this is not punitive, not absolute. Genesis itself demonstrates alertness to the literature and religion of Egypt as well as Babylonia, and appropriates from them, after its manner, quite freely. Are we to understand that God resents human brilliance? Considering the question from the perspective of contemporary history, and speaking in the language of the fable, there are grounds for believing He might fear it for our sake. Our tenure on this planet might have been brief indeed if our peculiar genius had had a more hectic flourishing. As it is, our hopes of survival may depend, in bald fact, on the discovery, somewhere, of a new heaven and a new earth, which our great brilliance makes remotely possible in theory. If God had dispersed the collaborators who made up the Manhattan Project, or any analogous project, this earth might be the better for it, or at least viable in the longer term.

The use of contemporary history in explication de texte amounts to finding fulfillment of prophecy in the Bible, if prophecy is basically an understanding of the one great variable, human nature, what it is and where it tends. Things seem to have taken an especially apocalyptic turn in recent decades, when every one of the proverbial horsemen comes thundering toward us armed with the effects of our presence on the planet, our choices. There are startling moments in Genesis that suggest the overplus of human ability the Babel story names outright, that nothing will be impossible for us. It is important to remember that not only we are threatened by our gifts.

Just after the Fall and its consequences,

> And the LORD God said, "Behold, the man is become as one of us, to know good and evil: and now, lest he put forth his hand, and take also of the tree of life, and eat, and live for ever . . ."
> Therefore the LORD God sent him forth from the garden of Eden, to till the ground from whence he was taken.

It is a convention of Genesis that God's thoughts and intentions are sometimes expressed as if to a companion or peer. Here the language suggests a family or community of gods who share a defining quality Adam threatens to acquire. Perhaps this phrasing is used to divert the narrative from saying that Adam might become too much like God Himself, which would not be consistent with the conception of God that pervades the literature. It would be strange that a transgression should bring him to that point. All the same, it is amazing to consider that only our mortality constrains our nature from whatever could complete that broken sentence. Adam is driven out of the garden, yet cherubim and "a flaming sword which turned every way" were set "to keep the way of the tree of life." Adam is not changed, only prevented.

There is a strange little passage at the beginning of Genesis 6, just before "God saw that the wickedness of man was great" and determined to send the Flood. Chapter divisions are a late addition to the text, and the division here encourages the thought that the intermarriage of "the sons of God" with "the daughters of men" is a part of the wickedness.

However, the passage goes equally well with the genealogy that immediately precedes it, which gives the ages at death of Methuselah, nine hundred sixty-nine years, and Lamech, seven hundred seventy-seven years. In response to these intermarriages, the Lord says that mortals' days "shall be an hundred and twenty years." This is another declension. The children of these marriages were "the mighty men that were of old, the men of renown." So the passage accounts for the difference between the great figures of legend on the one hand and humanity after the Flood on the other. As in the matter of the Tree of Life, humankind is inhibited from being whatever it might be by a limited span of years. The Flood and yesterday's newspaper are there to remind us that what it might be is not necessarily good. Israel will nevertheless continue to have and name its mighty men of valor.

"Good and evil" can be read as a merism, a figure of speech in which opposite extremes imply everything between them, here the whole of experience. The Hebrew can be translated "good and bad." So can the Latin, though theology seems indifferent to the moderating possibilities this translation would offer. *Yfil*, the Middle English word that became *evil*, can also simply mean "bad," without the very dark overtones for which the modern word is virtually unique. Choosing between these meanings appropriately takes account of the world Adam can anticipate and the children of Adam will know. A great deal that has happened here is far worse than bad, appalling at the level of motive in a degree the merely bad does not approach. Bad does not always suggest a motive or an adversary—bad harvest, bad accident—but evil certainly does. The "knowledge of good and bad" means we have had wide experience. The "knowledge of good and evil" means we are competent moral actors. I think it is clear from which of these understandings the biblical epic flows.

The way concepts like evil and fallenness have been received in Christian culture—the only branch of the Abrahamic tradition for which I can speak—has tended to set the Old Testament in opposition to humanism, though passages like the one quoted above express an extraordinarily lofty view of Adam, humankind. As in the tale of Babel, they/we must be inhibited, in this case through the expulsion from Eden and by consignment to a life of toil and to death. Also as in the tale of Babel, nothing is done to disable humankind or to deprive them of the brilliance and knowledge that make them "like one of us." The obstacles God sets to His Adam's strange grandeur are external. This is consistent with His unvarying loyalty to His creature.

All this is seen in another light in Psalm 8, a psalm of David, which asks, "What is man, that thou art mindful of him?" The psalmist sees this singular bond as an exaltation, owed to God wholly, that brings humanity within this same high sphere, almost "like one of us." He says, "Thou hast made him [humankind] a little lower than the angels." This is how it appears when it is quoted in the New Testament book called Hebrews. This seems like more than sufficient praise.

However, sometimes these words are translated as "a little less than God." In the Hebrew Scriptures, the word in question here is *Elohim*, a word closely associated with the Tetragrammaton, the name of God, and often paired with it. In the first great statement in Genesis it appears alone: "In the beginning God created the heaven and the earth." Throughout the first Creation narrative the word translated as God is *Elohim*. The verbs in the passage are singular, which suggests that the plural form of the noun here is honorific, like a royal plural. The word can mean authority or power, even in secular contexts.

David, whom I take to be historical and also the writer of Psalm 8, has the first Creation narrative in mind, clearly. It is Elohim in whose image we are made, God in the widest, least anthropomorphic sense of the word. "So Elohim created man in His image, in the image of Elohim He created them, male and female He created them." David's language proceeds very naturally from these verses. We are not the images of angels or lesser gods but of the Creator Himself. And we are crowned "with glory and honour." I propose that our conception of *humankind* is too anthropomorphic, too narrowly defined—as physical, mental, or moral—as mortal, either damned or saved, but not as the overwhelming power we are as a creature, a species. Every day we are confronted with the actual and potential effects of this power, but we are never properly in awe of it. As the tale of Babel tells us, it is collective, collaborative. None of us alone could by any means approximate the complexity of our presence on this planet, and none of us can materially effect its tendency toward change that exceeds our control. Only God Himself could alter Creation as we threaten to do and have done.

Psalm 8 takes account of the sun and moon, "the work of thy fingers," and also of the gift of "dominion over the works of thy hands," including our fellow creatures, the beasts of the field and the birds of the air. How vast is our dominion? Have we found our way to its limits? Shall we bring back the dinosaurs? Shall we colonize the moon? We know that humans somewhere are devising possibilities that will escape the laboratory, so to speak, and sweep the planet, and for weal and woe obstacles will fall and our dominion will have new expression. If we could step back from the dread we now stir in ourselves and look at all this with some objectivity, would we not feel awe? Would we not be struck by how absolutely unlike everything we are, excepting God Himself? What account can we make of humanity that does not imply another order of being than the brilliant natural order can contain? This granted, the grandeur of God can be assumed to exceed the honor and glory and the dominion of humankind in an infinite degree. They do, after all, derive from Him. Earth is a small theater for this great drama of encounter of God with humankind and of Adam with Adam, reality scaled to our capacities, which are immense within the profound limits of our creatureliness.

After Babel comes a genealogy of the descendants of Shem. Lives are very long by our standards but not nearly as long as they had been in Noah's day. The list of generations arrives at the family of Abram, who will be Abraham. Nahor was his grandfather, Terah was his father. He had two brothers, Nahor and Haran. Haran died, leaving a son, Lot. Abram's wife Sarai was childless.

We have arrived at a recognizable world where genealogy gives way to biography. We are introduced to a family on its way to Canaan but delayed in their travels at Haran, where Terah, Abram's father, dies. There were no doubt any number of families more or less like this one, wandering Aramaeans. But the family of Abram are singled out among humankind for all time to come, by a command and an extravagant promise: "Get thee out of thy country, and from thy kindred, and from thy father's house, unto a land that I will shew thee: and I will make of thee a great nation, and I will bless thee, and make thy name great; and thou shalt be a blessing. And I will bless them that bless thee, and curse him that curseth thee: and in thee shall all families of the earth be blessed." The God of History sounds ebullient, full of that first joy, full of vast and generous intent that can only unfold over centuries of human time. Where do these words come from? The story of Abram from this moment forward makes much of the fact that for him these words were not fulfilled, nor did they seem likely to be, even when at last he had been given his promised son.

Paul in the New Testament book of Romans says, "Abraham believed God, and it was counted unto him for righteousness." People often say that they believe *in* God, as if His existence were a hypothesis they are willing to accept. Abram has been told something directly by God, something unbelievable, and believed it. He leaves his father's house, takes his family to Canaan, where he cannot stay because of drought and famine, and drifts on into Egypt, where he does a thing that comports oddly with the promise that has been made to him. Sarai, who will be renamed Sarah, is so beautiful that Abram is afraid the Egyptians will kill him to take her from him. So he tells them she is his sister, which is half true. She is taken into Pharaoh's house, the Lord plagues his house, and Pharaoh understands the problem—Sarai is another man's wife. He is quite appropriately angry at Abram for deceiving him and sends them away in what must have been disgrace.

Would a man who believes he has a great destiny awaiting him fear for his life? Would a righteous man deceive Pharaoh and put his wife in a deeply compromising situation? This story must be important. The same situation occurs three times, twice involving Abram, once involving his son Isaac. If it tells us anything about Abram, it must be that after God has spoken to him, he is still an ordinary man, liable to fear and deception. About Egyptians it tells us that they honor marriage and that they expect divine punishment if it is violated. In all three recurrences of the story, the patriarchs act badly and the pagans act well.

The same point is made more dramatically when Abram again passes off his wife as his sister, this time to Abimelech, a Philistine king. In this story God speaks to the Philistine in a dream, saying bluntly, "Behold, thou art but a dead man, for the woman which thou hast taken; for she is a man's wife." Abimelech says he was misled and "in the integrity of my heart and innocency of my hands have I done this." God says, "Yes, I know that thou didst this in the integrity of thy heart; for I also withheld thee from sinning against me: therefore suffered I thee not to touch her." Nevertheless he warns him again that he and his will die if the woman is not returned to her husband.

Then Abimelech, full of indignation, summons Abram. "What have I offended thee, that thou hast brought on me and on my kingdom a great sin? Thou hast done deeds unto me that ought not to be done . . . What sawest thou, that thou hast done this thing?" Abram's reply is weak, but very meaningful: "Because I thought, Surely the fear of God is not in this place; and they will slay me for my wife's sake." We learn that God is aware of this Philistine's integrity and knows that his sense of sin is strong and controlling. Abram again shows little understanding of the nature of God. In imagining his relationship with God as exclusive, he denies respect to these strangers whose righteousness God Himself recognizes, values, and protects.

The moral appears to be that fear of outsiders, which amounts to contempt for them, leads to unrighteous behavior, and also that God is attentive to them, too, and will not let them be deceived into acting in a way they consider wrong. The encounter with the Egyptians comes immediately after Abram is told that he will become a mighty nation. Clearly this should not be taken by him to imply disrespect for other nations.

Considering the claim made in Genesis for the ancestor of the people who recorded and preserved the tradition of the Abrahamic covenant, and for themselves as his descendants, these stories must be seen as an impressive correction against a narrow conception of God and of humankind as well. Readers can be shocked by the fallibility of Abraham, Isaac, and Jacob. But the patriarchs are not offered as paragons. And when they err, the generous consequence of the text's attention to the fact is an assertion of the breadth of God's loyalty to all the descendants of Adam.

God's intention for Abram/Abraham is that he should be a blessing to all the families of the earth, very much including the Egyptians. Centuries on, when the history of Israel and the surrounding nations will have become long and painful, conflicts by no means resolved, the prophet Isaiah foresees a time when Israel will be "a blessing in the midst of the land; whom the LORD of hosts shall bless, saying, 'Blessed be Egypt my people, and Assyria the work of my hands, and Israel mine inheritance.'" This vision proceeds very naturally, as prophecy will, from the blessing God placed on Abraham.

This interest in the outsider arises in another narrative that raises troubling questions, the expulsion by Abram of the Egyptian servant woman Hagar with Ishmael, Abram's son by her. Abram and Sarai are childless, and Sarai says to Abram, "I pray thee, go in unto my maid; it may be that I may obtain children by her." This was a recognized form of surrogacy at the time, formally and properly arranged: "Sarai Abram's wife took Hagar her maid the Egyptian . . . and gave her to her husband Abram to be his wife." Hagar's pregnancy and then her child make Sarai jealous, and Abram, regretfully, casts them out. There is a tendency among modern readers to retroject onto our ancestors the faults for which we blame ourselves, and to blame them or to find them crude by our enlightened standards. However, there is no reason to think of Hagar's ethnicity as stigmatizing. For Hebrew hearers or readers, the association of the word *Egyptian* with the word *slave* would surely bring to mind the memory of their long passage as slaves to the Egyptians, just foretold in Abram's vision. It is notable that the behavior of Abram and, especially, Sarai is by no means idealized in the story, and notable, too, that Sarai has chosen this woman as her surrogate, and that Abram will ask God to accept her child as the long-awaited son.

None of this suggests anything invidious in Ishmael's having an Egyptian mother. As the story of Hagar develops, it becomes even clearer that Hagar the Egyptian, Hagar the slave, is singularly valued by God. The story, which knows utterly more than Abram and Sarai can know, tells us this very clearly.

There are two episodes centered on Hagar, each describing her encounters with an angel. They are so similar in form and substance that they might be two versions of one story. That they were once at least continuous is suggested in the fact that Ishmael seems to be an infant in the second telling, though the chronology provided for Abram would make the boy an adolescent when he and his mother are cast out. The text says, "Abram was fourscore and six years old, when Hagar bare Ishmael to Abram," then that he was ninety-nine when the Lord appeared to him, promising him a son by Sarai within a year. Certainly, if there were any intention to minimize the importance of Hagar, the two stories about her could have been combined. Hagar is important and is recognized as important in figuring in the first of the biblical annunciations. An angel who speaks for God finds her near a spring in the wilderness where she has gone to escape Sarai's ill-treatment. He tells her, the handmaiden, "I will multiply thy seed exceedingly, that it shall not be numbered for multitude," and, "Behold, thou art with child, and shalt bear a son, and shalt call his name Ishmael." These words resonate through both Testaments. This is the first appearance of an angel in the Bible.

In the second narrative Hagar is not a runaway but an outcast, this time stopping near a well, though she is not aware of this. The two parts of the story allude to each other so strongly that they might be two parts of an *inclusio*, the framing by repetition or parallelism of a section of narrative for consideration on its own terms. Several disparate and important events pass between them, making any significance they might have as interpretive markers less than clear. In any case, this placement of the stories of Hagar among major events elevates her. If, at a minimum, they tell us, as the Abimelech story does, that God is lovingly aware of the lives of pagans, kings, or slaves, this by itself is full of meaning with regard to the nature of God and His relationship with humankind.

Readers can feel that Hagar is unvalued because she is a woman, a maid, a foreigner, and these are indeed the conditions that make her vulnerable to mistreatment by Sarai and Abram. But what actually matters is the value the *text* finds in her, and in her life, which, humble as it may seem to us, can be called her destiny. People behave badly here. Abram and Sarai are not being held up to us as models of righteousness, even reasonableness. Hagar can't help gloating when she conceives a child, as her barren mistress cannot. Sarai turns her resentment of her maid against Abram, saying "the LORD judge between me and thee," though the arrangement was her idea. Abram does nothing to intervene when Sarai is so harsh to her maid—pregnant with his child—that she runs away. They all must be aware of her pregnancy, since it is the reason for Sarai's cruelty.

This is another situation in which it seems the judgment of God might be looked for. Wrong is being done, as in most human turmoil. Like Abimelech's justified rage against Abram, this moment, highly imaginable as ordinary household conflict and misery, has the inflection of the human. Its realism puts before our eyes the two tiers of being that are interacting when the immortal God works His will among mortals. He is bestowing blessings that will shape the history of humankind. He is giving universal meaning to obscure lives that might not feel much changed in being made bearers of divine intention, of promises that will work themselves out over millennia. Abram will still be childless, Hagar will still be serving a barren and resentful mistress.

Abram's great covenant blessing occurs in the text immediately preceding the first story of Hagar's surprising encounter with the angel, whom she calls God: "Have I also here looked after him that seeth me?" This encounter of Abram with the Lord has the quality of an archaic ritual. He is told to bring to the Lord, then to cut in half, a heifer, a she-goat, and a ram, all three years old, and to lay each half "one against another." A turtledove and a young pigeon are brought but are not cut in two. When the sun is fully down, "behold a smoking furnace, and a burning lamp that passed between those pieces." This cryptic event is traditionally called "the covenant between the pieces." It is the moment in which Abram is set apart to take his singular role as father of nations and blessing to all the families of earth. It is also the moment in which he is made aware that a great burden of grief will be entailed upon his descendants in their living out of this blessing. "When the sun was going down, a deep sleep fell upon Abram; and, lo, an horror of great darkness fell upon him. And he [the LORD] said unto Abram, 'Know of a surety that thy seed shall be a stranger in a land that is not theirs, and shall serve them; and they shall afflict them four hundred years.'" Remarkably, this great scene closes with a reason for the long sojourn in Egypt. Abram's descendants "in the fourth generation they shall come hither again: for the iniquity of the Amorites is not yet full." The Amorites are the Canaanites. The implication is that God is on terms with them, which He will honor until they have become excessively sinful, as He knows they will. Until they do, the Hebrews will remain in Egypt.

And after this second scene of Hagar and the angel, or the Lord, God appears to Abram again, renames him Abraham, and tells him when a child will finally be born to him and to Sarah, the new name He has given Sarai. The placement of these scenes side by side, the interlacing of them, is an instance in which the literary character of the text is especially clear and important. The extreme compression of biblical narrative is achieved in part by the setting or framing of its stories to invite comparisons among them. How are these encounters with God alike, and how are they different? They are alike first of all in that they involve promises made by God to women. Though the Lord speaks always to Abraham and only once to Sarah, in the last of these visitations, in Sarah's skeptical hearing, He promises her a child, celebrating the vast consequences over time of this birth: "I will bless her, and give thee a son also of her: yea, I will bless her, and she shall be a mother of nations; kings of peoples shall come from her." Hearing this, each of the two ancient half-siblings laughs at God's assurances, a striking response He might be expected to reprove. They are like a couple who have been married so very long that they react to things almost as one person. As His promise requires, God rejects Ishmael as the child of the covenant in favor of the son old Sarah is yet to bear. Ishmael's descent from Abraham, though God is attentive to him, and though he is destined to have a dozen princes among his own descendants, does not make him the fulfillment of the promise. This awaits the utterly impossible birth of the son who will be Isaac, the least interesting of all the patriarchs.

Descent from both Abraham and Sarah makes a very narrow window for the covenant to pass through, so that it can exist to be carried on by later generations. Isaac's two sons, Esau and Jacob, engage in guile and conflict that threatens to become another fratricide. Jacob's sons come near killing their brother Joseph, who will save them all from famine. The covenant would be in continuous peril if it depended for its survival on human loyalty rather than on God's steadfastness. From a scriptural point of view, this could be said of everything that matters.

If it had happened that Ishmael rather than Isaac had

been accepted by God as the promised son, Hagar would have been the first of the foreign wives whose children perpetuate the line of Abraham and Sarah. The genealogy of Jesus in the first chapter of the Gospel of Matthew names Tamar as the mother of Perez and Zerah, Rahab as the mother of Boaz, and Ruth as the mother of Obed— two Canaanites and a Moabite in the Davidic line. There is no mention of Sarah or of Rebekah, the wife of Isaac. In a traditional genealogy, only fathers are listed. Perhaps the inclusion of these women makes the point that the claim of descent from Abraham should not be understood too narrowly. These are important women in the Hebrew Bible, as bearers of important children and as exemplary figures in their own right. The appearance of their names among those who can be invoked to give Jesus a rightful place in the narrative of descent demonstrates that they and their stories are still well known in first-century Judaism. In every case they are essential to the survival of the direct line of descent from Abraham because there *is* a story—of deception that proves righteous, of extraordinary loyalty and generosity. In the cases of Tamar and Rahab, if not Ruth, there is also an element of the morally questionable. The writer of Matthew would have known that Jesus, while he lived, was criticized for associating with "sinners" and that he taught and befriended women. In recalling Tamar, Rahab, and Ruth he would preempt these criticisms and contextualize Jesus's example by reminding readers and hearers of the latitude contained in their own sacred history.

Questions about the covenant of Abraham that complicate its meaning arise from its very beginning. For example, the sign of the covenant is circumcision. Abraham
is told that every male in his household must be circumcised, including slaves born in his house and those bought
with money. This clearly anticipates the inclusion in the
covenant of a community of people not descended from
Abraham. Though infants are to be circumcised at eight
days, circumcision can be undergone at any stage of life,
as in the cases of Abraham himself, who was ninety-nine,
and of Moses, and of these servants, whenever acquired.
They seem to have no choice in the matter, but on the
other hand nothing more is required of them, no proof of
worth or belief. On this one condition, according to the
law of Moses, they are included in the profoundest and
most joyful rituals and festivals of the community. The
covenant is exclusive in that it is identified with a specific
history and family, and inclusive in that, as is foreseen already in Genesis, it can absorb and naturalize outsiders.
So with the genealogy that is said to bind the generations
to their father, Abraham. Providentially it has been carried on from time to time by foreigners, who are remembered and recognized as intrinsic to it. Hagar should be
seen in the light of this openness. I dwell on this, as on
other proofs of the generosity of God's attention, first, because it reflects on the nature and will of God; second,
because these stories are taken by persons who respect
Scripture as establishing norms, which can influence rela-

tions among groups; and finally, because the text deserves a fair interpretation.

The narratives of Ishmael and Isaac are another instance of scenes placed side by side so that they can be understood in terms of their likeness and their unlikeness. Both of these sons of Abraham are named, and accounts are made of their names. Ishmael, like Jesus and John, is given his by an angel, that is, by the Lord, before he is born. It means "God hears." Isaac is named by his mother, remembering her laughter and the improbable joy that still makes her laugh. If the Gospels can be taken as evidence of the persistence over many centuries of motifs of the Hebrew Bible, and of the resonances they carry, then this first divine naming of a child should be considered significant. This is truer because his descendants will be known by his name, as Ishmaelites. The two stories that root their existence in divine attention and blessing would be brought to mind whenever they were encountered or spoken of, presumably. In any case, the etiology of the name shows a respect consistent with the belief that they participate in the bond between God and humankind personified in Abraham. The angel tells Hagar that her son will be "a wild man," in the closer Revised Standard Version "a wild ass of a man," which does not sound to the modern ear like praise. But a wild ass in the biblical world is a free and untamable creature. The Hebrews, though always tending toward settled life in a fixed territory, wrote beautifully, in the Psalms and in the great

poem at the end of Job, about the wild, free, and powerful beasts of the wilderness. There are men who have elements of this wildness about them—the hunter Esau, son
of Isaac, whose garments smell like a sun-warmed field; the
patriarch Judah, the "lion's whelp," whose eyes "shall be
red with wine, and his teeth white with milk." Samson will
be another such figure. John the Baptist, dressed in skins
and eating locusts, is in this tradition, as Jesus might be also
after his forty days of fasting in the wilderness. The aus-
terity and intensity of this life disciplined later factions of
Judaism and early Christianity. If neither Esau nor Ishmael
is among those ordinarily thought of as holy men, their lives
seem to touch on another, primordial order of holiness.

Isaac is not a figure of this kind. There is nothing vivid
or unruly about him, even as a grown man. If in his child-
hood he suffers in comparison with Ishmael, this might
be the cause of the resentment in Sarah that leads to Ishmael's being cast out with his mother—into the desert
that is in fact his patrimony, where he will flourish with
God's blessing. In this way the story functions like the
tale of Babel, as an account of the dispersing of the family
of humankind through the world as distinct tribes and
nations.

All this raises the question of point of view. As in any
suspenseful folktale, the drama of the ending is not diminished by its familiarity. The story knows what the reader or
hearer does and doesn't know, that a cruelty at the scale of
human behavior can open on a providential rescue, a crux
in time becoming an epiphany. Hagar sees God and lives.

It seems fair to assume that the word *God* and the sense of the presence of God would have been vastly more powerful to the early tellers of these stories, and here to Hagar herself, than modern readers can imagine. Not much has been done in our period to magnify the Lord, maker of heaven and earth, or to enlarge our imagination to begin to comprehend the Godhead as an idea. So it is surely an error to imagine that Hagar, after her first encounter with the angel, could have felt poorly compensated for her days of anger and grief. Yet when she finds herself cast out, this time with the son to whom blessing and descendants were promised, she feels and expresses an even darker grief, unrelieved by the memory of the angel and his promises. When she has no more water to give the child from the skin Abraham had put on her shoulder, "she cast the child under one of the shrubs. And she went, and sat her down over against him a good way off, as it were a bow shot: for she said, 'Let me not see the death of the child.' And she sat over against him, and lift up her voice, and wept. And God heard the voice of the lad." Here an angel speaks from heaven to save the child's life, exactly as an angel will speak from heaven to stop the near sacrifice of Isaac.

There is another famous instance of a weeping child who has been cast out to die: the infant Moses. These wonderful, small details always mean that the narrative unfolding behind human circumstance is not only grander than it can appear to us but also qualitatively different. At the same time they make the humanity of these ancient souls present and undiminished. The God who has seized on the lives of Abraham and Sarah, taking them away from family and country, dazzling them again and again with great promises of land and descendants while they grow very old as childless pastoralists, this God comes to them to promise a child by Sarah in a year's time. And they laugh, despite themselves. It isn't hard to see why. The Lord they have believed has told them something preposterous. Their patient hopes, even their obedient lives, must finally have seemed like mockery to them. God loves them anyway.

Poor Hagar cannot bear to see what "the God of seeing" seems about to permit, the death of her son. Abraham, Sarah, and Hagar want one thing, a living child. They are told they will have innumerable offspring while they are fearfully at risk of losing or never having even one. This is so powerful a strand of the narrative of Genesis that it is worth pausing over.

After he has received the blessing of Melchizedek, the priest of El Elyon, God Most High, "the word of the LORD came unto Abram in a vision," promising descendants against Abram's lament that he has no heir. "And he [the LORD] brought him forth abroad, and said, 'Look now toward heaven, and tell the stars, if thou be able to number them': and he said unto him, 'So shall thy seed be.' And he believed in the LORD; and he counted it to him for righteousness." I include the final sentence here because it is theologically momentous and can fairly be taken as underscoring this moment. "The word of the LORD," "in a vision"—this language maintains a tactful ambiguity, as do the mentions of angels in these narratives. Someone walking by Abram's tent that night would presumably have seen him standing there alone, gazing at the night sky, rehearsing to himself, or prayerfully, the one sorrow that made his wealth and good fortune meaningless to him. But we are told God stood beside him, showing him the plenitudinous universe, stars lost in the light of stars, dimmed by nothing else. Then imagine, in God's sight, every star a human soul. If ever God exulted in His power to create, if ever the sons of God shouted for joy, surely it would be in His foreseeing this second universe of minds and spirits, whom, in fact, only He knows how to value.

This moment addresses a great mystery—how is one unique life to be thought of over against God's intention that there should be, as there have been and are, uncountable multitudes of lives? Is the meaning of a single soul diminished by sheer numbers of souls? Do any of us exist in excess of God's capacity for awareness, compassion, or love?

Nothing is more classically ancient Near Eastern than pondering the stars. The ancients can be said to have made a science of it. But against the background of the sidereal host the distinctiveness of the Abrahamic tradition stands out sharply. The myths of the Babylonians tell of gods who find people intolerable in too great numbers and cull or destroy them on these grounds alone. Those who live are useful to the gods, supplying them with food and building their temples. Whatever Abram thinks about the utterly unfathomable numbers of spiritual progeny that are being prepared for him, this vision, not of gods or angels but of all the families of earth, is meant to prefigure something truly wondrous, like Creation itself. God sees, through Abram's eyes, beauty that might seem an arbitrary display of divine power if it were only a throng of stars. He shows him what will unfold over eons of time among humankind. And all this will be blessed by the birth of that one child.

Between the two stories of Hagar and Ishmael comes the narrative of Sodom and Gomorrah, which might seem to be of an entirely different spirit. Or it might pose the question of the importance of a single life in other terms. It begins with the arrival of three travelers whom Abraham welcomes with ceremonious hospitality. Events make clear how vulnerable ancient travelers were to every kind of abuse, and why courtesy and generosity to them were great virtues. One of the travelers is the Lord Himself, who tells Abraham He has come to see if Sodom is as evil as it is reputed to be. As the other travelers go on toward the city, He stays behind to confide His full intention to Abraham. "Shall I hide from Abraham that thing which I do . . . ? For I know him, that he will command his children and his household after him, and they shall keep the way of the LORD, to do justice and judgment; that the LORD may bring upon Abraham that which he hath spoken of him." The other two walk ahead, angels who will put the city to the test.

Abraham makes bold to ask the Lord if the city might be saved by the presence among its people of fifty, then forty-five, then forty, then thirty, then twenty, then ten who are righteous. The Lord answers in every case that for the sake of such people, should they exist, He will not destroy the city. Then He destroys it utterly. Some interpreters say that Abraham has bargained with God. However, nothing indicates that God's intention has in any way changed, or could change, unless His intention to destroy the city could be understood to mean that He was willing in fact to destroy the righteous with the wicked, which, Abraham says, would be unbecoming in "the Judge of all the earth."

But this issue does not actually arise here. The text tells us that there were no righteous. The mob that surrounds Lot's house are "the men of the city, the men of Sodom, both young and old, all the people to the last man." This language is clearly intended to exculpate no one. The exchange between Abraham and the Lord might establish in principle that God's punitive judgment is never indiscriminate, even when it is wholesale. Some will object that, in any group of reasonable size, there are likely to be individuals who are worthy of consideration. This is true in fact, but need not be true hypothetically, if the question posed is philosophical or theological.

Sodom and Gomorrah were whatever remained of an apparent scene of desolation so absolute that they are a byword throughout Scripture. This account seems to answer questions raised by these ruins and by disaster in general—yes, the destruction was an act of God, and no, it did not destroy the righteous with the sinners. The assumption, which must reflect on the folklore surrounding the site, seems to be that the catastrophe was so sudden and overwhelming that the entire population would have been destroyed together. Abraham's questioning elicits a scriptural statement about the nature of God—not that He would spare the righteous in punishing sinners but that He would instead spare sinners in protecting the righteous. His care for the good exceeds His readiness to punish evil. If anyone in the city had satisfied this standard, no brimstone would have fallen. This is not a position arrived at by negotiation. If Lot should be considered righteous, a real question, the Lord removed him and his from Sodom, making the question moot. The same might be said of Noah and the Deluge.

In references to these cities in both Testaments there is the assumption that communities as a whole are subject to judgment, one of the most difficult and most frequently recurring subjects in Scripture. The text explains Sodom's relevance to this moment in the story of Abraham. The Lord says that He will tell Abraham what He is about to do, to destroy Sodom, "seeing that Abraham shall surely become a great and mighty nation, and all the nations of the earth shall be blessed in him." In Deuteronomy, where the promised nation, shaped by its history and its laws and instructions, is taking form under the guidance of Moses,

Sodom and Gomorrah are invoked by Moses as portend-
ing the fate of Israel, should it ever be unfaithful, "the
whole land thereof is brimstone, and salt, and burning,
that it is not sown, nor beareth . . . Even all nations shall
say, 'Wherefore hath the LORD done thus unto this land?
What meaneth the heat of this great anger?' Then men
shall say, 'Because they have forsaken the covenant of the
LORD God of their fathers, which he made with them
when he brought them forth out of the land of Egypt.'"
Here Abraham is being instructed in the profound weight
of the covenant relationship with God, a bond that we are
assured again is meant to have consequences for the whole
world. Should the covenant ever be forsaken, his people
will suffer disaster. As Moses and the prophets view the
matter, Abraham is not looking on as a righteous outsider
while an alien and wicked city dies in its sins. Rather he is
witness to the fact that nations, first of all his own, though
it can hardly be said yet to exist, have communal identities
and obligations and vicious tendencies as well, and that as
cities or nations they are liable to judgment. Abraham has
seen his descendants in a dazzling night sky, and dreamed
of their sufferings in a terrifying vision. Here he sees them
in the judgment that would await them should they not
"keep the way of the LORD, to do justice and judgment."

In Ezekiel, the Lord says, "Behold, this was the iniquity of thy sister Sodom, pride, fulness of bread, and abundance of idleness was in her and in her daughters, neither
did she strengthen the hand of the poor and needy."

There are many contending views about what the

sinfulness that doomed Sodom actually consisted of, though one idea has dominated the discussion for a very long time. There is no reason to suppose that the guilt of Sodom took only one form. In the narrative of the Flood, God says the world He condemns is "filled with violence," a word that comprehends evil of many kinds. It is certainly of interest that a relatively late prophet like Ezekiel would treat the nature of the city's sin as an open question. Post-biblical Jewish commentators associated Sodom with extremes of selfishness and cruelty. Failure to be hospitable is clearly one factor, bearing in mind that the attempted assault on these strangers would fall under this category. The barbarous attack on strangers is framed by the loveliness of Abraham's cordial and attentive welcome to his three visitors. The respect and disrespect they encounter, with their divine identities concealed, heighten the meaning of the courtesy of a righteous host or the brutishness of someone who would exploit a stranger's vulnerability.

Interpretation of this story has been very much affected by two words, first *sodomy*, a sexual practice forbidden in Leviticus that has taken a name from the doomed city and therefore is generally thought to have doomed the city. Then *abomination*, a misreading of a phrase in Latin, *ab omen*, which means contrary to a prohibition of more than merely legal or customary authority. There were no spaces between written words in ancient Latin, but at some time an aitch was inserted there, so that the word seemed to mean something like "inhuman." Over time the aitch vanished, but the implication of something unspeakably condemnable has adhered to the word. My concordance offers "loathsome" or "detestable," which seems not quite right, considering the great variety of things, foods, and behaviors, from shellfish to child sacrifice, that Leviticus calls "abomination." Attention to the law of Moses was a little too random in the Western church to provide context for those few, dramatic laws that were given authority by them. There was certainly an awareness, strenuously acted on, that witches should not be allowed to live. In any case, the distance is very great between "not propitious," which I take to be Jerome's translation, and "detestable," the assumed meaning of the word now and for centuries. All this is to say that the emphasis of the story is inappropriately placed on sexual transgression.

The much greater issue, the attempt to justify the ways of God to man, the question of whether divine justice in the world can be reconciled with individual human deserving, is among the preoccupations central to the whole of Scripture. When Abraham has his dark vision of the enslavement of his descendants, they do not yet exist except as God's intention. So when they do pass through their centuries in Egypt, they certainly are not being dealt with according to any ordinary idea of deserving.

Jesus comes down on both sides of the question of divine justice, rejecting the idea that one can read back from suffering or misfortune to unrighteousness and God's disfavor. Speaking of eighteen people killed in Jerusalem when a tower fell, he says, "Think ye that they were sinners above all men that dwelt in Jerusalem? I tell you,

'Nay: but except ye repent, ye shall all likewise perish.'"
He seems to say that God does indeed execute judgment
in the world, but that events are not interpretable in these
terms—except, perhaps, in one's own case, since one is,
with God, the only possibly competent judge of one's own
spiritual state. Jesus will become an epitome of righteousness held up to contempt and affliction, which is certainly
the ultimate No in response to the thought that, in this
world, God spares the innocent and punishes the guilty.
That his gospel culminates in a great exploration of this
question of cosmic justice, and its implications, argues for
its importance in the whole history and culture of biblical
thought.

I am assuming, always, that there is a point of view *of
the text*, that these stories have been considered together,
seriously and reverently and in the light of experience, that
their antiquity does not mean they are naïve, and that the
homiletic traditions that isolate them within the text, that
impose the convention of pericope on them, should not
be allowed to make them seem simple. Relative to what
God knows, and what the text knows, that is, the future
history of the covenant people, Abraham is naïve. He asks
the wrong question, a very human question: Will the innocent die with the guilty? The Lord replies, in effect, that
the innocent sustain, even shelter, the guilty: For ten, I
will not destroy the city. Unbeknownst to themselves or
anyone else, presumably, the innocent stay the hand of the
Lord. Abimelech, the pagan king who thought Sarah was
Abraham's sister, is kept righteous by the Lord because

he *is* righteous, and this protects his people from the consequences that would otherwise befall them. This is not analogous—it is pointless to imagine the effects of a righteous presence in a city that, axiomatically, has no such presence—except to say that Sodom would have persisted in its noxious ways, whatever they might have been, still arrogant and rich, never dreaming all this depended on some quiet soul or household who rejected its corruptions and, like Lot's wife, loved it anyway. One old wandering man and wife, one child, one family, one clan, one people, one promise, one singular destiny—it is all fragile at every point. And individual lives and characters are crucial at every point.

How to think about feckless Lot. He offers hospitality to the strangers just as Abraham had done earlier, repeating the formulas of courteous welcome. That he takes very seriously his duty to the travelers who have come under his roof is clear. The desperate expedient he lights on, of giving his virgin daughters to the mob in order to protect the strangers, may be understood as a failure to know what righteousness would be in this terrible situation. Perhaps the attack on Lot's house exemplifies the wickedness of Sodom because it allows no possibility for a righteous response. Only the intervention of angels can resolve it.

At the end of the book of Judges there is a story called "the Levite and his concubine" in which a woman is surrendered to a mob to protect her husband or master, and is abused and killed by them. This happens in a city of the tribe of Benjamin. The Benjaminites refuse to surrender the guilty men, the other tribes muster their forces to take them, and a catastrophic war is fought among the people of Israel. This outrage happened when "there was no king in Israel," and explains in some part the desire of the people to be given a king. There is nothing for which the Hebrew writers were more remarkable than their willingness to record and to ponder the most painful passages in their history, even the desperate, brutal confusions of the early period in the promised land. Whether this story or the story of Sodom is earlier, it is clear that these mob assaults were unrelievedly horrible and Lot's offer to give up his daughters was part of the horror.

Lot's character is never impressive. When he was given his choice of grazing land by Abraham, he chose the plain, the more verdant part, without demurral or hesitation. He was captured and carried off by enemies and had to be rescued by Abraham. When he is again rescued, this time by angels, he begs off going as far from Sodom as they want him to go. In fact, after this outrage, he and his family are oddly reluctant to leave the city. The angels have to remove them physically. He insists on stopping at Zoar, a little town nearer by, then stays in a cave because he is afraid to stay in Zoar. Finally, in a drunken sleep, he impregnates his daughters. His one redeeming trait, assuming fecklessness is not redeeming, seems to be that Abraham is his uncle: "God remembered Abraham, and sent Lot out of the midst of the overthrow." This would be an instance of righteousness sheltering the morally doubtful.

After the tale of Sodom and Gomorrah comes the second of Abraham's encounters with a ruler who seizes his wife, Sarah. He anticipates that this will happen because she is very beautiful, and fears that he will be killed if he is known to be her husband. The events at Sodom make it plausible that they are traveling through a world in which such an act of violence might be local custom, a sort of droit du seigneur. But this possible point of similarity makes clear that Sodom and the land of Abimelech are utterly different. The Lord knows the king as a righteous man. So the text establishes that it is not as a pagan city that Sodom is condemned, since pagan Abimelech is known to God and kept in His care. The text teaches and Abraham learns something of great importance—that the Lord is not a local or a tribal god. It cannot be assumed that the fear of God is unknown in foreign places, or that His power to protect has boundaries. The wonderful exasperation and offense captured in the voice of Abimelech make it clear that his views on right and wrong are not lightly held.

In gathering these formative stories, the traditional accounts of the life of the great ancestor by whom they define themselves as a community and people, one method of interpretation that would be available to these redactors would be juxtaposition, for example the placing side by side of stories that can be taken to refine a point by presenting different views of it. I assume that these traditions had value and authority that would make editorial intrusions on them very much to be avoided, a potential diminishment of the sacredness of memory preserved in them. At the same time, they are meant to be taught. Abraham is not so much an exemplary figure as a man under the immediate tutelage of the Lord, "for I know him, that he will command his children and his household after him, and they shall keep the way of the LORD, to do justice and judgment." Scrutiny to help focus the meanings to be taken from the account of Abraham and his heirs, to understand how righteousness and justice are to be defined and lived out, would be an implicit obligation for redactors and readers.

Interpretation by placement, without reconciliation of narrative detail or chronology, would explain anomalies in the text. For example, Abraham is said to have been ninety-nine when he laughed at the Lord's last promise of a child. After this comes the story of Sodom and Gomorrah, then of Abraham, Sarah, and Abimelech. If this sequence is chronological, Sarah is awfully old for her beauty to be so disruptive. If youth was miraculously preserved in her, presumably she would have been less amused and astonished at having borne and suckled a child. The story of a wife's capture is repeated three times in Genesis with little significant variation. In this iteration it makes no sense chronologically, has nothing to contribute to the flow of the narrative, and is in no way modified to reconcile it with its context. But it does address an issue Sodom raises, the privilege accorded to righteousness by the Lord. There is an addendum in which Abimelech promises to deal in good faith with Abraham, and Abraham reciprocates by coming to a generous understanding regarding the use of a well, demonstrating how others are to be dealt with by those who identify with Abraham.

A question hovers behind all this. What does the fact of a covenant exclusively carried forward by the line of Abraham and Sarah mean for the rest of humankind? Not so many chapters earlier, after the waters of the Flood have withdrawn, the Lord makes a covenant with the whole earth, saying to Noah and his sons, "Behold, I establish my covenant with you, and with your seed after you; and with every living creature that is with you, of the fowl, of the cattle, and of every beast of the earth with you." His promise is that "the waters shall no more become a flood to destroy all flesh." He also establishes a law requiring a life for a life, a sad concession to the human penchant for violence. Strikingly, this law is based on language more absolute and heartening than promise or covenant, for "God created man in his own image." This statement of relationship between humankind and God, which applies to every individual and to humanity as a whole, is unique in the Scriptures of the ancient Near East and Mediterranean. So the world outside the covenant family cannot be thought of as an object of indifference to the Lord. Indeed, He has said that Abraham's covenant will bless it all.

Abraham is being instructed in the nature of this God who has singled him out with the intention of establishing "his children and his household after him, . . . [to] keep the way of the LORD, to do justice and judgment." To know the nature of any god or goddess is to know what he or she requires. Much later the prophet Micah will ask, "Shall I give my firstborn for my transgressions, the fruit of my body for the sin of my soul?" No. He says, "What doth the LORD require of thee, but to do justly, and to love mercy, and to walk humbly with thy God?" Child sacrifice, driving children through fire, offering them to Moloch, is mentioned from time to time in Scripture as if it were a hidden crime or compulsion that was sternly forbidden and never finally quelled. One ancient Mediterranean civilization, Carthage, in modern Tunisia, was notorious for a large-scale ritual practice of child sacrifice. Carthage was the loathed and threatening rival of Rome, and its historical reputation has reflected Roman polemic against it. Archaeological evidence is open to interpretation on this matter but does not foreclose the possibility that this was indeed a rite of the city and its colonies. In any case, the old and persistent habit of separating classical antiquity from biblical antiquity tends to obscure the fact that for centuries Carthage was a great presence in the biblical world, sophisticated, rich, and influential, a sea power in the Mediterranean and up the Atlantic coast to Britain. It was an offshoot of Tyre, Canaanite, a Semitic-language culture that practiced a variant of Canaanite religion. Since there is, remarkably, no direct, unambiguous reference to Carthage in all of Scripture, it seems that serious religious and cultural defenses must have been reared against it. Carthage is not even acknowledged to be denounced. Dysphemism, the substitution of derisive epithets for the names of foreign gods so that their actual names need not be uttered, would be a comparable strategy. This occlusion would be consistent with the uneasy, unwilling acknowledgment that comes with stern prohibition. The scene of the near sacrifice of Isaac is a startling rupture within this averted awareness, this careful silence.

The Lord commands the sacrifice of Isaac without explanation. He does it to test Abraham, according to the text. From his leaving Ur of the Chaldeans to the birth of Isaac, the narrative of Abraham has been all faith and patience and longing. Everything he is promised is contingent upon the son he does not have. Then, when finally, miraculously, a son has been given to him, the old man is told to kill him. This must be called the climax of the Abraham narrative, a stunningly ironic reversal on the movement of the story to this point.

In what state of mind or soul does faithful Abraham lead his son to the place of sacrifice? He is the first man after Noah to whom God has chosen to make Himself known, at least for the purposes of the biblical account. (Melchizedek and Abimelech suggest there might be more to the story.) Abraham has encountered God directly, but we have no sense of what this experience would have been, except that it elicits a calm and steadfast obedience in him. "Now the LORD had said unto Abram, 'Get thee out of thy country, and from thy kindred, and from thy father's house,'" a very quiet theophany, considering that it is meant to, and will, set off a new era in the history of humankind. Through Abraham we first know the presence who is known sufficiently as the God of Abraham, who will instruct him so that his children will follow in His way. Part of this instruction is necessarily to distinguish Him from the throngs of false gods that swarmed the imaginations and fed the fears and hopes of ancient humanity.

Aside from the accumulation of wealth and household that marks Abraham as blessed in the eyes of the Philistines, God intrudes invisibly on these Bronze Age lives. He does not instruct Abraham to recruit other believers or to create a cultus of some kind. He expects some degree of righteousness on earth, as the destruction of Sodom and Gomorrah makes clear, and as His protection of Abimelech makes clear also. Mysterious Melchizedek, who appears and blesses Abraham after his rescue of Lot and others, invokes God, "possessor of heaven and earth," in words Abraham accepts and repeats. El Elyon, God Most High, is a variant of Elohim, the name used for Him by Abraham. This, together with the fact that Abraham in all his wandering never encounters any sign of adherence to another god, neither idolatry nor alien religious practices, suggests an original monotheism, however implicit.

As a strategy of narrative, the background, the terrain of Abraham's world, is silenced. There were an Ur and an Egypt, but for the purposes of this story there is Abraham, with his kin, his servants, and his flocks. Other nations and the pressures of their ambitions and their influences and examples will be constant presences in the chronicles of the nation this clan will become. Here there is the silence of Abraham as he walks with his son toward the place of sacrifice, and there is the silence of God.

It is amazing to consider what would have died under that knife if it had not fallen from Abraham's hand—the promised nations, and with them history as we have in fact known it. Why are we to believe that God Almighty is so invested in the emergence of nations, which are often enough troublesome and dangerous? They are lesser Babels, within which human capacities are discovered and expressed that we would never realize on our own. Because we can be beautiful collectively as we are singly— God is enthroned on the praises of Israel. Isaac embodies the future in which all of this will eventuate.

Sacrifice arises here as if without context. In pagan practice it was believed and intended to please the god to whom it was offered, to sway or enlist or mollify. In other words, it was meant to give human beings some degree of influence over divine sympathies and actions. It was transactional. When the Greek king Agamemnon sacrifices his daughter Iphigenia to the goddess Artemis, he does so to obtain winds that will carry his ships to Troy. This one favor is attended in due course by epic grief. Still, the sacrifice is made and the goddess obliges.

This sacrifice is not Abraham's idea. He has no purpose that would put him in the position of asking God for anything He has not already said He will give him.

He drifts over the land he has been promised, looking for grazing, leaving when famine requires him to, growing rich, growing old, living peaceably among the other sojourners in the land, encountering the Lord at the Lord's good pleasure, never summoning Him. The Lord speaks to him of an unimaginable futurity, assuming that Abraham will find the same joy He does in the prospect of innumerable descendants. Abraham asks Him how this promise can be fulfilled when he and Sarah have no son, but he never asks outright for God to give them a son. Somehow he is able to believe God long after belief seems impossible. This is the quality for which he is uniquely revered, and one meaning of it is that he does not in any way attempt to bend God's favor and power to his purposes, to impose his very modest though very passionate yearning on God's will, even though his longing aligns perfectly with God's promise.

We know what Abraham's thoughts are because the Lord tells him and the text tells us. What could Abraham say to Him, if he were to attempt an appeal? He is my son, my only son, whom I love. But this appeal is precluded— God knows what He is asking. Abraham's love for his son is precisely the measure of his obedience in acting on what he takes to be God's will. Then what of the covenant? What of those teeming nations, waiting to exist and to be blessed? These seem not to be considerations. What of the promises that were the bond between us, which I believed? Abraham might have challenged God in these terms. He could have said, as he had done before, attempting to intercede for any righteous there might be in Sodom, "Shall not the Judge of all the earth do right?" But God knows that the crux of it all is that Isaac is Abraham's beloved only son, and Abraham understands this. The stars of the heavens and the dust of the earth and all the generations that equaled their numbers would seem remote indeed beside this boy struggling under his burden of firewood. The irony of God's seeming readiness to make all those promises null might correspond to an indifference on Abraham's side to everything but the loss of his child.

That the very particular history of the Lord's relationship with Abraham falls away in this long moment makes the story universal. Abraham could have been any ancient worshipper who believed his god or goddess demanded his or her child. Archaeological remains in Carthage include the bones of young animals among those of small children, suggesting the hope that these substitutions would be acceptable, though they seem never to have become customary. In the New Testament, in accordance with Mosaic law, two pigeons are sacrificed in the place of a first male child, the infant Jesus.

If the story of the binding of Isaac is cruel, the cruelty it exposes plagued the lives of those who felt compelled to sacrifice children, whether Carthaginians or those unspecified others who are mentioned among the idolators of that world. The one God, Elohim, might have mourned this suffering and chosen to correct this misapprehension of His nature and His will. The plain statement of the tale is that the Lord does not want the sacrifice of a child, but that He is pleased to accept an animal, here a ram that He Himself has provided.

The God of Scripture tolerates sacrifice rather than requiring it. The festivals established in the laws involve sacrifices that are also feasts, in which the widow, orphan, and stranger are to take part. They define community. We moderns like our turkey dead and plucked before we have anything to do with it, but we know what it is to gather around a turkey and to bond in some way with the community who also participate in the secular consecration of the creature. But actual sacrifice was prone to excesses of every kind. It was thought to be effectively offered, that is, given, to a god or goddess and, at best, to put him or her under a kind of obligation. In *The Iliad*, the old priest Chryseis prays to Apollo, saying, "If I have ever decked your temple with garlands, or burned for you thigh-bones in fat of bulls or goats, grant my prayer," and avenge me. Prometheus had tricked Zeus into accepting thighbones wrapped in fat as the gods' portion of a sacrifice, securing the better part for human consumption. All the same, Apollo is immediately enlisted.

The prophet Isaiah and others voice the Lord's impatience with the practice: He says to Judah and Jerusalem, "Hear the word of the LORD, ye rulers of Sodom; give unto the law of our God, ye people of Gomorrah. 'To what purpose is the multitude of your sacrifices unto me? saith the LORD: I am full of the burnt offerings of rams, and the fat of fed beasts; and I delight not in the blood of bullocks, or of lambs, or of he goats . . . Your new moons and your appointed feasts my soul hateth.'" As He does so often, He asks for justice rather than sacrifice: "Learn to do well; seek judgment, relieve the oppressed, judge the fatherless, plead for the widow." The Canaanite gods would languish if they were not fed by sacrifices. The Lord says in Psalm 50, "I will take no bullock out of thy house, nor he goats out of thy folds. For every beast of the forest is mine, the cattle upon a thousand hills. I know all the fowls of the mountains, and the wild beasts of the field are mine . . . for the world is mine, and all the fulness thereof." And, "Offer unto God thanksgiving; and pay thy vows unto the most High." Human autonomy is unlike all other things. No ritual can make any creature or object more the Lord's than it is in itself. But in bringing before God justice or righteousness or thanksgiving, we are offering what we might very well withhold. We all know this from experience and observation.

Ritual sacrifice is a difficult subject for modern Western readers. But then very few of earth's peoples have fallen into that category. It is surely reasonable to assume that we are not always the Bible's primary audience. The idea of child sacrifice seems to have been felt as a temptation, perhaps because it might have been thought to have a special efficacy. What could show more devotion than the gift of what is most beautiful, most precious to one-self? After Abraham has shown his willingness to carry out this appalling act, the Lord says, "Now I know that you fearest God, seeing thou hast not withheld thy son, thine only son from me." Now Abraham knows that the most passionate worshippers of Moloch or Anat are not more devout than he. The most excruciating sacrifice they made was no greater than the one he would have made if God Himself had not forbidden it. So the seeming cruelty toward Abraham is compassion toward those great nations who learned from him or modeled their piety on his. God's stated purpose in His dealings with Abraham is to teach righteousness to later generations. If the purpose of the story is to instruct, this puts it into a category readers resist—"didactic" is never a compliment. But it should be remembered that the text intends a God's-eye view, one meant to shape the nations He is creating. It is true historically that Abraham's people were spared a profound, self-inflicted misery, which is at the same time a profound misunderstanding of the nature and will of God.

This reading shifts emphasis away from Abraham's obedience and toward the sacrificial act itself, the killing of a child. Isaac is utterly singled out by the narrative of his father's life and the miracle of his having been born to a very old woman. Providential history has a role for him. But this does not so much make his death, should it have happened, exceptional as it draws on the singularity of any child, and of the bond of trust between any parent and child. It is impossible not to wonder what Abraham's thoughts would have been, what nihilism and despair at being brought to the destruction, by his own hand, of

hope and promise made flesh in his son. Nor do we know
what Isaac thought or felt. Nothing distracts from the un-
speakable imminent act. The point is not that Abraham
is exemplary in submitting to this demand but that other
parents do this also, often enough for the practice in whatever form to persist as a grim concern in Scripture.

In the somber book of Judges, a man named Jephthah
vows to the Lord that if he wins a battle he will offer as
a sacrifice the first creature that comes through his door.
Nothing suggests the Lord does or does not take note of
his oath. Jephthah's daughter opens the door, dancing in
celebration of his victory and homecoming. She piously accepts the consequences of his oath and is sacrificed in due
course. This is a terrible sorrow to him. "She was his only
child; beside her he had neither son nor daughter." God
does not ask for the sacrifice and He does not intervene in
it. But the fatherly grief of Jephthah and the unrealized life
of his virgin daughter are the burden of the tale.

A reading that sees in the dramatizing of child sacrifice something shocking and transgressive, rejected by
God, rather than one more proof of Abraham's patient
obedience, is supported by the two stories of Hagar and
Ishmael. Hagar the foreigner, the slave, the concubine, is
the one character in the text who is likened to Abraham,
and in no small way. She has a great historical destiny
through her son, which is announced to her by an angel
in exuberant terms that explicitly recall the Lord's promises to Abraham: "I will multiply thy seed exceedingly,
that it shall not be numbered for multitude." Weary of

her mistress's bitter resentment of a situation her mistress has brought about, her pregnancy, Hagar runs off into the wilderness. This is a text or a world where anything could be true and therefore nothing is without meaning. The angel, who is the Lord, knows where Hagar is and in what state of mind, and He is ready to comfort her. For her as for Abraham His assurances exceed belief—descendants who cannot be numbered can hardly be imagined—but first of all there will be a son. I have mentioned before that for Hagar this promise comes in the language of annunciation, its first appearance in the Bible.

Nothing is described to let us imagine her experience of these two theophanies. Hagar says she has seen God and lived. More to be noted, God has seen her. Abraham is a prince among pastoralists while Hagar is a slave sick of mistreatment. The Lord and the text create an equivalency between them that is unique in the Hebrew Bible.

The desire for children and the love of them is central to the Hebrew Bible, as is loyalty to them despite all and grief at their loss. Like Abraham, Hagar comes near losing her son, in her case because the godly father of the child, to be rid of him, sends the two of them into the wilderness. Ishmael is born because Sarah and Abraham are desperate for a son, and now they send him away, perhaps to die. This is as perverse in its way as the Lord's demanding the sacrificial death of the long-promised Isaac. We see the grief of the slave Hagar in a choice that seems characteristic of her, to attempt to distance herself, to make at least a gesture toward escape from the unbearable. If the narrative were chronological, Ishmael would be an adolescent at this point, but Hagar "cast the child under one of the shrubs,'" language that suggests he is very young, a babe in arms. There is rage suggested in the possibly ungentle word *cast*, and care in the fact that she places him in the shade. "And she went, and sat her down over against him a good way off, as it were a bow shot: for she said, 'Let me not see the death of the child.'" But she cannot leave him, either. Whether she hears the cries of the child from this distance is not clear. But "God heard the voice of the lad; and the angel of God called to Hagar out of heaven."

The story of the binding of Isaac follows that of Hagar and Ishmael, after some brief business about the use of a well. And just at the point where "Abraham stretched forth his hand, and took the knife to slay his son," the Lord intervenes again, and in the same way. "The angel of the LORD called unto him out of heaven." Hagar sees a well of water, Abraham sees a ram caught in a thicket. The parallel is very close.

At any time before the era of mass literacy, say before the seventeenth or eighteenth century, the habits of attention to a narrative would have been aural, so repetition and its near equivalents would have been important and welcome. The Baal Cycle, a series of boisterous tales of the

Canaanite gods, is full of repetition, speeches, and scenes recounted verbatim and recounted again. The cycle is very unlike Hebrew Scripture, dramatic and incantatory, mythic in the strict sense, having only gods among its characters. The Canaanite pantheon were a turbulent lot. It is easy to imagine a crowd of worshippers chanting along with the more stirring threats and denunciations.

Hebrew Scripture is intended as history, a very different thing. But the conventions of its telling can reasonably be seen as influenced by the cadences of myth. Parallelism is a sophisticated form of repetition used very characteristically in Hebrew poetry for emphasis, clarity, or contrast. These lines are from Isaiah 29: "Thou shalt be brought down, and shalt speak out of the ground, and thy speech shall be low out of the dust, and thy voice shall be, as of one that hath a familiar spirit, out of the ground, and thy speech shall whisper out of the dust." Each varied repetition reinforces the thought. The story of Ishmael prepares our understanding of the more complex and epochal story of Abraham and Isaac. Both reflect on the nature of God, the first in its intimate care for a very humble woman, the second in its rejection of child sacrifice, and both in that they are instances of God's ultimate faithfulness to His promises. If the point were to create a flawless narrative, changes would have to be made so that both Ishmael and Isaac could plausibly be older than these narratives suggest they are. Instead the stories are placed together at the climax of the epic of Abraham for the emphasis created by their comparability, without respect to chronology and without change to their traditional form. This combination of freedom and conservatism in the use of traditional materials would be consistent with the historical method of Genesis.

The Baal Cycle is myth and the Genesis stories are history because Scripture is about human beings in human circumstances, which are not only continuously changing but also oriented toward a future time from a basis in a known past. "I will make of thee a great nation," says the Lord to a man with one child. Obviously a great deal must happen before this promise can be fulfilled. The text, the redactors, the community know that what was needed has happened, that the sacred past makes significant everything that has, and will, come after it.

In the narrative of Isaac's adulthood, repetition and parallelism are strikingly important elements, leading up to a scene of deep emotional complexity, as great a scene as any in the Hebrew Bible. Before it, Isaac is characterized as a kind of absence. We are told that Abraham's brother Nahor has had children by his wife and his concubine. This is the beginning of the story of Isaac's marriage and the next generation of the covenant family. Then we are told that Sarah has died at one hundred twenty-seven years old, the only woman in the Bible to have her age at death recorded. Abraham negotiates with the Hittites for a burial place for her. The Hittites courteously offer to give him the cave, and he courteously insists on paying them for it. Then Abraham, "old, and well stricken in age," sends a trusted servant to find a wife for Isaac among the family of Nahor. The life of Abraham, first of the patriarchs, has reached its denouement.

Since Isaac is forty, certainly old enough to marry, he might be expected to have some part in arranging his marriage. The servant asks Abraham whether Isaac should return with him to the house of Nahor if the girl will not follow him, the servant, back to Canaan. Abraham says no, he should not. So the servant is to act as proxy. The success of his journey rests entirely with him. He is as richly equipped and attended as if he himself were the prospective groom. This servant might be or might as well be the Eliezer of Damascus who childless Abraham feared would become his heir. The wealth of his entourage will be more remarkable over against the desperate journey of Isaac's son Jacob to the same family, where he will find two wives, one more than he intended. Here it is contrasted with the meager welcome Isaac will offer his bride.

This is the first time Abraham's great wealth is made visible—ten camels, weighty gold bracelets, a troop of followers. Rebekah draws water enough to slake the thirst of camels and men, a truly prodigious feat, which it is probably fair to interpret as excitement at all this. The text pauses over and repeats the ceremonious speeches and courtesies that pass among these stranger kinfolk, a status the servant enjoys as proxy. At their first meeting he puts a nose ring and bracelets on Rebekah, like a suitor or a husband. Rebekah's family ask whether she agrees to this marriage. Then "the servant brought forth jewels of silver, and jewels of gold, and raiment," and gives "precious things" to her mother and brother. Her family urge her to stay with them a little longer, but she follows the servant without hesitation, accepting the assurance that is intended by all this decorum and munificence.

Rebekah and the servant arrive at the place where Isaac is staying, apparently unannounced. He is walking in the field, meditating. "He lifted up his eyes, and saw, and, behold, the camels were coming." On his part, no words, no gestures, no gifts for Rebekah. He takes her into the tent—the Jewish Publication Society translation has "the tent of his mother Sarah." She became his wife and he loved her, "and Isaac was comforted after his mother's death." The journey of the servant is the longest continuous story in Genesis. Its ending is an abrupt anticlimax.

The Jewish Publication Society interprets the detail about the tent being Sarah's to mean that continuity is preserved. This may be true. This understanding of it is not inconsistent with the fact that Rebekah is an unhappy woman, and that her household, the first generation to carry forward the covenant and the tradition of Abraham, is also unhappy.

What is theological about watching domestic malaise and turmoil work its way through these lives? Let us say that God lets human beings be human beings, and that His will is accomplished through or despite them but is never dependent on them. The remarkable realism of the Bible, the voices it captures, the characterization it achieves, are products of an interest in the human that has no parallel in ancient literature. The Lord stands back, so to speak. The text does not blur the unlikeness of the mortal and the divine by giving us demigods. Its great interest is in the children of Adam, who are in every way a mystery, and the singular object of God's loyalty, which is another mystery. The covenant having been given to Abraham with the understanding that his descendants would learn justice and righteousness through him, these few people, Isaac and his family, then Jacob and his, might be expected to be governed by his history and example. Instead they seem as adrift in error and circumstance as anyone else.

Theology is the study of God; anthropology is the study of humankind. Why are we so brilliant? Why are we so self-defeating and self-destructive? How is the diversity of languages to be accounted for? How do tribes and nations form and spread themselves over the earth? What constitutes a religious culture, and how does it perpetuate itself? These are all questions of anthropology, using the word in the modern sense. The Hebrew Bible raises them and responds to them in its own terms. The questions themselves indicate where the interest of the text lies—with humankind, God's image, among whom words like *justice* and *righteousness* have meaning, as they do when they are used of Him. Modern anthropology has tended to build upward or outward or downward from reductionist definitions, humankind as naked ape, as phenotype of the selfish gene. Biblical anthropology begins with an exalted conception of humanity, then ponders our errors and deficiencies and our capacities for grace and truth, within the world of meaningful freedom created for them by an omnipotent God. This seems paradoxical, but sustaining paradox is the genius of the text.

Near the end of Genesis, Jacob stands before Pharaoh. He has been saved from famine in Canaan by his son Joseph, who has become powerful in Egypt. The great man asks him, How old art thou? Jacob answers that he will not live as long as his fathers did. He has grown very old in fewer years, enduring a life of poverty and sorrow. He is the third patriarch, the eponymous ancestor of the nation Israel, which at that time will not exist for centuries. He has received the great promises of the covenant, including possession of the land he will only return to as an embalmed corpse. His narrative is written from the perspective of history, in the knowledge he does not share, that, long after the days of Abraham, Isaac, and Jacob, their faith will be vindicated. Therefore at every step of the way it is vindicated, though rarely apparently or intrusively. The covenant will endure through a thousand difficulties that make the life of Jacob seem a most improbable part of providential history. In the text, his life is a brilliant working out of the interaction of human freedom and divine will, the first of these leading to error, guilt, and misfortune, answered by a kind of divine tact that allows the wonderful character of Jacob/Israel to assume its full pathos and dignity within His gracious purpose.

Isaac's wife is barren, as biblical women tend to be whose children when they come will be people of great consequence. An aspect of the humanism of Scripture is its awareness that history and everything borne along in history, nations and cultures and the lore that sustains them, proceed life by life, generation by mortal generation. In the case of Rebekah's children, the covenant line seems threatened not because it depends on a sole inheritor like Isaac but because there are two potential heirs, twin brothers, who contend with each other even in the womb. Rebekah, alone in Scripture, laments the discomforts of her pregnancy. She is the vigorous girl who was able to draw hundreds of gallons of water for a stranger's camels, the bride wooed by a courtly servant and by the display of his master's great wealth and munificence, the beautiful wife seized by another Philistine king named Abimelech, who, in an abbreviated repetition of this story, does not touch her and responds with indignation to the lie he was told, that she was Isaac's sister—which was not true in this case as it was, strictly speaking, in the case of Abraham and Sarah. This Abimelech is terse and harsh in dismissing Isaac, and as certain as the other kings have been that sleeping with a married woman "shouldest have brought guiltiness upon us." The king figures things out for himself. When Isaac "had been there a long time," the king sees him "sporting with Rebekah his wife" and sends them away. Isaac's accumulation of wealth is seen by the Philistines not as a blessing of God, though it is, but as a threat, and he is asked to leave. Comparison of this incident with the earlier version of the story suggests that Isaac, within a way of life that is generally his father's, is a lesser personage, at least in the view of his world. His major act is to restore wells Abraham had dug and restore the names Abraham had given them. This does not mean that his place in the succession of patriarchs is less worthy or essential than that of the others, since the will of God is as active as ever in his generation. Its steadfastness is proved in the unremarkable adulthood of the endlessly promised and awaited Isaac.

Did Abraham send his servant to find a wife for Isaac, and forbid him to take Isaac with him, because Isaac himself was unprepossessing? Did the servant mislead a little, allowing it to seem that the master for whom he acted was Isaac rather than Abraham? Would the bride have been pleased to be brought to Sarah's tent, and to comfort Isaac for the death of his mother?

The text perfected very early the art of showing rather than telling. These are interesting details, certainly available to misinterpretation thousands of years after the mores they reflect have passed out of all memory. But in a long and telling scene we find Rebekah putting the covenant succession at great risk, having contrived a scheme that will play cruelly on the helplessness of Isaac's old age. Bitterness might lie behind this, and determination to win at an old game of favoring one son over the other. Rebekah's voice is heard in her distress at the miseries of her pregnancy: "If it be so, why am I thus?" In the Hebrew, her sentence is unfinished. The word *live* is normally supplied in translations—Why do I live? But the break, as if her feelings exceed her power of expression, seems in character.

Rebekah speaks a second time in terms of existential despair or exasperation about Esau's foreign wives. "I am weary of my life because of the daughters of Heth: if Jacob take a wife of the daughters of Heth, such as these which are of the daughters of the land, what good shall my life do me?" Here she is trying to create a pretext for Jacob to flee the homicidal rage of his brother. Still, this is a very distinctive voice. She has expectations she cannot bear to have disappointed, though, I speculate, they have been disappointed since she first saw Isaac walking in that field. Disappointment is a very familiar turn in human affairs, therefore always relevant to the larger question of the divine providence at work in it.

Rebekah takes the question of her pregnancy to the Lord, whose reply is distant, oracular, a poem. Two nations struggle within her, the older will serve the younger. No angel speaks, no comfort is offered beyond the assurance that history will follow from the struggles in her womb. In general, He seems to be stepping away from these mortals who are the bearers of sacred history, giving latitude to their humanity but, crucially, providentially, remaining loyal to His purposes. It is not always obvious that God does love humankind as such or that He should, but this is, of course, a human view of the matter. Abraham was coaxed along in the way that he should go with visions and promises. For the generations that follow, divine intent has a subtler but no less efficacious touch.

On what may have seemed a day of no special moment—Esau coming in famished from hunting, Jacob among the tents, cooking a pot of lentils—a momentous thing happens. The birthright, which conveys leadership of the family, passes from Esau to Jacob. Esau declares he is dying of hunger, Jacob sees leverage in his brother's demand for food and offers him a mess of pottage, as the old translation has it, in exchange for his birthright. Esau agrees, eats, and leaves. There is no sense here that there is much in the way of family to lead. Isaac has one wife and two sons. There are no servants to be seen. The family prepare their own food. This is striking, since Isaac is wealthy enough in his own right to alarm the Philistines and he is Abraham's heir as well. A throng of servants attended Abraham, a small army when needed, circumcised whether purchased or born in his household. They all vanish, from the point of view of the text, along with the wives and concubines and their children. This might help account for Esau's indifference to the role birth order had given him, making it seem a fairly minor thing. It also prepares for the years of stark and lonely poverty that will await Jacob, birthright and blessing not at all withstanding. If Jacob had simply been one more princely pastoralist, the meaning of his place in providential history would be very different.

The covenant relationship between the Lord and the children of Abraham is defined again and again by the elimination of what might be considered intrinsic to it, the right of an eldest son as inheritor, for example, or the orderly and conscious movement of this unique honor and responsibility from generation to generation. In the case of Esau and Jacob, primogeniture is as murky a principle as could well be imagined. Jacob is born holding on to his brother's heel and is given a name that means "supplanter." So, from the beginning, birth order is not a reliable predictor of status. This deviation from presumed custom will recur in various ways throughout the Hebrew Bible. Here it has a special character, a surprising element of calculation. There is little reason to suppose that Esau is really at the point of starvation. He is brusque with hunger and impatience, rude and demanding toward Jacob, gone as soon as he has had his fill. For Esau to have accepted this meal at the price of his standing and his responsibility within the family does, as the text says, show contempt for his birthright. Jacob might have been surprised at the effect of what was meant only as a bitter little joke. It was brought on in that moment by Esau's self-engrossed impulsiveness, hardly a promising trait in someone destined to act as a figure of authority. Jacob's behavior is not handsome, either. Yet this is providence working itself out. Esau with his craving for "the red pottage" might have caught Jacob brooding on the thought that he had the favor of his mother only because his father so strongly preferred Esau. And here he was among the tents, stirring a pot, while his robust and hairy brother was off in the fields with quiver and bow, doing just what his father loved him for. If Jacob had been a little less envious, if Esau had been a bit less boorish, this epochal turn of things, this wholly unimpressive moment, would never have entered sacred history. This is an instance of the fact that the covenant is not contingent upon human

virtue, even human intention. It is sustained by the will
of God, which is so strong and steadfast that it can allow
space within providence for people to be who they are, for
humanity to be what it is.

Esau is the father of Edom, a country with whom Israel in the future would have a contentious history. If their
ancestor appears primitive here, it is worth remembering
that the Bible's other great Edomite, Job, represents the
wisdom tradition at its most rigorous and eloquent. The
book of Job is set in patriarchal times, which suggests that
the association of Edom with wisdom was considered to
be very ancient. There is also the characteristically biblical awareness that even an inveterate enemy is a brother,
to set limits to the interpretation of Esau's character as
primarily a disparagement of Edom.

"When Isaac was old and his eyes were dim, so that
he could not see, he called Esau his eldest son." Isaac's
intention is to give Esau his blessing before he dies. In the
Jewish translation, it is his "innermost" blessing. First he
wants Esau to prepare a meal of game for him, "savoury
meat, such as I love." Typically for the Hebrew Bible, gaze
is averted from the question of the kind of wild creature
Esau will hunt and kill.

Rebekah is listening. She has a little window of time
for a scheme to defeat her old husband's intention and
secure the blessing for Jacob. She says, embellishing a little, that Isaac wishes to bless Esau "before the LORD." So
she "commands" Jacob to bring two kids from the flock
that she will prepare, savory food for Isaac. She can do

this more quickly than Esau, who has to stalk and kill a wild animal before he can prepare it. Jacob objects that his father will detect the ruse when he touches him, since he is not hairy like Esau. He is afraid that if he is found out by his father he will seem to be mocking him and be cursed rather than blessed. Rebekah has a solution. She dresses Jacob in Esau's best garments, and she puts the skins of the freshly slaughtered kids "upon his hands, and upon the smooth of his neck."

In all this Jacob obeys his mother. He could only be grotesque, decked out in a disguise that will work if it does only because his father is blind and frail and defenseless. The ruse is needed because Esau is the older son and also because he is the son Isaac loves. Clearly his craving for the wild game Esau provides as hunter can be satisfied by Rebekah's preparation of animals from his own flocks.

Isaac is doubtful, when Jacob first speaks to him, wary of a deception of exactly the kind that is being perpetrated on him. But the skins persuade him. When he embraces Jacob to confer the blessing "he smelled the smell of his raiments, and blessed him, and said, 'See, the smell of my son is as the smell of a field which the LORD hath blessed.'" Jacob, in the course of this shameful deception of his dying father, hears his father praising Esau, expressing love for him, loving the thought of his open, vigorous life, those ways in which Esau is unlike Jacob. And he learns or is reminded that his father distrusts him, Jacob.

Isaac's very deep suspicion suggests that relations

among his family were, at best, strained. We learn in this scene that Jacob with those lentils has indeed possessed himself of the birthright. The new scheme of deception is devised and effected by Rebekah, who, events will suggest, might be as much motivated by malice toward her husband as favor toward her son. Jacob, the supplanter, the supposed beneficiary of the ruse, may have forgotten the meaning of the blessing. The story of Abraham's family to this point has been that, through them, the world would learn justice and righteousness, and that the Lord's gracious intervention in the life of the world would eventuate as blessing through their lives and generations, the birth and life of Isaac being crucial. And here he is, at the end of a relatively uneventful life, vulnerable to being deprived of his last powerful and loving act, and knowing it: "The voice is Jacob's voice, but the hands are the hands of Esau."

The text itself is a gracious and divine act, so the ways in which it is remarkable merit consideration. Here two of its great figures are determining the course of history—on one side weakness, custom, and fond partiality, on the other, deceit and shame and, no doubt, filial reverence and simple pity, divine intent embracing it all. The very existence of the Hebrew Scriptures, as much as the narratives they contain, testifies to the steadfastness of the God of Abraham, Isaac, and Jacob, a name the Creator of heaven and earth has chosen for Himself. The text, in its great interest in humankind, looks on from a greater distance, with an eye toward unrealized history, and also from a nearer proximity, at the level of "innermost" feeling, than any merely human observer could approach.

Jacob will not be a conventional national hero. He will be exceptional for shrewdness, usually deployed to achieve or secure what the Lord intended for him in any case, as in the matter of the birthright and blessing. (Could history have taken its appropriate course if the supplanter had not agreed to engage in this deceit? If he had dealt righteously with his father? Did he have that option? What becomes of moral judgment if an unrighteous act works for good, without or despite the actor's intention?) In his turn Jacob will be the victim of the shrewdness of Laban, brother of Rebekah, which, for all the vexation it costs him, will also work out as it should. He will be estranged from his father, mother, and brother but will be the loving father of twelve sons, some of whom will cause him grief as great as his love but who, in their descendants, are the beginning of the promised multitude.

Jacob has stood by his father's couch, just sufficiently disguised to fool a blind man, finding his father a little harder to dupe than he could have hoped and knowing Esau might return at any time. The old man asks, "Who art thou, my son?" In that moment, he is neither Esau nor Jacob, since as supplanter he rejects his given role and pretends to a role that is not his. He answers that he is Esau "thy firstborn" and offers him the game that is not game. Isaac is suspicious. He asks how he could have found it so quickly. Jacob replies, "Because the LORD thy

God brought it to me," invoking the name of God in a lie, implying that the Lord had a part in this moment—as, in a larger sense, He did have. Even after Isaac has felt Jacob's hands and decided to bless him, he asks once more, "Art thou my very son Esau?" Assured that he is, he kisses him and blesses him with "the dew of heaven, and the fatness of the earth . . . Let people serve thee, and nations bow down to thee: be lord over thy brethren, and let thy mother's sons bow down to thee . . ." These blessings sound like the dreams of the boy Joseph, also not a firstborn son, that made him so odious to his brothers, and were, finally, fulfilled. Primogeniture in the Bible is important chiefly for the disruption and discord the notion causes.

Jacob goes away, blessed, but not in a state of mind normally associated with that word. Esau enters with the savory food he has prepared for Isaac, and the scene is recast, father and son—and no blessing, in its place only grief and outrage. This paralleling, repetition with a difference, brilliantly frames an essential question: What is this blessing, if it can be stolen? More questions will arise in the course of time. What is the blessing if it makes its possessor a desperate fugitive? If he is reduced by poverty to a kind of debt bondage while his defrauded brother flourishes in his own country? Taking Isaac's blessing to be a sign of the Lord's faithfulness to Abraham's descendants through generations, it is above the reach of human malice, error, or incomprehension. It concedes little or nothing to human expectation. That God intends the unfolding of His blessing through human history, to all

the families of earth, means that in its nature it anticipates what for human purposes is unforeseeable, that it
does not reveal its whole meaning in the course of any life
or generation or era. This is the freedom of God within
which humankind is free. Jacob has a great destiny, which
is entangled with great sorrow and difficulty. We know, as
this man could never know, what consequences would follow from his struggles and even the apparent rescue from
his struggles, when he and his family make their descent
into Egypt.

Jacob is sometimes seen as a picaresque figure, the
kind of prankster found in folktales. It is likely that stories
about him were part of an oral tradition and were influenced by its conventions, and equally likely that the writers
who created the written literature would have been influenced by these same conventions. But writers understand
and use the methods of storytellers. These ancient writers
would surely have listened to the lore of their culture with
intense interest, and reverence, as well, and have found it
authenticated by signs of ancient origins. Our "popular"
culture is the product of capital and technology and mar-
keting. It is a best guess at interests and tastes that it also
instills and exploits. It has only accidental points of contact with collective identity or memory. At the same time,
a modern prejudice, to associate a theologically important
narrative with folklore is often to diminish its capacity for
meaning.

If the episode were only a tale about how Jacob the
supplanter stole his brother's blessing, the second itera-

tion, the scene between Esau and Isaac, would not have such weight as it does. The voices of Esau and Isaac are very striking, significant because voices full of human passion could have been heard in any number of tents and dwelling places across the ancient world, as in our world. The narrative of Scripture has moved with astonishing speed from "Let there be light" to this intimate scene of shared grief and haplessness. There is no incongruity in this. Human beings are at the center of it all. Love and grief are, in this infinite Creation, things of the kind we share with God. The fact that they have their being in the deepest reaches of our extensionless and undiscoverable souls only makes them more astonishing, over against the roaring cosmos. That they exist at all can only be proof of a tender solicitude.

When Esau comes to his father with the game he has prepared for him, Isaac "trembled very exceedingly," telling him someone else has come with game and he has blessed him, "yea, and he shall be blessed." At these words Esau "cried a great and exceeding bitter cry . . . 'Bless me, even me also, O my father!'" The son who despised his birthright is deeply anguished at this loss. The first words Isaac has said to Jacob in blessing him, that he loves the smell of Esau's garments, means that the blessing would have been, whatever else, an act of love toward a dear son, and toward sensuous memory. His craving for game is a kind of engagement in Esau's life, which savors of life itself to an old man who has lost most of the threads of connection to the world.

But this blessing does not belong to Isaac, or arise out of his great love for Esau. His son asks him, "Hast thou not reserved a blessing for me? . . . Hast thou but one blessing, my father? Bless me, even me also, O my father." And Esau "lifted up his voice, and wept." Isaac tries to give Esau a blessing of his own, but it is very different from the one Jacob has taken from him. The translations of Isaac's blessing by the Jewish Publication Society and the Revised Standard Version of the Bible differ sharply, for a very interesting reason. The JPS translation is as follows:

> See, your abode shall enjoy the fat of the earth
> And the dew of heaven above.
> Yet by your sword you shall live,
> And you shall serve your brother;
> But when you grow restive,
> You shall break his yoke from your neck.

The RSV has:

> Behold, away from the fatness of the earth shall your
>   dwelling be,
> and away from the dew of heaven on high.

The remaining lines are substantially the same in both translations.

According to the JPS note, the preposition *min*, which appears twice in these phrases, may or may not be "understood to express deprivation." English has no way of expressing the ambiguity of this utterance. But Esau would, of course, have heard it. I have no name for the emotion I imagine coursing through him as he heard this equivocation from his father's mouth. Given the oracular character of these words, which seem to foretell more than to bless, the ambiguity may have surprised Isaac himself. Altogether, Esau's expectations are bitterly disappointed, and he reckons up the harm his brother has done him, first depriving him of his birthright, then his blessing. Word comes to Rebekah that Esau plans to kill Jacob after Isaac has died and the period of mourning for him has ended. Once again she takes a crucial, if discreditable, part in sacred history. She tells Jacob about Esau's intentions, that he "doth comfort himself, purposing to kill thee." She tells Jacob to flee to her brother Laban and stay with him until Esau's wrath has cooled. "Then I will send, and fetch thee from thence." Here that important literary structure, parallelism, again comes into play. Jacob retraces the long journey made by the nameless servant sent to find a wife for Isaac. This same purpose is now only a pretext invented by her so that Isaac will agree to let Jacob leave. She is tormented, she says, by the thought of his possible marriage to "daughters of the land," and Isaac therefore blesses his journey to Padan-aram.

There is an irony here that deserves to be savored. Rebekah has shattered the covenant family, alienated its sons. She has, to all appearances, defeated their father in his desire to perform the signal act of his life, the conferring of the blessing he received from Abraham to another generation. She has potentially released the uncontrollable energies of revenge, threatening the covenant as an ongoing heritage. She asks Jacob, "Why should I be deprived also of you both in one day?" as if she had no part in the matter. Endogamy, or at least marriage within a cultural or religious group, is very common historically. The capstone of Hagar's happiness is that she can give Ishmael an Egyptian wife. But it is hard to imagine a wife and mother of any sort more profoundly disruptive to her family than this close kinswoman, Rebekah. Nevertheless, Isaac agrees, Jacob obeys, and birthright and blessing are carried away from the tents of Isaac in the person of a resourceless fugitive.

Repetition and parallelism are also framing devices that encourage particular attention to what they enclose. These two journeys enclose the life of Isaac from his marriage to his death. The contrast between them, opulence in the first instance, desperation in the second, indicates a decline of fortunes, certainly. There seems to have been a radiance of blessedness, a flourishing visible to the world in Abraham, and, in a lesser degree, in Isaac. For Jacob there are poverty and obscurity. Yet, over time, he also flourishes.

The *inclusio* might also be intended to invite our attention to Rebekah, who lurks and listens and schemes to great effect. Though the text says that Isaac loved Esau and Rebekah loved Jacob, there is really no evidence that she loved anyone. Playing on the helplessness of the patriarch as he approaches death is abysmally unloving. She is ready to defraud Esau, supposedly to benefit Jacob, but she sends Jacob off without bride price or gifts to make himself welcome in Padan-aram, with no more than his staff. She tells him she will summon him back home when it is safe, but there is no evidence that she ever contacts him, not in all those years he was indentured to her brother. Unlikely as it seems, and this is surely the point, the Jacob of indolence and guile, through his singular life, emerges as a towering figure among the patriarchs. This is not to say that he became a self-made man but that the Lord was faithful to His promise to Abraham. Odd words like *feckless* and *hapless* can be applied to Jacob, and then, in time, words like *pitiable* and *tragic*. His greatness never transcends his humanity. And if it is bad feminism to say that Rebekah's liveliness and vigor turned to resentment, scheming, and manipulation, her role in this seeming disaster was providential. The very mingled characters in Genesis, in the fact of their flaws and errors, should give hope to us all.

The fugitive Jacob "lighted upon to a certain place, and tarried there all night, because the sun was set; and he took of the stones of that place, and put them for his pillows, and lay down in that place to sleep." The "certain place" will be called Beth-el, the House of God, an early shrine that will be destroyed by the reforming king Josiah centuries on. Here Jacob has his dream of angels ascending and descending a ladder whose top reached to heaven. He also experiences a full-fledged theophany, a vision of God making the promises to him that He had made to Abraham and Isaac. The land will be his and his descendants', who will be like the dust of the earth. All the families will bless themselves by them. To this lonely man, the Lord says, "Behold, I am with thee, and will keep thee in all places whither thou goest," with more assurances.

Jacob, waking, says, "Surely the LORD is in this place; and I knew it not." This is just the realization Abraham came to in his dealings with the righteous Abimelech. The notes in my Bible interpret the events at Beth-el in terms of ancient religious belief, which is, presumably, the state of belief to be assumed in a man of Jacob's time and place, and not to be considered individually meaningful—in a patriarch who has just had a vision of the Lord. "Ancient religious belief" of the kind that makes God limited and local, to be found in one place and not another, can also be called paganism. This distinction, between monotheism and polytheism, is so central to the Hebrew Scriptures that the appearance of pagan elements in the text should not be assumed to be naïve. Prevalent methods of criticism assume precisely this, claiming historicism.

Before he left for Padan-aram, Jacob received another blessing from Isaac, who prayed that El Shaddai, God Almighty, may "give thee the blessing of Abraham, to thee, and to thy seed with thee." Clearly Jacob is indeed the heir of the covenant despite all. What this means to him and how he understands it seems to me to be the question the text is posing here. This is another framing of the independence of the covenant from its human bearers, even while it is profoundly associated with this fallible and vulnerable little clan. Its aloofness has to do with the nature of God, His faithfulness, first of all, which could not be absolute if it could be affected by the thoughts and actions of creatures so volatile as these mortals are. A covenant, a bond of faithfulness, is the form of relationship the Lord offers humankind.

Then there is the fact of His oneness and His omnipotence. I may appear to be imposing terms not appropriate to the religious consciousness of a literature as ancient as Genesis. But this can only seem to be true if the first Creation narrative is excluded from a reckoning of the theological universe Genesis presents to us. Elohim speaks into being even Being itself. There is no other God, and there is no limit to God's effective power in a Creation that embodies the Will that brought it into existence. The elegance of this metaphysical poem is so striking that composition of it is assigned to a tradition of priestly writers in a later period. But there are real limits to how much would be gained by this. Nothing in antiquity could provide a context that would make it less singular. Our most contemporary cosmologists might say that the utterances of God are information and the moon and stars and the sea creatures are the hologram, at a sharp loss in poetry and implication.

The Hebrew Scriptures are consistent with this vision, except in the passages in Genesis where Abraham and his kin are being instructed by the Lord in the Lord's own nature. The creation of all humanity in the persons of Adam and Eve populated the world with one divine image.

The Flood narrative, in the Hebrew version, describes a humankind utterly known to God and an earth entirely exposed to His judgment. In the episode of the dream, Jacob is right that there is something holy in that place, and wrong to find the *place* holy rather than the moment and the circumstance of his own investment by God with the covenant of Abraham. The Lord tells Jacob that He will be with him wherever he goes. All places are the same.

There are Babylonian bas-reliefs of gods carrying bricks up ladders, building ziggurats that are meant to reach heaven. The "gate of heaven" recalls Babel, "the gate of God," which did indeed bring God to earth, so the story goes, but only in order to put an end to such presumption. These are names Jacob applies to the place where he has slept, an etiology of Beth-el that suggests uneasiness with the localism that is implied in it. Then, after God has essentially claimed him for the purposes of His covenant with Abraham and Isaac, Jacob makes a remarkable vow: "If God will be with me, and will keep me in this way that I go, and will give me bread to eat, and raiment to put on, so that I come again to my father's house in peace; then shall the LORD be my God: and this stone, which I have set for a pillar, shall be God's house." He seems to be making the Lord's status as his God conditional on God's good behavior, by the standards of what one might hope from a personal deity, a household god. Making an anointed stone His house is a miscalculation of the same kind. None of this suggests that Jacob, to this point, has given any real thought to God or to the covenant. This is another instance of assurance that the covenant can be in any degree of apparent peril and still be firm and safe because it is the will of God toward the patriarchs and their descendants, and toward all the families of earth. The covenant is much more the heritage of Jacob than it could ever be if he had had to deserve it.

I say this with all possible respect and reverence: The text has a sense of humor. Jacob, to escape the consequences of his trickery, flees to his mother's brother Laban, that is, into the arms of another trickster, one who is not at all above exploiting the necessitous state Jacob's mother has brought him to. Jacob has gone along with a plot instigated by Rebekah, lying disgracefully, true, but doing no more than she has told him to do. This clan of Padan-aram folk are a slippery lot. Jacob might be said to have come by his foibles honestly.

The character of Laban begins to emerge in his response to the arrival of Abraham's emissary, the nameless servant who will bring Rebekah home to Isaac. When Laban sees the gold ring and bracelets the stranger has given Rebekah, and sees him standing with his camels, he welcomes him effusively. "Come in, thou blessed of the LORD; wherefore standest thou without?" It is as if the wealth and munificence were the servant's, though the servant, so scrupulous in carrying out his mission, makes clear that he is only acting for Abraham. When Jacob arrives with nothing but kinship to recommend him, Laban runs to embrace him, kisses him, and brings him into his house, saying, "Surely thou art my bone and my flesh." Then we learn that for a month Jacob has been making himself useful, serving Laban in ways for which he would normally receive pay. Since he has no gifts to offer the family this would be a form of compensation for their hospitality, the best equivalent he can offer to the servant's costly ornaments. Laban formalizes the situation. "Because thou art my brother, shouldest thou therefore serve me for nought?" Jacob, perhaps still thinking of himself more as kinsman than hireling, says he wishes to marry Rachel, the daughter of Laban whom he has met at a well, as happened with the servant and Rebekah. Laban agrees that this would be highly appropriate, and Jacob, in the exuberance of love, offers to serve Laban seven years for Rachel. Rebekah has sent him to Padan-aram with the search for a bride as pretext for leaving his family. He actually, in his own person, finds the love of his life, and the prospect of marriage to her functions for him, and for Laban, as a form of debt that must be paid in full before they can be married. When that day, or evening and morning, comes, Jacob the supplanter will find that his chosen bride has been supplanted by her older sister, Leah, with whom he has consummated marriage. Laban has arranged this, he says, on the grounds that custom in his country did not allow a younger daughter to be married before an older one, and this could be true, though he might have mentioned the problem to Jacob seven years earlier. In any case, Jacob—a surprisingly trusting man—agrees to serve Laban another seven years, still for the hand of Rachel. Unfavored Leah will be the mother of most of Jacob's children. She will be essential to the emergence of a Hebrew people and the unfolding of the covenant. Providence is active in all this, perhaps itself the ultimate trickster. It even drops the veil of misfortune from time to time to show an unexpected face.

The Lord has compassion on an unloved wife, and great names enter history—Reuben, Simeon, Levi, Judah. This is a beautiful detail, the kind of thing that is to be found only in the Hebrew Scriptures. God is not so engrossed in His own will that eponyms of the twelve tribes are not first of all the pride and comfort of a sorrowful woman. The interactions of human circumstance, providence, and grace are pure mystery, but great futurity does not minimize the power of Leah's sorrows or her hopes by exposing the workings of inevitability.

Rachel, whom Jacob loves, is childless. As Sarah had done, she gives him her maid as a wife, to bear children for her. From this marriage came Dan and Naphtali. Leah does the same, and her maid gives him Gad and Asher. After a quarrel between Rachel and Leah over mandrakes, the Lord "hearkened unto Leah," and she bears Issachar, then Zebulun, and finally a daughter, Dinah.

The text says, "And God remembered Rachel, and God hearkened to her, and opened her womb." The word *remembered* seems strange in contexts like this. To say that someone is at some point remembered implies to us that he, she, or they were, up to that point, forgotten. After four hundred years in Egypt the Lord "remembered" the Hebrew people. But He told Abraham in his dark dream that the Hebrews would pass those years in Egypt. So, difficult as it is to speak of God in terms of time, it might be useful to consider a paraphrase that could take into account the role of time in the eventuation of God's intentions and promises, which are not contingent but are constant over time. Joseph is set apart from his brothers as the cherished only son of a favored wife. His relationship to his brothers, like the relationship of Esau and Jacob, will become a factor in the history of Israel. If this sounds like contingency, this is a consequence of the fact that God realizes His purposes in and through the lives of human beings. Scripture is centered on human lives.

The infant patriarchs of the next generation enter the story in a kind of competition for the love of Jacob, which Leah cannot win no matter how many sons she has and Rachel cannot lose although she is angry with him out of grief at her childlessness. If the passage sets these women in an unflattering light that might not seem to serve the interests of the narrative, it also poses a philosophical question, or perhaps suggests a philosophical answer, having to do with causality. First, from the point of view of the women, births or barrenness are matters of the body, whence the quarrel over mandrakes. Second, the text speaks of them in terms of God's kindness to a despised wife, then to a childless one. Third, the very names of their children invoked here recall the covenant and the imminent, crucial movement of sacred history into Egypt and beyond. The etiologies of these names associate them with the old grief and struggle in Jacob's household when he had not yet extricated himself from the snares of Laban. They record detail as quotidian as dust. Yet the fact that there was once a child whose mother named him Judah has had far-reaching consequences, an instance being my writing this book, one of hundreds or thousands with the same ultimate origin, Israel and Judea, being produced in any given year. This is objectively remarkable.

As to causality, the text offers three models, each arguably sufficient—human experience, divine act, and sacred history—which differs from history as it is usually understood in that it has all the reality of things passing or past irrespective of the fact that in any particular the history may not have happened yet. Here, in this modest domestic turbulence, its imminence is palpable. The habits of rationalism would prefer human experience, the model that is in principle verifiable, or falsifiable, which may mean only accessible to our methods of inquiry as the others are not. The hypothetical rabbis I imagine as the mind brooding on such questions, good realists all, would have been interested, I believe, in pondering the three models together. God's covenant and God's active grace are profoundly implicated in—braided into—plain human physicality. If God is a given, then Being should be expected to bear the mark of a complexity that exceeds our understanding. As it does in any case. So contradiction and anomaly should not act as pretexts for excluding evidence that any given conception of reality is too simple. How can the constancy

of God's historical intention be reconciled to the freedom
of His grace? The rabbis might say: As they are with Rachel and Leah. And what do these lofty things have to
do with human procreation? The rabbis might say: You
haven't been paying attention.

The tale darkens. Rachel at last bears the child she has
longed for, Joseph. The name rings with import concerning the future of Israel, and it is also a woman's prayer for
a second son. In the birth of her second son she will die.
Jacob has served out his time and more with Laban, caus-
ing him to prosper. He asks permission to separate from
him and take his family with him to Canaan, to the home
he had fled years before. Laban tries to argue that there
is a part of the debt still to be paid. By custom a departing servant should be given something from his master's
wealth. Jacob says he will take as his own the animals from
Laban's flocks that are "speckled and spotted" as well as
"all the brown cattle among the sheep." He will continue
to care for the animals that will be Laban's, to be paid on
the basis of their thriving. Jacob is acting very honorably,
accepting the terms of the exploitation he has suffered
from his uncle and trying to make the best of them. His
mildness is heroic. It is as if his former indolence has become a rare virtue. His early guilefulness distracts attention from his Abrahamic readiness to be more than just.
But Laban is always the trickster. He agrees to Jacob's
offer, then goes through the herd to find every creature

with a fleck of white and all brown lambs and sends them away with his sons, "and Jacob fed the rest of Laban's flocks." In response to Laban's bad faith, Jacob plays another trick. He takes partially stripped "rods" of poplar, almond, and plane and puts them by the wells, where the animals breed, taking care that the strongest of Laban's animals will see them. Thus, it seems, he creates herds for himself, spotted and striped. "The man increased exceedingly; and had much cattle, and maidservants, and manservants, and camels, and asses."

Jacob realizes that he has lost favor with Laban and his sons. He confers with his wives in an open field, so as not to be overheard. He tells them that the God of his father has spoken to him in a dream, telling him that it was actually He who gave him Laban's flock by making their offspring spotted and striped, and that he should return home now. The wives agree. They have their own grievances. They were sold by their father, they say. They and their children have been given nothing of the vast bride prices Jacob has paid for them in his many years of profitable labor for Laban. Laban reduces relationships to forms of servitude, and Jacob is reduced to fleeing from Laban, as if he were escaping indenture. It is pleasing and interesting that Jacob consults both of his wives, that he does not simply announce his intentions to them. Presumably they could have chosen to stay with their father's people rather than following Jacob to his.

This is the first instance in Scripture in which a vision or dream is reported to someone, rather than being evoked as if the text could give the reader or hearer a direct experience of it. We see the burning torch and smoking furnace of Abraham's dream vision. We hear the urgency of the words the angel of the Lord speaks from heaven to Hagar, then Abraham. Here we are told that Jacob reports a dream to his wives. Reported dreams will become very important as events unfold. They will lose the visionary character, the presence in them of the Lord, that Jacob has experienced here. The narrative as a whole is carefully shaped to allow for the subtlety of such change, of movement away from the world of the early patriarchy, which reflects the continuing relationship God maintains with the generations of the covenant family until they enter on those mysterious centuries in Egypt.

Jacob's tolerance of Laban's treatment of him is consistent with signs that his brother Esau is on his mind. He might feel uneasy, rebuking anyone else for guile or theft. In his dream, the Lord tells him that his trick with the stippled rods didn't actually work, or that it was so consonant with God's will that it had no independent meaning. Perhaps Jacob yearned to be unburdened in his own mind of his identity as trickster, though this trick had been his first impulse, and it had served Laban exactly right. Retaliation could hardly be more condign. Then "Jacob stole away unawares to Laban the Syrian, in that he told him not that he fled." How to react to the affronts and injuries others offer is a profound concern of Genesis from this point on. Jacob must respond to a harder question—how to react to those he himself has offended and injured.

In the case of Laban, who feels he, Jacob, is in the very act
of stealing his substance and family, he has rancor to deal
with, however unjustified.

Rachel and Leah answered, "Whatsoever God hath
said unto thee, do." So Jacob mustered his household and
the herds that were his and they fled. "He fled with all that
he had; and he rose up, and passed over the river, and set
his face toward the mount Gilead." From the Euphrates
to Gilead is a very great distance. But when Laban hears
he has left, he pursues him all that way and overtakes him.
This is another parallel structure, Laban behind him, Esau
ahead, both of them powerful, Laban furious, Esau with
much better reason to be furious. God intervenes in the
potential strife with Laban by sending him a terse dream
to the effect that he should leave Jacob unmolested. "Take
heed that thou speak not to Jacob either good or bad."
Esau is a special problem. Jacob cannot give back what
he has stolen from him nor can he offer any equivalent for
it. We are not told that God has said any word to Esau to
temper his anger. The dramatic tension is very high.

Laban must be dealt with first. Jacob camps in the hill
country of Gilead, and Laban does, too. When they speak,
Laban accuses him of theft. By his stealthy leave-taking,
Jacob has supposedly deprived Laban of the pleasure of
sending him away "with mirth, and with songs, with tabret, and with harp." And his gods have been stolen. Jacob
declares his innocence and makes one of those terrifying
vows, that "with whomsover thou findest thy gods, let him
not live." Rachel has stolen them and, child of Padan-aram

that she is, has thought of a way to trick her father by hiding them in a camel's saddle and sitting on it. She tells him that she cannot rise because of her menses, so his search is unsuccessful. We learn from this odd little episode that the Aramaeans were idolators, which might be expected of anyone at that time, and that Rachel was not one, since her ploy involved an insult to these gods that would seem dangerous to someone who believed they had power of any kind. So Rachel did not steal her father's gods because she valued them. She was moved by pique or spite, presumably. From the point of view of the text, her prank might mean that these exotic wives had become naturalized to the religion of their husband. In any case, a favorite polemical point is made, that idols are mere blocks of wood, helpless in the face of abuse. It should be noted that Jacob has no part in the theft and assumes no one in his company would have stolen them.

Laban's search of his possessions finally angers Jacob. He has tried to make his case calmly against Laban's accusations, but this blatant disrespect is more than he can tolerate, and he makes a lengthy, passionate statement of his grievances, all to the effect that he has toiled in Laban's service and made him blessed and rich, a fact Laban has confirmed independently "by experience" Laban answers, "These daughters are my daughters, and these children are my children, and these cattle are my cattle, and all that thou seest is mine." This would be true if Jacob were a departing slave. His wife and children and all the wealth his work had produced would remain with his master, excepting whatever severance custom and honor induced his master to give him. Acquisitiveness and selfishness could hardly have a broader license. Laban has insisted on seeing his nephew Jacob in this light, which if it were acted on would make slaves of his daughters and their children.

Laban's argument seems to have reached a reductio ad absurdum, its implications suddenly clear to him. "What can I do this day unto these my daughters, or unto their children which they have born?" So he proposes a covenant with Jacob, which makes argument moot, in effect a truce that God is to oversee. They share a meal. They erect a pillar and a heap of stones and agree to stay each on his own side of them. Laban makes one demand of Jacob. "If thou shalt afflict my daughters, or if thou shalt take other wives beside my daughters, no man is with us; see, God is witness betwixt me and thee." This is a wise, fatherly concern. It suggests that in their case Laban's legalistic possessiveness is a crude expression of the fact that he hates to lose them, a bully's version of an ordinary parental regret. Jacob offers a sacrifice and shares bread with "his brethren," an acknowledgment frequent in the Hebrew Bible that adversaries are, after all, family. The next morning Laban kisses his grandchildren and his daughters and blesses them and departs for Padan-aram.

• • •

The habit of reading Scripture piecemeal, whether for preaching or for the purposes of scholarly argument, or because it is considered to have its full meaning in isolated phrases or verses or episodes, is so deeply engrained that the larger structures of the text, its strategies of characterization, its arguments, can be completely overlooked. The theme of the loving father, so central to its vision at every level, from the transcendent God who loves the world to Laban, the grasping scoundrel whose love for his children finally forbids him to do them harm, is densely threaded through these stories, with all the varieties of sorrow and anguish that attend this love. That Laban is moved by feelings that stir in the heart of God is a deep statement about the metaphysics of being human.

Jacob does not win this argument. He makes his case. Laban refuses to concede anything. Mere equity is not of interest to him, nor is the fact that Jacob has done and suffered much more than even righteousness would ask. There is no leverage to be had while Laban insists on viewing Jacob as a thief who has no right even to his wives and children. Jacob does not mention to Laban that he is threatening injury to his own family, perhaps thinking this argument will have even less weight with him. Laban arrives at the realization himself.

If the strategy of the text were to make Jacob heroic in the classical style, shrewd and dominant, Laban would not have had his moment. The great figures of Scripture are not at all Homeric. They do not absorb the energies of the narrative into themselves. Granted that, when he first met Rachel at the well, Jacob performed an act of heroic strength, just as his mother had done at the same well when she watered her proxy-suitor's camels. For Rachel and her flock Jacob lifted a very heavy stone from the mouth of the well, defeating for the moment a local arrangement for sharing access to the water. But aside from this his strength is mainly to be inferred from his endurance. After the strange, sad business of the deception of Isaac and the supplanting of Esau, Jacob is patient in the face of injury, not a very zealous defender of his own interests. This may reflect the guilt he feels. Or it may be patriarchal patience and restraint. The same might have been seen in Isaac, who blesses Jacob once more, even after he knows the wrong he has done him.

On the one hand, Jacob relinquishes nothing to Laban, it being very clear to him that he owes Laban nothing. All his assessing of bride prices and time of service, including payment for his herd, shows a balance much to his credit. On the other hand, there is the incalculable debt to Esau.

I speculated earlier that Jacob may not have been deeply instructed in the conception of God that his family received through Abraham, because he thought it was exceptional for God to be in a place Jacob did not associate with Him, and because he sets conditions for God to satisfy before he will agree to accept Him as his God—food to eat and clothing to wear. But the Lord is always faithful to His own intention, and to those who must live out His purposes. God appears to Jacob in a dream, identifies Himself in terms of the conditional vow and the anointed stone, and tells him as He had told his ancestor Abraham to leave the house of his kin and go, in his case return, to Canaan. That very long journey one more time. What state of mind and comprehension a vision of God would create in anyone is beyond my ability to imagine. Jacob, like Abraham, obeys. He has many reasons to wish to leave Padan-aram, but does so only in obedience to God's command, which comes at the time of the birth of Joseph. In any case, in the vision God makes clear that Jacob is the heir of the covenant. This can only mean that God intended this to be so and has ratified it, no matter the scurrility involved.

Jacob seems to have interpreted the vision in another way. It is as if the grandeur of it all is the measure of his crime against his brother. Certainly there is no loftiness or presumption in anything Jacob says or does. He is terrified for the safety of his wives and children. Everything he has acquired in his years of service and through the grace of God appears to him as at best a great ransom and at worst an appalling vulnerability. He sends a message to his "lord Esau" in Edom that Jacob his "servant" is returning and hoping to find favor in Esau's sight. The messenger returns with the grave information that Esau is approaching with four hundred men. Considering that Jacob's great wealth includes menservants, it is striking that no defense that would involve violence seems to cross his mind. He divides "the people" and the rest into two companies, so that if Esau will "smite" one, the other can escape. This hardly merits the word *defense*. He prays to the God of Abraham and Isaac to be delivered from the wrath of

Esau, acknowledging the grace and faithfulness God has shown him but fearing "lest he [Esau] will come and smite me, and the mother with the children." He reminds God in his prayer that his descendants are to be like the sand of the sea in their numbers, and still he fears for his children's lives. The text tells us nothing about Esau that leads us to suppose he would be merciless, that his anger would lead to enormity. Word comes to Rebekah that he says he will kill Jacob after their father has died. That he delays out of respect for his father means his rage is under some control, assuming that the report his mother has heard is true and is an indication of what he would in fact do. Justified or not, these fears are the measure of Jacob's feelings of guilt. They correspond to the loss he feels he has inflicted on his brother, which does exceed in degree and kind any possible estimate of its value.

Jacob sends droves of animals ahead of him—"thirty milch camels with their colts"—very rich gifts that he hopes will appease Esau. Then perhaps, he thinks, "I will see his face; peradventure he will accept of me." He has no illusions about making amends with these presents, about balancing the scales. He is simply using what he has, offering what he can, as if he were settling an enormous debt. Jacob takes his wives and maids and their children and all his possessions across the Jabbok River. "And Jacob was left alone; and there wrestled a man with him until the breaking of the day."

This is one of the most famous and mysterious passages

in Scripture. The scene is often called "Jacob and the An-gel," but the Hebrew word is not *angel* but simply *man*. It is a story that the redactors clearly took to be ancient, since they use it to account for a custom observed among the Israelites "to this day." Interpretation aside, the strug-gle is a wonderful image of lonely anguish, utter bewilder-ment, and profound determination. I take it to be a sign of the reverence with which ancient sources were used that this "man" did not become an angel at some point in the history of the text.

Once again, Jacob's strength is endurance. "When he [the man] saw that he prevailed not against him, he touched the hollow of his thigh; and the hollow of Jacob's thigh was out of joint, as he wrestled with him." Jacob is injured but he struggles on. The man said, "Let me go, for the day breaketh." But Jacob said, "I will not let thee go, except thou bless me." This is a beautiful and surpris-ing turn in the story. Jacob has prevailed, in that the man cannot escape his hold on him. It is Jacob who sets the conditions on which the struggle will end. But blessing is what he asks of his adversary, not help or safety or power. While it is true that these things might be implied, the word has a special context here. To be blessed is Jacob's oldest longing, perhaps powerful enough to have drawn him off the path of a generous righteousness that would otherwise be characteristic of him, and which has with-stood many tests. This is to read a motive into his decep-tion of Isaac, beyond Jacob merely abetting his mother.

The blessing he stole from Esau is at issue in this narrative moment, together with the many kinds of struggle it has cost Jacob, and will cost him.

"And he [the man] said unto him, 'What is thy name?' And he said, 'Jacob.' And he said, 'Thy name shall be called no more Jacob, but Israel: for as a prince hast thou power with God and with men, and hast prevailed.'" If this is a folk etymology, it is also a traditional interpretation of this story as well as of the larger narrative of Jacob. The Lord changed the names of Abram and Sarai to Abraham and Sarah as they became the bearers of the covenant. Certainly the imminent emergence of the Israeli people out of the household of Jacob would account sufficiently for his being given this eponymous name. At the same time, the name Jacob, according to the text, has an invidious meaning, the suggestion of a character and a fate he has lived out—on only two occasions, but both of them of absolute significance. It might seem to him that as often as he says his name he is making a confession or giving a warning. The new name would relieve him of this.

If it is theologically possible to say that Jacob really did defeat God's intention in stealing birthright and blessing from Esau or, more probably, that he fulfilled His will in taking possession of them albeit without apparent thought for His will, and though by guile, with poverty and exile and the disruption of his family as consequences, then the name Israel reframes all this as a heroic and triumphant struggle. If, at the Jabbok River, Jacob had claimed this

name for himself, it would have been an impious, hercu-
lean boast. Instead, the name is given to him, making it,
so to speak, a blessing on his life, ideally timed to ease
his meeting with Esau. But his anxiety and anguish, and
perhaps his shame, seem undiminished. Jacob/Israel asks
the man's name. The man evades the question and blesses
him. Jacob names the place Peniel, "for I have seen God
face to face, and my life is preserved." As with Hagar in
the wilderness, who also saw God and lived, the distinction between God and angel is blurred. Here there is also
the figure of a man whom Jacob and the text understand
as God. That these identities can be so fluid is significant
in itself.

Jacob's dread at the approach of Esau makes him put
the least loved of the mothers, a maid, with her children,
toward the front of his company, then the second maid
and her children, then Leah and hers, then Rachel and Joseph, in a declining order of exposure to attack by Esau
and his men. This is a miserable expedient, the kind of
thing that might lead to the resentments among brothers
that torment Jacob's family into his old age. Jacob, making
himself most vulnerable, goes ahead of them all, then
"bowed himself to the ground seven times, until he came
near to his brother." The man, or angel, or God Himself,
has blessed the striving of Jacob by which he supplanted
Esau. He himself has thanked God for his great prosperity
and his return to Canaan. Yet he takes what might well be
his brother's view of it all, as a theft for which no restitu-

tion is possible, which would be only more galling for the fact that the thief has become extraordinarily rich.

But "Esau ran to meet him, and embraced him, and fell on his neck, and kissed him: and they wept."

This is a beautiful break in the narrative tension, wholly unprepared except in all the carefully established dread that heightens the surprise. Jacob's dealings with Laban were complications surrounding an odd version of debt bondage. Even though there was finally no resolution, only a truce, there were at least terms in which the dispute could be carried on that allowed Jacob to justify himself amply, to his own satisfaction. But how to describe what has passed between Jacob and Esau? There is a famous verse in the New Testament Epistle to the Romans, about God's freedom to choose as He will. Paul says that when Rebekah had conceived children but before they were born, "neither having done any good or evil, that the purpose of God according to election might stand, not of works, but of him that calleth; it was said unto her, 'The elder will serve the younger.' As it is written, 'Jacob have I loved, but Esau have I hated,'" quoting the Hebrew prophet Malachi. Both texts are extremely complex. But in this they make the point that whatever happened between Esau and Jacob is not to be understood in terms of birth order, merit, or desert. If God simply chose Jacob, then he is not at fault in his supplanting of Esau. The oracle seems to have foretold this in any case, though its primary reference might be to conflict between Edom and

Israel expressed in terms of their eponymous ancestors. To say God "hated" Esau rather than Edom seems inconsistent with the fact that Esau has clearly enjoyed wealth and prosperity in his own country, and that he is capable of the act of grace that sweeps aside Jacob's terrible fear.

Jesus is attentive to the matter of debt. It figures often in his parables. He teaches his disciples to say, "Forgive us our debts, as we forgive our debtors." To some traditions, and to the translators of the King James Version, his language must have seemed unpoetical or inexact, and they have supplied *sin* or *trespass* in place of this blunt word, which, in context, might imply that we should, ahem, forgive our debtors. *Trespass* is an ancient term in European property law. It need not imply that any harm is done as ordinarily defined, only that there has been an undesired intrusion of some kind. Whether this is an appropriate metaphor here—those without property rights cannot be intruded upon, which certainly does not mean they cannot be injured—I leave to others. *Sin* is anodyne. The word in the version in the Gospel of Matthew 6:12 is the Greek word meaning "debt," which is the word that also appears in the parables of Jesus where debt figures. The difference is significant. To forgive a trespasser might cost nothing. The law of Moses gives the poor and strangers access to fields and vineyards and the right to gather food in them, so the legal protections of property that lie behind trespass as a concept are biblically dubious. On the other hand, to forgive a debt means first of all to abandon the expectation of repayment of money or goods, at a cost that could be substantial. This sounds more like Jesus.

There is another, briefer version of this prayer in Luke 11:4. In it, Jesus says, "Forgive us our sins, for we also forgive every one that is indebted to us." The word *sins* here is used elsewhere for violations of the will of God, which arguably do not include trespass. Jesus himself, on a Sabbath, leads his disciples through a wheat field where they pluck and eat the grains. To me the word *trespass* seems like an accommodation to the world that should be reconsidered, especially in light of the important context in which it occurs.

Who are our debtors, literal or figurative, and what do they owe us? Most of us could probably come up with a list. The verse makes us God's debtors. What do we owe Him? Everything. More than we can conceive of. But a debt is an obligation. The prophets make it clear that sacrifice does not satisfy the Lord's requirement of us. Doing justice and loving mercy in practice might mean, among other things, the forgiving of debts. In the nature of things we cannot possibly pay God Himself what we owe Him. We do not deal in the same coin. Our debts must be forgiven by our Creator, by His grace. In the same way, we see Jacob offering a flood of wealth as wealth was reckoned among ancient pastoralists. He does not deceive himself that he is compensating Esau for the things he stole from him, the blessings and promises that are on the one hand a unique and sacred heritage and on the other hand unspecifiable and indefinable except as they emerge out of a history already known to extend over dark centuries. His debt cannot be repaid, but it can be forgiven. This is the economics of grace.

These two clans confront each other, one threatening, the other thought of only as threatened. The gesture of reconciliation is Esau's to make because he is the more powerful, at least in his willingness to threaten, and because he, along with his clan, his descendants, has been wronged. The two chieftains embrace. Then Esau notes the presence of women and children in his brother's company—a vulnerability that has haunted Jacob. In their order they kneel to him. Esau is accompanied by four hundred men, a war party, Jacob by his whole household, including his animals, including the children he will call "tender." Esau's notice of them might be ominous. Then he mentions the droves of animals Jacob has sent ahead, gifts he at first declines to accept, saying, "I have enough, my brother; keep that thou hast unto thyself." His demurral doesn't withstand a little insistence on Jacob's part. Then he suggests that the two companies travel on together. Jacob says no, he must move very slowly out of concern for his children and his herds. Then Esau suggests that some of his men travel with Jacob. Jacob, out of excuses, simply begs off. "What needeth it? Let me find grace in the sight of my lord." Jacob does not trust Esau, and Esau is either devising ways to do him harm or teasing him with his fearfulness. Jacob tells Esau that he and his company will "come unto my lord unto Seir," in Edom. "So Esau returned that day on his way unto Seir. And Jacob journeyed to Succoth," in Canaan. If Esau or his men had stayed with Jacob, they could have prevented this parting of the ways, with what consequences no one will ever know.

The ambiguities that surround this apparent reconciliation isolate the embrace of estranged brothers as something true and right. It ought to be what it appears to be. Because it stirs this recognition it cannot be diminished, even by doubts or mixed intentions. Jacob says to Esau, "Truly to see your face is like seeing the face of God, with such favor have you received me." His relief by itself would justify the comparison. Still, the comparison recalls the scene before this one, where he found himself in a wrestler's embrace at the Jabbok River, and came away from a crippling struggle having seen the face of God. Formally, the visual parallel might be meant to reenforce the power of the fact of embrace, the element of divine meaning in it despite every element of threat it brings with it.

Jacob's life will make more and more extreme demands on him. The Lord has chosen to call Himself the God of Abraham, Isaac, and Jacob, yet the text does not give us any simple way to understand how this inexpressibly rare distinction aligns itself with the course of his existence, except in its setting the conditions for a turn in history Jacob will not live to see.

Jacob camped before the city of Shechem. As scrupulous as Abraham, "he bought a parcel of a field, where he had spread his tent, at the hand of the children of Hamor,

Shechem's father, for an hundred pieces of money. And he erected there an altar, and called it El-elohe-Israel." But his adult sons do a terrible thing, rationalized as revenge for the rape of their sister, Dinah. In the way of vengeance, it overwhelms any notion of justice or proportion. Hamor, the prince of Shechem, and his guilty son, also named Shechem, try to make things right by marriage. Hamor proposes that intermarriage between the Israelites and the people of the land as well as full freedom for these strangers within the land and whatever marriage gifts they ask for should compensate for Shechem's crime. Jacob's sons agree on the condition that Shechem and all the men of the city be circumcised. They comply, and before they have recovered and can defend themselves, "two of the sons of Jacob, Simeon and Levi, Dinah's brethren, took each man his sword, and came upon the city boldly, and slew all the males." Then they plundered the city, taking "all their wealth, and all their little ones, and their wives," as well as their flocks and herds. Jacob tells them they have made him "stink among the inhabitants of the land," who might decide to destroy all of them. God tells him to leave the place and go to Beth-el.

This is the epitome of the stories that seem far too ugly to be in the Bible. This is not trickery but treachery at its most abysmal. It should be said, first of all, that the Hebrew Bible does not romanticize the history of the people who create it, to whom it is addressed, and who have preserved it faithfully over millennia. It is as if America had told itself the truth about the Cherokee removal or England had confessed to the horrors of slavery in the West Indies. History is so much a matter of distortion and omission that dealing in truth feels like a breach of etiquette. However, if a people truly believed that it interacted with God the Creator, it might find every aspect of its history too significant to conceal. In this case, circumcision, the sign of the covenant given to Abraham, which identified the covenant people and was the means by which others could be brought into the community, is viciously and cynically abused. Yet God does not treat the covenant as violated. Jacob and his sons remain under His protection. In this sense, the story is another approach to defining the covenant. It is secure in that God is faithful to His intentions despite appalling human crime, even sacrilege.

Consistent with other encounters of the covenant people with outsiders, and with the habit of honesty, Jacob knows that "the Canaanites and the Perizzites" will be enraged and offended by his sons' actions. No moral superiority is claimed on the part of the Hebrews in what is wholly their narrative to record, interpret, and preserve. This is remarkable. Also to be noted: There is no mention of comparable transgressions of surrounding peoples, no mitigating context, though ancient history and human history make it certain that there were stories to tell. The creators of Genesis are not interested in others' vices or crimes, only their own. This is again remarkable. Say the text believes what it records, that out of the inconceivable assertion of power from which everything has emerged and will emerge there came a small family of herdsmen who were of singular interest to the Creator despite much and who over time would be His means of shaping history. Then amazement, which is closely allied with candor, would be inevitable.

This episode anticipates dark passages in Joshua and Judges. In terms of narrative, the covenant people will pass through their centuries in Egypt, a highly ordered and refined civilization. They will emerge with a leader and lawgiver who has been schooled in the ways of Egyptian governance, an example he sometimes emulates and broadly rejects. Once they are on a terrain that they consider their own, they sink into violence and disorder until finally they decide they must have a king. This proves a mixed experience. Over time law will come to have its central place in their individual and collective lives. The intense valorization of law, or instruction, is the obverse of the chaos into which human beings fall in its absence. It is law, not patriarchy or monarchy, that is the essential structuring force in what will be Israel. Kings and prophets and high priests come and go, but the law, like the covenant, does not pass away.

The Lord tells Jacob to return with his household to Beth-el, where He had appeared to him as he fled from Esau and to Laban. So Jacob tells them, "Put away the strange gods that are among you." Jacob has, at this point, eleven sons, youths and young men whose names will be the names of eleven tribes of Israel. Their father has had several encounters with God and is acting under His direction now when he tells them to purify themselves and change their clothes in preparation for this return. Yet his sons and those with them have idols among them, and Jacob is apparently aware of this. Shechem is the first indication of how unruly these sons are, and how little Jacob does or can do to control them. As always, insofar as the covenant might seem to be dependent on human beings, it is imperiled, even lost.

As Jacob and his clan journeyed to Beth-el, "the terror of God was upon the cities round about them, and they did not pursue after the sons of Jacob." After the Fall, from the beginning of the human narrative, vengeance has been a subject of the text. Why did God not avenge the murder of Abel? Lamech boasts of avenging injuries done to him "seventy and sevenfold," epitomizing, for the purposes of midrash or parable or myth, the violence that led to the Flood. As the world was restored, Noah was given a law that permitted the taking of a life for a life. A different crime has been committed here, a rape and abduction. Without speculating on the severity of this act in the reckoning of the ancient Near East, it could hardly justify the destruction and looting of a city. The vengeance of these sons of Jacob exceeds all proportion. Pride drives it: "Should he deal with our sister as with an harlot?" There is a special casuistry that means matters involving women can seldom be aligned with any standard of equity. And again, God prevents the punishment that might reasonably be exacted in response to flagrant guilt. When we benefit from or approve of His restraint we call it grace.

In their wanderings the Hebrews dealt with the imagined threats of murder by Egyptians and Canaanites

because of the beauty of Sarah and Rebekah. There was
the fear that Laban would seize his daughters and their
children. And there was the terrible dread of Esau and his
possible vengefulness. In no case was there a suggestion
that these Hebrews themselves did anything threatening, or that the cities they passed would consider pursu-
ing them. But after Shechem they are a band of outlaws
who could be attacked lawfully for their crime, like Cain
himself. Like Cain, they are protected by God. They no
doubt terrified the cities they passed in any case, and an
added "terror of God" assured their safe passage. This
is very different from the safety God has promised His
people to this point. The change in the life of this family,
the darkening of it, might be indicated in the noting of
the death and burial of Rebekah's nurse, otherwise unmentioned, who would have traveled with her many years
before from Padan-aram. Jacob remembers the times
when his life was very different—his flight from the wrath
of Esau with only his staff, and the theophany and blessing he was given on his way to Padan-aram. To note an
obscure death in a narrative so marked by economy might
mean that stories about this Deborah made her a personage in family memory. This was a family, after all, with
many more tales among them than have come down to us.

Jacob and his people arrive at Beth-el. Jacob raises
an altar. Then the text does something very beautiful. It
restates the blessing and the promise—the covenant—at
length and in terms that have become familiar, as if nothing had happened to raise any question about Jacob's or

his sons' status as heirs. Without comment, it establishes God's great constancy. The emotion with which Jacob experiences this vision and hears these words might be compared to his joy and relief at his encounter with Esau. He is still Israel. God has not forgotten his promises to Abraham, or to him. This passage reads as reiteration, as if earlier narrative has been patched in by redactors. I suggest that this is the point.

As they travel on from Beth-el, Rachel goes into labor and dies in the birth of her second child. She has been essential to the narrative from the moment Jacob first saw her at the well. For her, he indentured himself for seven years, then another seven. For her, he accepted marriage with her sister Leah, even though he was tricked into it. Granted, Jacob might not have felt comfortable making much objection to the ploy of concealed identity, one sibling disguised in order to take the rights of another. In any case, it was because of Jacob's love for Rachel that the Lord gave Leah her sons. Because of Rachel, if indirectly, Jacob acquired family and, finally, wealth, and was ready to return to Canaan. She has given the covenant family its twelfth son, Benjamin. Then we are told that Isaac dies, "and his sons Esau and Jacob buried him." Many things are brought to an end, or prepared for a beginning.

One verse foreshadows the turbulence that will plague Jacob and his family—and carry forward providential history, since their conflicts bring them into Egypt. We are told that Jacob's oldest son, Reuben, "went and lay with Bilhah his father's concubine: and Israel heard it." The text has established repeatedly that the world of their wanderings did not approve of relations with a married woman. A concubine was a wife of lower standing, but a married woman all the same. Leah had married her maid to Jacob so the maid, Bilhah, could bear children to him and, by the custom of the time, for her. Moses would forbid this relationship of a man with his father's wife, as he would also forbid Jacob's marriage to sisters. But before the law of Moses, what Reuben has done was already clearly scandalous. The words "Israel heard it" imply ongoing consequences, not only for Reuben's good name but for Jacob's status as the leader of Israel, which seems to be cohering as a political community. In antiquity a claimant to leadership might seize the ruler's concubines, as Absalom will do in his attempt to supplant his father, King David. So, more than moral issues are involved here.

In his old age, Jacob will "bless" his sons. More precisely, he will tell them what he thinks of them and what they can expect. Reuben, though Jacob calls him "the beginning of my strength," is told "you shalt not excel; because thou wentest up to thy father's bed; then defiledst thou it: he went up to my couch." Among other things, this episode touches on the question of primogeniture, which, as in the case of Jacob, counts for nothing against countervailing circumstances.

How can it be that a God of righteousness can be forgiving to the point of permissiveness or indifference? Is the destruction and looting of Shechem a pattern of behavior acceptable to God? Jacob fears, very reasonably, that con-

dign vengeance will be inflicted on him by the people of
the land, the destruction of *his* people and all that *he* has.
But the Lord protects him from any consequence at all,
except his own fear and shame. Abraham is notable for
the careful equity with which he deals with strangers. He
worried that righteous people might be caught up in the
destruction of Sodom. There is no reason to assume that
Shechem was an evil city, yet it is looted even of its children. This comparison is unfair to Jacob, who was aware
of the crime only after it was committed and was appalled.
Still, how can those who have departed so far from any
standard of righteousness be protected by God?

We are being told a story different from epic or fable,
and different from conventional history. The mind of the
text hovers over a very long span of time, during which an
absolutely singular providence works itself out through and
among human beings who are fallible in various ways and
degrees and who can have no understanding of the part
their lives will play in the long course of sacred history. The
scale of the unfolding of this history is touched on in the
genealogy of Esau, which is also the emergence of Edom
as a people. It names "the kings that reigned in the land of
Edom, before there reigned any king over the children of
Israel." The first Israelite king was Saul, the second was David. From the narrative point of view, clearly kingship was
an established custom in Israel when these old stories were
recorded in their present form. So they are seen in deep
retrospect, as they appeared after the descent into Egypt
and the captivity there, after Moses and their wanderings

in the wilderness, after the claiming of Canaan and the period of the judges, and into the period of the kings, that is, after a number of eventful centuries. Providence can become visible in retrospect. It might seem especially clear when Israel was prospering under David and Solomon, when the king was writing brilliant poetry or building a glorious temple. Or the text might have a deeper insight into a grander providence, not transitory, as history and prophecy both tell us the greatest epochs are. In any case, granting that this narrative concerns itself with the singular history of a chosen people, one not primarily meant to offer examples of virtue or heroism or to support generalizations about ethical conduct but meant instead to trace the workings of God's loyalty to humankind through disgrace and failure and even crime. Again, my old rabbis practice a generous rigor in not having obscured this essential meaning by editing or eliding the tales on which it depends. They have preserved the world's best hope.

The genealogy of Esau closes a series of stories centered on Jacob. The next section is introduced as "the generations of Jacob." In the stories that follow, his sons, especially Joseph, assume great importance, though Jacob is always there in the background, gravely aware of what might be passing among his sons. The narrative takes up when Joseph is seventeen, already officious, bringing bad reports about his brothers to their father. He is not an unfamiliar type, currying favor with authority, antagonizing his peers. The situation is worse, more galling in his case, for several reasons. He is the son of the beloved and deceased Rachel, which gives him status his older brothers do not enjoy, favor signified by the splendid coat his father has had made for him. The text mentions that he made an ill report against "the sons of Bilhah, and . . . the sons of Zilpah, his father's wives," who were the maids recruited to supply the family with more sons. Notably, the mothers, not the sons, are named here. If Jacob's tenderness toward Joseph, which is understandable and touching, created perceived ranks of preference among the brothers, this would no doubt exacerbate their irritation with Joseph, who would always come first in their father's eyes. Joseph is young, bright, and self-infatuated, blind or indifferent to the resentment that is stirring around him, though his brothers "hated him, and could not speak peaceably unto him." He is, in literary terms, a great character.

Joseph has a series of dreams, which he describes to his brothers. They seem to require little interpretation. Certainly his brothers have no doubts as to their meaning. He and they were out binding sheaves. His sheaf arose and stood upright and theirs all bowed down to it. His brothers say, "Shalt thou indeed to reign over us?" And more to the same effect. But he dreamed again and described the dream to his brothers. This time, "the sun and the moon and the eleven stars" bow down to him. Even Jacob reacts. "Shall I and thy mother and thy brethren indeed come to bow down ourselves to thee to the earth?" His brothers are more resentful after hearing this dream, but Jacob "observed the saying."

Joseph's dreams are prophetic rather than visionary. These two seem at first to be projections of his own nature and preoccupations, his own egotism. The Lord does not appear in them, as He did in the dreams of Abraham, Isaac, and Jacob. In the course of the narrative their meaning will become complex and deeply refined, visionary in another sense. Here they only exacerbate a conflict among brothers. Joseph will make his way in the world without angelic voices, but he will receive much practical help from the riddles that come to him and others in their sleep. He is the resourceful man, the problem solver, who, all unawares, first to preserve his life, then to enjoy the benefits of his competence, will carry forward God's intention for Israel. As always, the path is not straight and Joseph's success in Egypt is not entirely admirable. This is to say that providence, whose operations are of another order and scale than these mortals can imagine, is the crucial factor in it all.

We are told that Joseph's brothers are pasturing their flock near Shechem. Jacob sends Joseph to see how things are with them. It is understandable that Jacob might worry, since the attack on that city seems entirely unresolved, and it had offended the people of neighboring cities. The text does not address this concern explicitly, but it does name Shechem three times in a brief passage that ends with the information that the brothers had gone elsewhere. Joseph manages to find them. They recognize him and begin scheming against him while he is still at a distance. Their first thought is to kill him "and cast him into some pit." They will say that a wild animal has eaten him, "and we shall see what will become of his dreams." Literally true. This is the irony of providence, that it is served by just those steps that are taken to defeat it.

Antagonism between or among brothers has recurred in Genesis, beginning with a first statement of the theme in Cain's murder of Abel. It is assumed that Esau really might kill Jacob. The issue in both cases is a yearning for the blessing and approval of the Father or father, and bitterness that another enjoys it. So Joseph, in the coat that never lets his brothers forget he is the favored one, wanders into a very perilous situation.

People can indulge violent fantasies they have no intention of acting on. But the mentions of Shechem, which serve no other purpose, call to mind the fact that these men can indeed be violent, even murderous. In their assault on the city, they acted on intention, not impulse, as Cain did also in asking his brother to meet him in a field where his crime would not be seen. Only Simeon and Levi are mentioned by name in the narrative of Shechem. Dinah is their sister, so their desire for revenge would have been especially intense. In this case, a warm hatred for Joseph is shared by his brothers, so it is only in the course of the story that we find out which of them would kill him. Reuben, the eldest, talks them out of shedding his blood, quite easily, it seems. His intention is to return to the place on his own and help his brother out of the pit, and "to deliver him to his father again." Jacob's love for Joseph is a provocation, the source of extreme resentment and jealousy in them. It is also a great joy and tenderness in the life of the old man, whom they love.

Having put Joseph in a pit, "then they sat down to eat." We have no idea how Joseph would have been reacting to all this. Resented as he was, and younger than his brothers, he had presumably been tormented by them before. He might have waited quietly in the pit for the joke to be over. Or he might have cajoled them, or wept and pleaded. They ate their supper as if nothing of particular moment were happening, a taunt. Then some Ishmaelites appeared with camels carrying trade goods to Egypt, and Judah struck on the horrible, and providential, idea of selling Joseph to them. "Judah said unto his brethren, 'What profit is it if we slay our brother, and conceal his blood? Come, and let us sell him to the Ishmaelites, and let not our hand be upon him; for he is our brother and our flesh.'" This is surely as shabby a moral scruple as is to be found in any literature. To give up a brother to slavery in a strange country for money is very, very nearly as abysmal as killing him outright. To put whatever harm might come to him out of sight, to make it the work of other hands is, for Judah, to lessen their guilt while satisfying the urge to be rid of him. In fairness, societies routinely manage to conceal from themselves profitable practices such as child labor by exploiting these practices in distant countries. The references to the spilling and concealing of blood, which they agree not to do, recalls the murder of Abel, whose blood the Lord heard "crieth unto me from the ground," making concealment of the crime impossible. Perhaps it was only caution they had learned from that old story. Reuben thinks of their father.

It must be noted how unsparing the text is in its treatment of these great figures, the sons of Jacob. Levi took part in the raid on Shechem. Judah proposed that they profit from the sale of their brother. These are the ancestors of two of the greatest tribes. Moses, Aaron, and Miriam are Levites. The tribe of Judah becomes predominant in the later history of Israel. Yet here are their eponyms, their darkest sins memorialized into a future they could not have conceived of, when no more would have been needed than a sympathetic redactor to obscure culpability a little. Much modern interpretation of Genesis has proceeded on the assumption that the text was composed and edited by redactors with political or other agendas. Such a text would not preserve traditions or invent stories that establish so vividly the mere humanity of its heroes. This is a consistent feature of Genesis going back to Noah. Consistency with variation is another feature of the text that argues against the theory of its being made up of disparate, unreconciled documents with no unifying vision behind them.

As it happens, Joseph's brothers don't kill him and they don't sell him, either. Passing Midianites pull him up from the pit, and a band of Ishmaelites buy him from them for twenty shekels of silver. The note in my Bible says that a merging of two traditions has occurred here, as it may have. Redactors may have exploited the fact that there were versions of the story that make either the Ishmaelites or the Midianites Joseph's captors.

For all this to have happened without their knowing, Joseph's brothers must have been a considerable distance away from the pit. The same is true if Reuben thinks he can come back alone to rescue Joseph. Surely his brothers would not have stood by passively had they known this sale was occurring. Judah and presumably some of the others were moved by the thought of profit. And Reuben, when he returns, is surprised to find the pit empty. The text, being so precise about the amount of the sale, assures us that a transaction did take place, if not between Jacob's sons and one of these tribes, then between the two tribes. The Midianites have Joseph, the Ishmaelites have the shekels, and Joseph's brothers have nothing but the coat that is the sign of their father's love for him and the miserable scheme they devised in the first place to conceal his murder. If they had told their father that Joseph had been abducted by a band of foreigners, or had simply vanished on his way home, they could have left their father with the hope that he might still be alive. Lie that this would be, it would not be as black a lie as the one they tell him. They could have simply disposed of the coat somehow, since Joseph's absence would be proof enough that something had befallen him. Instead, they bloody his garment to show to the old man as proof of this unbearable death.

There is nothing in these anomalies to indicate that they

are more than a lapse in the narrative, except that they are so interesting. Reuben, when he finds that Joseph is gone, goes to his brothers and says, "The child is not; and I, whither shall I go?" As he is the eldest, he may feel and be considered especially at fault for not keeping his brother safe. He thought of the rescue he intended as returning Joseph to their father, and now he must see his father's grief, and must maintain this deception for as long as his father lives. The words "Whither shall I go?" suggest that he has lost his place in his father's house, whether expelled from it or unable to live with the old man's grief and the lying he must trust his ten unruly brothers to sustain, for years. The family is poisoned by the deception. The effect of the truth would be unimaginably worse.

Strikingly, among the brothers it is as if they had acted on their first and darkest impulse, the murder they had intended before second thoughts, qualms, and calculations began to enter their conversation. The ritual quality of their killing a goat for its blood, which is not an act the loss of Joseph required, simply a reenacting of the original homicidal plan, might appear as a substitutionary sacrifice, an animal dying in the place of "the child," as Reuben calls him. I suppose it could be an attempt to undo the death, pouring the lifeblood of the creature onto the coat that epitomized their brother. The blood is the life, the old law says.

Then again, they are preparing to present their father with evidence that Joseph has suffered a terrible death, bloodying that coat and filling his mind with an image of mortal suffering that is purely their invention. Either/or are not categories that apply to motives or emotions. And Jacob's favoring of Joseph is the grounds for their bitterness. So guilt and dread could involve vengeful anger toward their father: See what you did by slighting the rest of us. Did Jacob believe what they told him? If he did not, he lived for years among sons who he thought did away with their brother. Later events suggest he suspected them. He knows as well as anyone could that fathers are sometimes bitterly deceived.

Things that were indeterminate would have taken what seemed to be their definitive form during this episode of the selling of Joseph. Joseph, standing among these haggling traders, must have looked around for any sign of his brothers, hoping that he had not been utterly abandoned. While his purchaser checked his limbs for soundness, a thought with the force of realization must have overcome him. They really did hate him this deeply. His father, Jacob, must have thought, while he sat pondering the bloody coat, Perhaps my sons really are murderers. Perhaps the kind of provocation that lay behind their attack on Shechem was not required to bring out viciousness in them.

But if the Midianites and the Ishmaelites had happened by a day later, Reuben would have rescued Joseph from the pit. The brothers would have arrived at a reconciliation of some kind, telling themselves that the worst kind of evil was never really intended, as even Joseph would be ready to believe. Events are conditioned by accident. The Midianites might have chosen to treat "the child" as a youth in need of help rather than as abandoned property, theirs to sell. The text has established repeatedly that the people of the land could be honorable. Because these particular traders happened along, Joseph will be confronted years later by brothers who, so far as he could know, had agreed to leave him to die. He might have experienced captivity itself as a rescue and adapted to it on these terms. In any case, his father would live out long years among sons who were burdened with secrecy and guilt, always suspecting them, his divinely promised descendants, of a crime he might detest them for. Now his comfort would be Benjamin, Rachel's other child, who would have been too young to have any direct knowledge of these events but would have felt their effects all around him. If all of this were explored as fiction, he would be a great point-of-view character.

When Jacob's sons return to him and show him Joseph's coat, the old man says, "'Joseph is without doubt rent in pieces.' And Jacob rent his clothes, and put sackcloth upon his loins, and mourned for his son many days. And all his sons and all his daughters rose up to comfort him; but he refused to be comforted; and he said, 'For I will go down into the grave unto my son, mourning.' Thus his father wept for him." Then we are told in a single verse that, in Egypt, Joseph has been sold to Potiphar, an officer of Pharaoh.

At this point the narrative takes a very odd turn. It tells how it came about that Judah, a widower, had sons by his Canaanite daughter-in-law Tamar. Tamar has been married to one and then another of Judah's sons. Both have died childless. She has a right to be married to Judah's remaining son, Shelah, to bear children who would be treated as her first and second husbands' offspring. When his son has grown to a marriageable age, Judah still withholds him, afraid he will meet the fate of his brothers. The brother (or brothers) of a man who dies childless must enter into levirate marriage with his widow to produce a son that will be treated as his. Judah prevents this. Therefore Tamar veils herself to look like a harlot—disguise is important again—and seduces Judah. The relationship would normally be forbidden. When he is told that his daughter-in-law is pregnant, Judah is full of indignation and orders her to be burned. But she proves that she was the harlot he lay with. Judah says, "'She hath been more righteous than I; because that I gave her not to Shelah my son.' And he knew her again no more." There is righteousness in honoring righteousness in someone else, especially at a cost to one's own good name. So, however obliquely, this tale redounds to Judah's credit. The fact that he is the one who suggested that Joseph be sold makes another light on his character welcome. Again, the traditions behind both this story and the selling of Joseph must have been solid and much respected for Judah to have been identified as the originator of that scheme, and then in the matter of Tamar to have been in some degree rescued—from his own hypocrisy, true, but by his realization and confession of his own guilt.

A creative redactor could have suppressed these embarrassing details. But, as always, despite and through the human turmoil another thing is happening. Tamar bears twins. One, Perez, manages to emerge before his brother. He becomes a name, that is, a link, in the genealogy that leads to David in the book of Ruth and to Jesus in the Gospel of Matthew. Tamar is determined to carry out her widow's obligation to her husbands, even though both were so offensive to God that, in a departure from usual practice that suggests the influence of folktale, He slew them. Tamar does what she can for them at obvious risk to herself, and providence rewards this twice-widowed Canaanite woman with two sons, one for each of her odious husbands. This is more remarkable because the lethal sin of the second husband was his refusal to father a child for his childless brother. There is something to ponder here about faithfulness to one's obligations even to the dead and irrespective of what might seem their deserving. In any case, sacred history unfolds in these morally confounding events as surely as it does in the saga of Joseph in Egypt.

Joseph in the service of Potiphar, like Jacob with Laban, brings great prosperity to the man whose steward he is, and therefore he enjoys trust, responsibility, and wealth. Potiphar's wife wants to sleep with him, but he refuses to betray his master. She takes hold of his clothing, he escapes, leaving part of it behind, and she shows it to her husband as proof that Joseph has attacked her.

This story closely resembles a passage from a long Egyptian text called "The Tale of the Two Brothers." The Egyptian story features self-mutilation, the killing of the faithless wife, resurrection, the creation of a semidivine woman, metamorphosis—all of which draws attention to the rigorous realism of Genesis. Human beings come into existence only through birth. Men do not become trees or rise up from drops of blood. Every creature exists "after its own kind." Ultimately the two brothers, who are the adversaries in this story, reconcile. From their struggles they emerge as the king of Egypt and his viceroy. So there is a broad similarity with the narrative arc of the story of Joseph.

The borrowing, assuming this is what it is, explains the imprisonment of Joseph that leads finally to his encounter with Pharaoh. It preserves the virtue and integrity that are central to his character, and underscores them, while he is given the problem of imprisonment to deal with. Egyptians did indeed use dungeons. Hebrews did not. But the Hebrew version adds this detail, which is not found in the Egyptian story. The tower of Babel and the Flood were Babylonian and the world of the text was oriented toward Mesopotamia. The dungeon and the borrowing from an Egyptian tale are appropriate to the change of scene to Egypt. Exotic elements might have heightened the pleasure of tellers and hearers, and might have added a kind of verisimilitude. They might have functioned as interpretive cues, or they might have established comparisons that used likeness to demonstrate unlikeness, for example the magical or fantastical narrative elements mentioned above beside the biblical realism. For weal or woe, there is no institution or authority in the world of the patriarchs to visit punishment on whoever might offend a superior, as the unfortunate baker has done. Egypt is all about captivity. Joseph, son of Jacob the wandering herdsman, is caught in the toils of a highly ordered, hierarchical society.

He seems to give no thought to resistance or escape. Instead he benefits from his competence and trustworthiness. He becomes the perfect prisoner, once again so good in his role that he displaces the jailer, as he had Potiphar before him. He does this with no hint of insinuation or of calculation, no harm to any competitor. It happens that two fellow captives have dreams he can interpret with the help of God, help he does not request but assumes. His interpretations are borne out by events. Then he is forgotten for two years. When Pharaoh has two troubling dreams, Joseph is remembered. He is brought before Pharaoh, predicts a famine, and recommends the storing of grain in anticipation of it. He begins the ascent that brings him finally to the point of displacing Pharaoh—after his fashion, by being such a good steward that his master keeps his office in perfect security while he is relieved of all the burdens of it. The great irony of all this is that, meaning well to his master as always, but proceeding with more zeal than reflection, Joseph enslaves the Egyptians. He does not ration out to the Egyptians the grain he has taken from them. He sells it to them. Their utter destitution is the only limit to his demands.

To explore the larger meaning of this I will look ahead to the law of Moses, which forbids just the kind of thing Joseph will do in his unhesitating determination to enrich quite possibly the richest man on earth. Mosaic law looms behind many of the stories that arise from the period before Egypt and Sinai. Jacob should not have married sisters, Judah should not have lain with Tamar his daughter-in-law. There are many irregularities in the history of Abraham's family, scrupulously remembered and recorded. But these minor divagations are taken up by the end of the tale as providential. They do not at all compare in terms of transgressiveness to Joseph's opportunistic reduction of a whole population to poverty and dependency. It is possible to speak of transgression against law that is not yet articulated and acknowledged only if the old values of justice and righteousness that Abraham and his descendants were to bring to the world are the basis of that law. In the matter of the distribution of property and of provision for the poor, Moses's instructions run entirely counter to the order of things established by Joseph.

We know that, before Joseph and the famine, Egyptians had wealth of which they could be dispossessed. Their impoverishment reaches finally to their own bodies, which they give in exchange for food. This is slavery. In order for it to have been arrived at by these increasingly radical dispossessions, the population must have been relatively prosperous. If they lived with some degree of oppression, as people usually do, at least they considered their bodies their own. In other words, Joseph brought Egypt into bondage to Pharaoh by putting into his possession everything of value in his land. Here is the warning God gives through the prophet Samuel, telling the people what it will mean to them if He allows them to have a king. "This will be the manner of the king that shall reign over you." He will take sons and daughters to be put to his uses. "He will take your fields, and your vineyards, and your oliveyards, even the best of them, and give them to his servants . . . And he will take the tenth of your grain and of your vineyards and give it to his officers and to his servants. He will take your menservants and your maidservants, and your goodliest young men, and your asses, and put them to his work. He will take the tenth of your heep: and ye shall be his servants." This is a milder regime than the one said to be established by Joseph, but the principle is the same. Joseph is the servant or officer who grows rich as the populace is made poor. The Lord says there is a time when the Israelites will "cry out in that day because of your king which ye shall have chosen you." In Exodus, the cry of the Israelites under bondage "came up unto God." Clearly slavery is understood as a consequence of impoverishment, as impoverishment creates and perpetuates slavery.

The narrative of the origins of kingship in Israel is not a rousing endorsement of the institution. In choosing to have a king, the Lord tells the prophet in 1 Samuel, "They have not rejected thee, but they have rejected me, that I should not reign over them." Yet the history of Israel, still sacred history, is very largely a tale of kings, some of them very great, all of them very flawed, as this understanding of king-ship allows the text and tradition to acknowledge. What-ever else he did, Joseph, with the help of God, anticipated a famine, responded sagaciously to the years of plenty that preceded the famine, and saved many lives, including those of his family, those ragtag aliens on whose survival the covenant promise rested. God gave Pharaoh these dreams to interpret. He also allowed Joseph agency—the problem of famine is one the managerial Joseph is perfectly suited to taking in hand. Dreams cluster around the narrative of Joseph, beginning with the ones he had as a boy that offended his brothers and even his father. They were prophetic, and not only in anticipating his rise relative to his family. They are also like the dreams of the Egyptians, little fragments of allegory with veiled meaning, rather than Hebrew dreams, in which God is a speaking presence. Joseph has something of the Egyptian about him even before he leaves his father's house. In any case, whether his dreams are visionary or allegorical, a difference that might allude to real cultural and religious differences, God is the giver of dreams.

Egypt at that time was already unfathomably old. It was vast, mighty, and self-engrossed. That its social order could have been transformed in the span of a few years by even the most enterprising foreigner, given its intensely theocratic foundation, is hardly to be imagined. More probable, since it is important throughout the Hebrew Bible, is a profound reluctance in the text to place blame. This may be the grandest moral instruction and example in the book of Genesis, strongly present in the teaching of Jesus: "He that is without sin among you, let him first cast a stone at her." In Exodus, the Egyptians make the condition of the Hebrews as corvée laborers intolerable progressively, depriving them of the straw they need to make brick so that they have to find it themselves, which is a demand on their strength and time that would have made it harder for them to find means of subsistence. The corvée system, in which laborers as members of a class are required to work without pay for intervals throughout the year, was broadly prevalent in the West into the modern period. It is consistent with the law of Moses having been a systematic rejection of the Egyptian social order that forced labor, the kind that built canals and pyramids and had an inexhaustible need for bricks, has no place in it. Compared with surrounding cultures, Israel put relatively little emphasis on building of the monumental kind. It had no spectacular tombs, no proliferation of shrines. Culture and religion would have seen to this, not only by centering worship in the temple but also, perhaps, in their having no corvée, no lawful and routine access to forced labor. The law of Moses that governs slavery seems to envisage it as a household arrangement, more or less, of a limited duration, rather than as the kind of gang labor used for building, mining, and other large-scale projects in the premodern world.

In any case, Joseph reduces the wealth of the Egyptian people progressively, until they must sell themselves for food. He does this without malice, without any apparent self-interest, guided by the advantage that he has over them because of his control of the food supply through years of profound famine. If this is thought of as an intentional parallel to the enslavement of the Hebrews, its effect is to establish an awareness that the Egyptians were not alone in the unrighteousness that underlay enslavement. The law of Moses would prevent such immiseration and its consequences by rooting a conception of justice and piety in social and economic relations that would obviate this brute opportunism. To forgive one's debtors is to free them from coercion, from impoverishment. Moses intended there to be forgiveness of debt every seven years and great festivals of forgiveness every fifty years.

The emphasis on economics and on debt will seem to some a secularizing approach to sacred Scripture. But it is precisely because I take Scripture to be sacred that I leave it to Scripture to establish the meaning of the word *sacred*. There are the soaring anthems of human art and imagination meant to evoke the majesty of God, and they are invaluable for framing a conception of the system of grandeur within which He has placed us. But as soon as the terms are set for our existence on earth, after the Creation, the Fall, and the Flood, the gaze of the text falls on one small family, people who move through the world of need and sufficiency, birth and death, more or less as we all do but, a difference less absolute than we might expect, having at intervals direct encounter with the Lord God.

I have dwelt on this sequence of stories, one after another, exploring the ways in which the faithfulness of God is manifest in the world of fallen humankind. This kind of interpretation might seem ingenious and little more if there were not essential truths lying behind it. The first of these is that these divine likenesses among whom we live are of the highest interest and value to God. We have been given the coin of wealth to barter among ourselves for the things we need or want. We assign worth to persons, consciously or not, and then to prestige and property and ease, all the things that compete so successfully with the claims of justice and righteousness, kindness, and respect, which would follow from a true belief that anyone we encounter is an image of God. And the second is that we do not know how to judge or where to blame because events are working themselves out at another scale and toward other purposes more than we can begin to grasp.

I am confessing my own anxiety here. I am as intent on magnifying the Lord as if I were a painter or composer, but my first obligation in commenting on the text is to be faithful to the text. Abraham and Sarah might be thought of as standing near the dawn with the brilliance of the original moment behind them. Their persons cast long shadows. This is a faulty metaphor for something true. The importance of the Abrahamic tradition, the billions of people who have variously claimed and revered the patriarch, is a matter of plain, historic fact. Much more is said about him in the Talmud and the Quran than in the Hebrew Bible, but all to the same effect, that he was a kind man, no idolator, faithful and obedient to the one God. In Islam, he is believed to have actively turned nations to monotheism. The Bible says nothing about this, but monotheism is firmly and uniquely associated with Abraham's name, so there is one important sense in which it is certainly true. Genesis tells us how this all began.

In the Letter to the Romans, Paul bases a crucial interpretation of God's way with humankind on the parsimony
of the biblical account of Abraham. He quotes Genesis:
"Abraham believed God, and it was counted unto him for
righteousness." Even Abraham did not achieve righteousness through his own virtues but received it in the eyes of
God as a gift of God. This implies, on the one hand, that
human meaning is not bound to what is done and suffered
in this world. On the other hand, God loves and demands
justice and kindness—Paul struggles with the implications of these apparently irreconcilable truths, reconciling
them in Christ. This is a difficult and contested locus in
Christian theology, which I mention here only to make the
point that the old Hebrew tradition of Abraham, carried
on in the New Testament, makes the meaning of mortal
Abraham rest in the choice and act of God. Abraham
"means" that the Lord has an intention for the world that
is to be realized through history. So Joseph, who finds favor with the powerful for the very good reason that he acts
purely in their interests, never looking right or left, is, unbeknownst to himself, creating the circumstances that will
induce his brothers, the sons of Israel, to leave Canaan and
settle in Egypt. If the text implies that Joseph establishes
servitude as a structuring element of Egyptian civilization,
lifting some part of the opprobrium from Egypt for the
ultimate enslavement of the Israelites, this would be consistent with the complication of blame that runs through
both the Hebrew Bible and the New Testament. This complexity is further compounded because, the text tells us,

even the enslavement is providential, shown in a dream to Abraham. It is a terrible dream, heavy with grief—in case *providential* might be taken as a synonym for *happy* or *propitious*. The long-term consequences of the choice to settle in Egypt will be—have been—unfathomably great. Debate about whether these events actually occurred, whether the figures involved are in any sense historical, can never be resolved and need not be. The great fact is the power they have had to shape history.

Because of Joseph's foresight and diligence, there is food to be had in Egypt and Jacob hears of it. He tells his ten adult sons, Joseph's brothers, to go there and buy grain so "that we may live, and not die." He keeps back his youngest, Benjamin, like Joseph the son of the beloved Rachel, "lest peradventure mischief befall him." This suggests a tension between father and sons in the years after the supposed death of Joseph. Jacob speaks of being bereaved of his children, and this alienation from ten of them would certainly make him mourn and fear for them, too. The brothers go to Egypt, encounter Joseph, the seller of grain, kneel to him like the sheaves in his boyhood dream, and submit to his questioning. He is clean-shaven, dressed in the manner of a high official, speaking to them through an interpreter as if he knows only Egyptian. He recognizes them, but he acts toward them like a hostile stranger. He accuses them of coming as spies.

They answer that they are twelve brothers, "and,

behold, the youngest is this day with our father, and one is not." A novel drawn from this brief account of a very freighted moment, their counting Joseph among their number after years of his absence, and pairing him with Benjamin, his full brother, would find guilt and deep regret. Whenever, during those years, Jacob showed some special care for Benjamin, some hint of anxiety about their dealings with him, they would be reminded of the terrible grief they had caused their father, sorrow renewed in his continuous awareness of the lad Benjamin's vulnerability. Jacob would inevitably seem to cherish Benjamin above his brothers, though the favor he showed to Joseph was presumably the provocation, if his brothers had indeed done away with him. A question too terrible to be asked, a confession too terrible to be made, and Jacob growing old in this silence.

The powerful stranger somehow knows where to touch the brothers' unhealed wound. He singles out the lad, Benjamin, and tells them they must do the thing their father dreads and will try to forbid: They must bring him to Egypt. At first Joseph says one of the brothers must fetch him; then he says one of them must remain as a hostage while the others carry grain back to their households, then return to him with Benjamin. They know what bitter doubt they will see in their father when they tell him the one condition Joseph has set in selling them the grain that will let them "live, and not die." This demand is perfectly calculated to call up in the minds of the brothers the thought of their crime and of the retribution they fear. Their response is not to the immediate situation but to the source of its disruption, the guilt that underlies it. They say to one another, "We are verily guilty concerning our brother, in that we saw the anguish of his soul, when he besought us, and we would not hear; therefore is this distress come upon us." They may assume that they are responsible for his death, however this might have happened. It is not the sin of manslaughter that haunts them but the memory of the lad's shock and grief. They all feel they saw his growing awareness of the reality of their betrayal of him.

If this were a Greek tragedy, and destiny had brought these protagonists to a place and circumstance where their transgression was made clear to them, there would be a chorus to help the audience ponder the complexity and potency of their recognition in that moment. No one could really know what it would be to realize, as Oedipus did, that they had killed their father and married their mother, and to learn this after a life lived to evade the oracle that doomed them to commit these acts they find abhorrent. In these tragedies horror lifts a veil that otherwise conceals the workings of the fates, the vengefulness of the gods, and the helplessness of the greatest mortal figures when these immortal forces touch them. A stunning recognition about the profounder nature of things is felt on human nerves.

Hubris is the transgression that offends the cosmic order in Greek tragedy. In Genesis the recurring sin is grievous harm to one's brother. Cain casts a long shadow. When Joseph's brothers are confronted with a situation that refers so powerfully to their crime, they assume that they are experiencing the justice of God. But in the Hebrew Bible, notably in the story of Cain, things are never that simple. The Lord is not Nemesis. He is free, acting toward His own ends, indifferent to the harsh symmetry of revenge. The brothers could not know that their distress brings them toward rescue from their most onerous regret and from some part of their father's sorrow. They anticipate the worst, taking divine justice to proceed as human justice would do. Reuben says their trouble is a reckoning for Joseph's blood, and Joseph, hearing these words, turns away to weep in secret. This is the beginning of his softening toward them and of the gradual transformation of their tense encounters with him into profound recognition, in the dramatic even more than the literal sense.

Joseph is very much a human being, not yet arrived at the realization that will liberate him from the impulse to avenge himself on his brothers. He keeps Simeon as a hostage, but he also provides food for his brothers' journey home, and he has the money they have paid him put into their sacks of grain. Without their consciousness of guilt, and despite Joseph's harsh manner toward them, this could be seen as a kindness. Instead, when they discover the money, they are terrified. "And their heart failed them, and they were afraid, saying one to another, 'What is this that God hath done unto us?'" It would be remarkable to see these ten nomad princes, terribly and furtively of one mind, all guilty and all witnesses of the others' guilt, looking to one another in shared dread and amazement. They may have seemed to the Egyptians to tremble at the power and grandeur of Pharaoh's viceroy. No, they are believers in the God of Abraham, the Fear of Isaac. Foreign potentates are impressive only as they might be His instruments. In this case, Joseph's importance to them is magnified and interpreted by their terror of God.

When Jacob first raised the matter of going to Egypt, he asked his sons, "Why do ye look one upon another?" Only the ten of them would know that, on account of them, any chance event might have terrible meaning. Because they have offended so gravely, any choice might open on exposure and humiliation. They may have made a practice and then a habit of consulting together wordlessly, hesitating for no clear reason, as in this case when the possible solution to a pressing problem awaits their decision to act. Was this deadly famine their punishment? If so, is there any use in trying to find relief from it? Will the departure from the familiar expose them to risks, stir judgment out of its long, haunting silence? This conspiracy after the fact would have been apparent to Jacob. Since the presumed death of Joseph, he would have noticed a grim bond among them, stronger than loyalty, that excluded him. And he would not have been able to put aside the bitter knowledge that sons can deceive their fathers. Alone as he had been with his guilt as he stood absurdly disguised, lying to blind old Isaac, he might find a semblance of it in the tense caution of their dealings with him.

Joseph has told them that he will have no further business with them until they come back with their youngest brother. On their return to Canaan they find money in their bags again and are again alarmed. Jacob finally speaks his heart. "Me have ye bereaved of my children: Joseph is not, and Simeon is not, and ye will take Benjamin away: all these things are against me." This deep disruption of Jacob's family was foreseen in Reuben's cry at the discovery that Joseph was gone from the pit, lost to them. "The child is not; and I, whither shall I go?" Back to their father, with proof of a violent death that did not happen, a confession of their intent that they felt somehow compelled to make though it could only darken his suspicions. They will go back to a family that will be grievously changed. On the one hand, a father in Jacob's situation might try to suspend judgment rather than bring on the cataclysm of accusing ten sons of fratricide. On the other hand, he had the fatherly problem of protecting Benjamin from the worst he suspected of them. Since the Lord put that mark on Cain, the gist of every story in Genesis is that human judgment is no equivalent of God's justice. Through his long trial, heroically, Jacob has almost suspended judgment.

The climactic scene of Joseph's encounter with his brothers is prepared formally, artfully. To suggest craft in the making of sacred text disturbs some people, as if the Holy Spirit would never descend to the strategies of nuance and emphasis that heighten the intelligibility of a story and are as much aspects of language as are words themselves. Imagine that the old rabbis of my speculations had told this story a thousand times, seeing its effect on their listeners. Three times they made the long journey to Egypt! Or imagine that it was enacted. "If I be bereaved of my children, I am bereaved!" The text does not tell us how Jacob reacts when Reuben offers his own sons to be slain if he does not return with Benjamin. Does he think Jacob could possibly be compensated for the loss of off-spring by the deaths of offspring? It all seems too rich for this narrative to be the only form in which it would be given to people who knew and loved it and saw their identity in it. The bereaved old man is Israel, after all, and his agonized restraint preserves the clan of twelve eponyms whose tribes will shape the future of the people of Israel.

As the ten brothers make the three journeys to Egypt, suspense develops with the varied repetition of detail. The stranger's insistence on seeing Benjamin plays out against the background of a famine in which they and their families could die, and the deeper background of the guilty act and their father's unassuageable sorrow, which might end in his death. Then there is the overarching suspense present to teller and hearer, a preoccupation of the text concerning the providential history that must somehow withstand and resolve all of this threat and fear within the limits of the tale. These repetitions, a familiar literary convention, are here made to emphasize Jacob's refusal to entrust Benjamin to his brothers, which is absolute at first and then, under the extraordinary pressure of cir-cumstance, becomes a tortured and weary concession to necessity. This family, of whom it is uniquely true that they are chosen by God to carry forward His will for human-kind, must be as unhappy as any family could be. When we consider what the favor of God can look like, Jacob and his sons should surely be borne in mind.

Judah reminds Jacob of what is at stake, that they might live, "both we and you and also our little ones." On the strength of his promise, "If I bring him not unto thee, and set him before thee, then let me bear the blame for ever," his father relents. Judah, like any of them, must make such a vow without any way of knowing what this presumably hostile Egyptian stranger intends. "Little ones" are mentioned in contexts where the tenderness and vulnerability of a group of people are thought of or appealed to. Judah gently reminds his father that there are other lives than Benjamin's to consider.

The brothers return to Egypt, and this time Joseph orders a feast for them in his own house. As always, they are surprised and frightened. Before Joseph appears they query his steward to find out if the money that has been returned to them twice is regarded as stolen. With the insight the text so frequently grants to pagans, the steward tells them, "Your God, and the God of your father, hath given you treasure in your sacks." In light of the fact that these events are so thoroughly providential, this is true. Then they feast, not together but in proximity to one another, they at one table, Joseph by himself at another, Egyptians at still another. The brothers do not yet recognize Joseph.

This seating arrangement is necessary because "the Egyptians might not eat bread with the Hebrews, for that is an abomination to the Egyptians." Presumably an *abomination* is something to be *abhorred*. Both of these potent words occur in Scripture, rarely elsewhere. Whether they are given weight in particular instances seems to depend on the preferences of interpreters, and this makes them hard to define. What is described here resembles a caste barrier. It is more or less the kind of thing that scandalized observers when Jesus broke bread with tax collectors and prostitutes, except in this case the line not to be crossed is ethnic. All-powerful Joseph is married to the daughter of the Egyptian high priest, and still he must eat alone. It appears that he is also too Egyptian to be seated at table with his Hebrew brothers. There is a law, Deuteronomy 23:7, that in effect responds to this practice and much else: "Thou shalt not abhor an Egyptian; because thou wast a stranger in his land." The fact that the sojourn in Egypt should remove stigma from the people who became the Hebrews' oppressors is remarkable, as is their open acceptance of those who stigmatize them. This is consistent with a general biblical freedom from the coercions and constraints of retaliation. Other laws concerning peoples with whom they have a history are less forgiving and therefore less surprising. But to dismiss what is atypical in the text is to misrepresent it.

Joseph is deeply moved by the presence of Benjamin. He goes to his chamber to weep, then washes his face and returns to his brothers. He favors Benjamin with generous portions of food from his own table. They "were merry with him." And then as they are leaving he has his steward put his silver cup secretly in the lad's grain sack. Claiming that the cup has been stolen, he sends pursuers after his brothers and has them brought back to him. Exactly why he chooses to keep his brothers in this state of terrified uncertainty is never made explicit, but it has the effect, finally, of moving them to make a passionate account of how things are with their father, a confession of sorts, their father's grief being the measure of their sin.

"They"—no speaker is named—make the kind of drastic pledge that is meant to insist in the strongest terms on their innocence. In fact it greatly heightens the suspense of the moment for listeners, who know what Joseph has done. The brothers say, "With whomsoever of thy servants it [the cup] be found, both let him die, and we also will be my lord's bondmen." The steward replies, "He with whom it is found shall be my servant; and ye [the rest of you] shall be blameless." This milder version of their pledge means nevertheless that they will not return to their father with Benjamin. The steward searches their bags, eldest to youngest. This would be an amazing scene. Each exoneration would bring the possibility of apparent proof of the theft closer to Benjamin. The brothers might hope that their innocence would be proved when the cup was not found with any of them, if the story had not established twice over that they could not know what might be in their sacks. Their guilt and their expectation that punishment might come in any form from any side would heighten

their dread. This is another of those moments when the
experience of the protagonists is not to be imagined in
other circumstances. Presumably as each brother is found
to be innocent and the odds improve that blame will fall
on Benjamin, relief at each vindication will become more
deeply mingled with sorrow and fear.

The cup is found with Benjamin. His brothers rend
their clothing with grief and return to the city, to Joseph's
house. He has played a trick on them, but he attributes the
discovery of the supposed theft to divination. Perhaps this
is a little satire on Egyptian sorcery. He rebukes them, and
Judah answers, "What shall we say unto my lord? . . . God
hath found out the iniquity of thy servants." This is the
retribution that they have expected to overtake them for
years. Their individual innocence of this supposed theft
is of no consequence to them in light of the guilt that has
burdened their lives. Judah tells Joseph that they will all
be his slaves. Joseph says no, only the one found with the
cup will be his slave, "and as for you, get you up in peace
unto your father." This is exactly what they cannot do.

Joseph has created a situation in which the ten brothers can abandon a cherished son of Rachel and return to
their father to make whatever account they can of the lad's
absence. He has given them a chance to act in their own
interests, at the cost of a brother's betrayal. This would be,
in effect, one interpretation of Joseph's own history with
them. The brothers clearly see this recurrence of the old
crime emerging out of circumstance, as if their punishment
for it might be their having to reenact it. The unbearable

consequence would be their father's grief, this time greatly compounded. The old man anticipated that these ten sons might again bereave him. The horror of Shechem would linger in memory. To have his fears confirmed would be the confirmation of his most painful suspicions about them, the collapse of the tenuous doubt that they would descend to fratricide against his most tenderly favored children. The loss of all possibility of suspending judgment would surely, finally, bereave him of these ten as well.

Judah makes a long appeal to Joseph, who is still unrecognized by him, describing the sorrow that will overcome Jacob, father of them both, if they do not return with Benjamin. "His life is bound up in the lad's life. It shall come to pass, when he seeth that the lad is not with us, that he will die." He asks to be made a slave in Benjamin's place. "For how shall I go back to my father, and the lad be not with me? Lest peradventure I see the evil that shall come on my father." Joseph can no longer conceal his weeping and he reveals himself to his brothers. "He wept aloud: and that the Egyptians and the house of Pharaoh heard. And Joseph said unto his brethren, 'I am Joseph; doth my father yet live?'" His brothers are speechless, "troubled at his presence."

He brings them close to him and reassures them. "Now therefore be not grieved, nor angry with yourselves, that ye sold me hither: for God did send me before you to preserve life." Elevating these events, bitter as they are in themselves, to the level of divine providence lifts them beyond the reciprocities of injury and revenge, beyond

the reach of justice as we mortals understand that word.
It is not inevitable, humanly speaking, that the providential turn of events should mean that the brothers go un-
punished, that they should even be treated as if they were
guiltless. This is not a pardon. It is grace.

The book of Genesis is framed by two stories of remarkable forgiveness, of Cain by the Lord, and of his ten brothers by Joseph. Cain was the father of saintly Enoch and
the ancestor of Noah, from whom all humankind is descended. Nothing in Scripture suggests that human beings
are interchangeable, so providence would act through the
life of Cain to arrive at Noah, Cain's crime notwithstanding. Cain's descendants, through vengeful Lamech, also included Jubal, "the father of all such as handle the harp and
organ." Considering the importance of music in the Hebrew Bible, this is no small thing. Psalm 150, the conclud-
ing hymn in the great book of worship, says, "Praise [the
LORD] with stringed instruments and organs. Praise him
upon the loud cymbals: praise him upon the high sound-
ing cymbals." It would be wonderful to have been there.
Jubal's brother, Jabal, "was the father of such as dwell in
tents, and of such as have cattle," like Abraham, Isaac, and
Jacob. Providence can be seen working its way through
very mingled human history, blessing it with music and
with drifting pastoralists and their herds, sometimes,
unpredictably, transmuting evil into good. Measured revenge, justice as it is understood among mortals, is rig-

orously queried in Scripture, challenged in the text by a higher awareness, a knowledge of what could be lost if small earthly dramas of action and reaction foreclosed whatever might come in the fullness of time.

I have argued that the Flood is the working through of a philosophical question raised in another belief system, an excursus that reshapes a Babylonian thesis to serve Hebrew purposes. So I take it that the human world forming before the Flood should not be thought of as swept away as if it were wholly condemned. These primordial tales tell us the origins of the world we know: Jubal gave us musical instruments, Noah was the first vintner.

The very Hebrew coda added to the Flood story responds to the evil to which humankind is prone with a set of laws, notably one that allows and restrains violence. Whoever kills a man will be killed by a man. Adam kills Adam for killing Adam, an image of God destroys an image of God for having destroyed an image of God. Even in permitting condign punishment, the law makes clear the fundamental absurdity even of punishment limited by strict equivalence. It views the matter from the perspective of Creation, the great expression of divine intent that so radically sanctified humankind. The law expresses a terrible anomaly that takes its power from the fact that even in the miserable business of homicide, criminal or judicial, this sanctity is undiminished.

In the story of the Flood, God Himself might be said to have modeled revenge and its consequences. Extinction would be just punishment for the abuse of existence.

But He repented of the destruction He had caused, and even though, being God, He could have remade the world so that evil and violence were excluded from it, He forgave, or forbore, the corrupt thoughts of human hearts, setting certain bounds around human conduct insofar as law and covenant have that effect. He chose to let us be, to let time yield what it will—within the vast latitude granted by providence. Joseph's brothers are epochal figures. The narrative records little about any of them that redounds to his credit. But their mere existence as the sons of Jacob/Israel, with the multitudes of their descendants, makes them crucial to the unfolding of human and sacred history.

To speak of these events as providential might seem to lift them out of the world of human meaning and experience. This is a problem that always attends the idea of providence, especially when it is called by its other name, predestination. The story of Jacob and his sons proceeds entirely on human emotion and motivation even while it tends always toward the descent of Israel into Egypt foreseen in Abraham's nocturnal vision. Jacob's supplanting Esau, stealing his father's blessing, is understandable as rivalry between brothers. His flight to Padan-aram in fear of Esau's wrath brings him to Laban's household, to Rachel and Leah. His great love for Rachel and his favoring of her child helps stir the resentment of Joseph's brothers and their abandonment of him. Tamar appears in the tale, absolutely intent on producing sons for her two dead husbands. The famine comes, threatening survival, stirring fears of divine retribution, making the brothers assume correctly that events are more than meet the eye, even while their great fear and guilt lead them to misunderstand the sense in which this is true. Joseph is surpassingly businesslike in his various roles—officious as he was as a boy. He yields finally to the great burden of emotion that builds up in his manipulative dealings with his brothers. At no point are the actors' motives insufficient to account for events, and at no point are their actions out of character. Few elements in this story suggest that divine providence has a part in them, though we know it is active in them all. The story could, no doubt should, function as a theological proof that the earthly and the providential are separate things in theory only. In fact neither can be distinguished from the other or exist apart from the other. The text anticipates a thousand questions about this view of human life, in which for most of us little seems like providence. It does this by reminding us that, from the time of Abraham's dream of "an horror of great darkness," the children of Israel are bound for Egypt and slavery. To the extent that these events might be called providential in a purely positive sense, this would be true for the thousands of generations of Abraham's children, for all the families of earth. As for the Israelites who will live out the time of Egyptian oppression, little escapes the darkness of those four hundred years.

After Joseph has revealed himself, "he kissed all his brethren, and wept upon them." This recalls another meeting of estranged brothers, when Jacob, returning home to Canaan, encounters wronged Esau, who "embraced him, and fell on his neck, and kissed him: and they wept." This might be conventional language or behavior in such circumstances, but it does not detract from the richness of the text, since in neither case are those who are embraced by their erstwhile victims wholly persuaded of the authenticity of the gesture. Jacob deploys a bit of his famous guile to put distance between his people and Esau's troops of fighting men. Joseph's brothers are alarmed to discover him alive, more concerned for their safety than moved by an alleviation of their guilt. They will worry that after Jacob's death Joseph will turn on them and avenge himself. Convention is the politesse of ambiguous relationships. Both of these moments look, and in some degree must feel, like grace. Grace, being apart from the calculus of deserving, is often suspect.

Here is another pattern that recurs through Genesis. The first instance of it is found in the second Creation narrative when the Lord tells Adam and Eve that if they eat the fruit of the forbidden tree they will surely die. This is a simple statement of an offense and its punishment, if this then that, casuistical in its finality. Adam and Eve taste the fruit—and they do not die. Satan is right to reassure them. They live on, chastened, in a harsher version of the created world. The Flood narrative begins with the Lord's resolve to end all life and ends with a great relenting, and a changed, harsher world that is nevertheless again the place of seedtime and harvest, where the children of Noah can

still be fruitful and multiply. The text raises the prospect
of punishment that would be appropriate to transgression
or corruption and then steps away from the execution of
it, though not entirely. Grace tempers judgment. In this
way the text conceptualizes the justice of God together
with His mercy or grace or His loyalty to Creation. The
anomaly of His restraint or His repentance in these stories
is not evidence of flaws in the text or in the theology of
the writers but of the difficulty of expressing the simulta-
neity of these qualities in Him. As in the matter of Cain,
the tacit withholding of expected punishment may be
the primary point of these stories. When Jacob wrestles
all night with a man at the Jabbok River, he emerges
from the encounter lamed. He is given a name, Israel, for
which the text provides an etymology—"for as a prince
hast thou power with God and with men, and hast prevailed." The mysterious figure has crippled him with a
touch, which suggests power that is not wholly brought to
bear on this struggle. Jacob says when day comes that he
has looked on the face of God and lived. When Hagar had
her encounter with an angel rescuer, she expressed this
same amazement—not that she had seen His face but that
the force of the experience did not destroy her. In other
words, it is not the near presence of God Himself that is
primary in their reactions but the restraint that allowed her
and her child's survival and Jacob's long struggle as if with
an equal. They are amazed by the restraint that allows the
Lord to interact with them. The great metaphysical statement of the first Creation narrative might seem to evoke a

God who would not, perhaps could not, comfort a desperate servant woman or challenge the strength of a frightened man and let him feel he had prevailed. But a given of the text is that God is interested in human beings. If they are to be granted individuality, agency, freedom, meaningful existence as human beings, then God must practice almost limitless restraint. My language is entirely insufficient to my subject, but I hope to draw attention to an important consistency to be found in Genesis. To refrain, to put aside power is Godlike. Jacob says that seeing Esau is like looking on the face of God. Presumably this would not be true if Esau had met him with the vengeance Jacob feared, and of which his troops would have made Esau capable.

There will be other pharaohs who do not know Joseph, but this one is pleased to hear that Joseph's brothers have come and is eager to settle his whole family in Egypt, sending wagons to ease the journey for the women and little ones, and for Jacob. He says they "shall eat the fat of the land," and to tell them "the good of all the land of Egypt is yours." Joseph urges his brothers to come to him so that he can provide for them through the five years of famine that remain. He sends them back to Canaan and to Jacob with lavish gifts that will persuade his father that he really is alive, and a great man in Egypt. As these men, fathers and grandfathers, heads of households, leave for Canaan, he makes a little joke, reminding them of the irksome boy he was once. "See that ye fall not out by the way."

"And Israel took his journey with all that he had." He will see Joseph before he dies. At Beer-sheba he offers the God of Abraham, Isaac, and Jacob a sacrifice, and God appears to him in "visions of the night," assuring him that he should go down to Egypt, that He will be with him and will "make of thee a great nation" there, covenant language, which means that Jacob is not leaving his God or his heritage behind in leaving Canaan. The Lord, Who, in Hebrew dreams, speaks, tells Jacob, "Joseph shall put his hand upon thine eyes." There is no aggrandizement of these epochal mortals, but sometimes a tender attentiveness to them.

Joseph presents his father to Pharaoh. Jacob blesses this mighty man, a gentle assertion of his own dignity. Pharaoh asks his age, and Jacob replies that his life has made him old. At one hundred thirty, he knows he will not attain to the great age of his ancestors. "Few and evil have the days of the years of my life been." Here is the realism that sets Scripture apart. Jacob has found Joseph, not only living but in a position to preserve the lives of his whole family. Benjamin is safe and favored by Joseph. But the days of many years have been full of dread and loss and grief and suspicion, and no ending can be happy enough to change this.

After Joseph's family is well situated, given grazing land where presumably they will be unmolested because their way of life as shepherds is an abomination to Egyptians, there comes the long passage in which Joseph dispossesses the people of Egypt of all money, then all cattle, then all land and their own persons. This might broadly reflect a state of things that was characteristic of Egypt at some time. But this does not account for the attributing of it to Joseph. Under the law of Moses, land, which is owned collectively by each tribe, cannot be alienated permanently but must be restored to the original owners every fifty years. Slavery, likewise a recourse of poverty, is not a permanent status but is to be limited to a period of seven years with a bonus for the slave at the end of it. Moses, whoever he was, clearly wished to create a property system antithetical to the one thought to prevail in Egypt. Since Genesis would have been written, or have received its last refinements, long after the time of Moses, the standards he established for land tenure would have been known if not adhered to. All this could have gone unmentioned, or Joseph given no role in it. But it is characteristic of Joseph, always shrewd in someone else's interest, to exploit an opportunity. "Joseph bought all the land of Egypt for Pharaoh . . . The land became Pharaoh's. And as for the people, he removed them to cities from one end of the borders of Egypt even to the other end thereof." Thou shalt not abhor an Egyptian. The Egyptian has grievances, too.

The ending of Genesis brings to a close two sustained narratives, one the story of Joseph and his brothers, the other the story of Abraham, Isaac, and Jacob, the patriarchs, men with whose names God ever afterward chose to identify Himself. Before the rise of Joseph, the children of Abraham drifted through the world as their flocks and their little ones allowed, as drought required, as God directed. They were dwellers in tents and keepers of cattle, unexceptional, perhaps, even in having a conception of God unique to them, drawn from the dreams and visions of the most revered among them. Abraham stood in the door of his tent and saw the heavens shining with their multitudes of stars, which were all the families of earth. Now we know that there are vastly more stars than he would have seen, even allowing for the purity of earth's darkness on an ancient night. And the earth has indeed been fruitful, bearing and nurturing families enough to justify the Lord's promise. That radiant futurity had nothing to do with grandeur of any kind beyond its own singular magnificence. Abraham was told that he would be a blessing to humankind. We can't well imagine that there was such a man, brought out into the night by his friend the Lord to consider the ongoingness of Creation at its most spectacular and to be told by Him that he has a part in its unfolding. This moment is like nothing I know of in any other literature or myth system. It is worldly in that the vision sees the glory of the heavens as like the families of earth, which are and will be numerous and also glorious. In this moment it might be possible to say that Abraham saw as God sees, valuing humankind as God does.

The book of Genesis begins with the emergence of Being in a burst of light and ends with the death and burial of a bitter, homesick old man. If there is any truth to modern physics, this brings us to the present moment. Disgruntled and bewildered, knowing that we derive from an inconceivably powerful and brilliant first moment, we are at a loss to find anything of it in ourselves. God loved Jacob and was loyal to him, no less for the fact that Jacob felt the days of his life, providential as they were, as deep hardship.

After the passing of Jacob/Israel and his son Joseph no more will be heard of the Israelites for four hundred years. Their descent into Egypt is carefully prepared in the stories of both Jacob and Joseph, and when it comes it is a descent into utter silence. This is remarkable. Captivity in Egypt is a very central part of Israelite identity, yet no tales of pathos or of heroism are given a place in Scripture before the birth of Moses. Historical, literary, or both, this dark passage defeats every question that might be asked about its place in the working of providence.

For the purposes of the law it rooted compassion in experience, as for example in Deuteronomy 24:17–18: "Thou shalt not pervert the judgment of the stranger, nor of the fatherless; nor take a widow's raiment to pledge: but thou shalt remember that thou wast a bondman in Egypt, and the LORD thy God redeemed thee thence." Or the beautiful Exodus 23:9: "Thou shalt not oppress a stranger: for ye know the heart of a stranger, seeing ye were strangers in the land of Egypt." Laws based on compassionate identification with those most vulnerable to abuse are vanishingly rare, in antiquity and in every subsequent era. It is a comment on human nature, presumably, that a captivity so long and profound would be required to introduce this kind of empathy into personal and social morality. And it is another comment on human nature that such a harsh experience could yield an ethic of justice and generosity rather than of insularity and resentment. If Israelites fell short of this high standard, notably after their entry into Canaan, so do we all, and in much less exigent circumstances. As always, to their great credit, they cherished their mingled heritage and preserved it.

Redemption is another central idea that emerged for scriptural purposes from the centuries in Egypt. To be redeemed means literally to be "bought back," to be freed from trouble, especially bondage, by a kinsman or benefactor. Poverty or debt often led to slavery, so to pay the debt was to restore the debtor to freedom. God presents His intervention in these human terms that, like a covenant, involve loyalty to the relationship on the part of the stronger party. The word and the relationship retain the memory of slavery and of a gracious act of liberation. This understanding of the bond between God and Israel remains important through the whole of the Hebrew Bible. Its significance to the New Testament can hardly be overstated.

There is a moment early in the story of Moses that might have been the beginning of his career as a revolutionary leader. "He went out unto his brethren, and looked on their burdens: and he spied an Egyptian smiting an Hebrew, one of his brethren." A young man brought up in the circles of power and privilege one day realizes his identity with an oppressed people and reacts to an act of violence with violence, no doubt thinking that in killing the Egyptian and concealing his body he has done something just, worthy of respect. Perhaps assuming this, when he sees two Hebrews fighting, he asks the aggressor, "Wherefore smitest thou thy fellow?" The solidarity he has begun to feel he wants to encourage in them. The Hebrew makes a startling reply. "Who made thee a prince and a judge over us? Intendest thou to kill me, as thou killedst the Egyptian?" Moses is not admired for the violent act but taunted with it. Farther on in the story Moses does indeed emerge as a prince and judge, but not as the leader of an insurrection. His killing of the Egyptian, personification as the man may have been of the brutality suffered by the Hebrews, does not at all redound to his credit. So Moses will become the leader of an exodus, not an insurrection. This exchange with a nameless man, long before Moses is given his role by the God of Abraham, Isaac, and Jacob, is remembered in the text, an isolated Hebrew voice speaking out of the Egyptian silence, expressing in his way the old belief that to kill any human being is to kill Adam, God's image. Clearly Moses, who goes into hiding, understands his words to mean he will be seen by the Hebrews as a murderer and not a hero— and perhaps not as a Hebrew, either, since he has violated this prohibition. This is remarkable in the circumstances and crucial to the form resistance will take. We are told that the Egyptians feared the Hebrews because they had become so numerous. But rather than turning to force, through Moses and Aaron they ask Pharaoh for leave to be gone, and only when they have received it—granting spectacular coercions—do they depart. This is a moment in which some Spartacan act of heroic rebellion would be satisfying. And this is an instance in which God repays evil for evil. But the Hebrew people simply gather themselves up and walk out of Egypt.

Genesis can hardly be said to end. In it certain things are established—the nature of Creation and the spirit in which it was made; the nature of humankind; how and in what spirit the Creator God enters into relation with His human creatures. The whole great literature of Scripture, unfolding over centuries, will proceed on the terms established in this book. So Genesis is carried forward, in the law, in the psalms, in the prophets, itself a spectacular burst of light without antecedent but with a universe of consequences. This might seem like hyperbolic language to describe a text largely given over to the lives of people in many ways so ordinary that it is astonishing to find them in an ancient text. This realism by itself is a sort of miracle. These men and women saw the face of God, they heard His voice, and yet life for them came down to births and deaths, love, transgression, obedience, shame, and sorrow, everything done or borne in the course of the characterization of God, for Whom every one of us is a child of Adam, made in His image. God's bond with Jacob, truly a man of sorrows, is a radical theological statement.

Herman Melville's Father Mapple calls Scripture "a mighty cable." Its intertwined strands of narrative exist in time, which they also create, or assert. There are the three overlapping generations of the patriarchs, which reach their mortal conclusion in old Jacob. There is the slow working out of the confrontation of Joseph's brothers with their crime, time as experienced under a burden of guilt and dread. At the height of Joseph's power in Egypt, there is imminent time, the four hundred years for which he, unbeknownst to himself, is preparing the prologue. And there is God's time, always tending toward a resolution or realization or culmination inconceivable to us. Within this great arc are the eras we live out as history, and within them the comings and goings of human life, and human lives—the generations passing one to another the lore they have about it all, as they emerge and as they vanish.

To speak about strands of scriptural time is too schematic. It is useful, nevertheless. There is the kind of narrative that allows for character, experience, and choice and will be expressed most vividly in the psalms and the prophets. There is the constancy of the covenant, the Lord's faithfulness, which makes Him a presence in every ebbing of faith and in all impending trouble. Then there are visionary moments, which seem to rise out of time and take on, however briefly, the character of truth, of goodness as the word is used at Creation.

Joseph does not see the face of God, not in a dream that affirms God's care of him, nor in an angelic intervention in his time of sorrow and peril, nor in his embrace of his alienated brothers. What he sees instead is the working of divine intention.

In his first encounters with his brothers, Joseph is in the role of disguised avenger. Odysseus likewise conceals his identity to deal with offenses against him. He returns unrecognized from war and wandering to find his house filled with his wife's suitors and hangers-on. In an ecstasy of rage he plans and carries out a great slaughter. His house runs with blood. Not even servant girls are spared. In another literature a character in Joseph's place could have made a choice of this kind, could have demonstrated wiliness and power while he satisfied a crude definition of justice. But this is Scripture, and in place of catharsis there is an insight that casts its light over the narrative of Joseph and over the whole book of Genesis. When Joseph has made himself known to his brothers he tells them not to be distressed, because "God did send me before you to preserve life." On these grounds, because he is able to save them from famine, he has forgiven their abuse of him, or he has seen matters in another light that made their guilt of no interest. As always in Genesis where revenge or punishment is an issue, the demands of justice in the human sense are not satisfied. God might have killed Cain, Esau might have killed Jacob, Judah might have condemned Tamar to death, and Joseph might have made his brothers feel his anger and his power by letting them and their families starve. It must be true that sacred history would have found its way to its ends even if these lives had been cut short, though the story is told in a way that makes every one of these lives seem absolutely consequential. This is something to consider, seeing that it occurs in a context that can be taken to mean that divine intent is altogether determining.

From a literary point of view, the fact that both can be true simultaneously is amazing, Father Mapple's mighty cable at its most impressive. God's humanism is so absolute that one particular Egyptian serving girl must be the mother of the Ishmaelites, one particular Canaanite widow must complete in long anticipation the genealogy of King David. By extension, any one of us, if we knew as we are known, would realize that there was a role that required our assuming it, uniquely, out of all the brilliant constellations of human families. I won't speak here of the possibility of falling short, since there are so many instances of rescue, compensation, or reversal in the Bible that we are not competent to judge sufficiency or failure. If tasting that apple was the felix culpa, the "fortunate Fall" that launched us into history, the crime of Joseph's brothers was comparable as the impetus that began the history of the nation Israel.

How to make moral sense of this is a real question. The next great phase in the history of Israel is God's giving of the law, which is far too revelatory of His nature to be thought of as a kind of patch on a deeper antinomianism. In Romans, the apostle Paul paraphrases the book of Proverbs, "Be not overcome of evil, but overcome evil with good." Our punitive bias, the legitimation of *vengeance*, in many cases the sanctification of it, which never means respect for the fact that God has claimed it for Himself, very much complicates the issue. If one wishes to align oneself with the will of God, granting every difficulty, grace, kindness is clearly the safer choice.

When Jacob dies, Joseph asks "his servants the physicians" to embalm him, and they put the mortal remains of the old herdsman through this very protracted, utterly pagan process, which, the text notes, takes forty days. Then, with his family, they deliver him with much ceremony and lament to the cave in Canaan where lie Abraham and Sarah, Isaac and Rebekah, and Leah, once again the wrong wife. Jacob must have seemed a strange intrusion, mummified and encased. Everyone meant well. Joseph is embalmed in his turn and placed in a coffin in Egypt. After Joseph the situation of the Hebrews worsens.

While he lived, at the pinnacle of authority, Joseph saw his dreams play out more beautifully than anyone could have imagined, not as foreseeing mere superiority or dominance but instead as giving him an occasion to comfort, sustain, and forgive. This is the climax the narrative has been building toward since Cain and Abel. I know of no other literature except certain late plays of Shakespeare that elevates grace as this book does. Joseph's brothers have brooded for years on the grievous harm they have done him and their father. But in their darkest moment they might never have thought that Joseph himself, clothed in power, would hold their lives in his hands. Certainly they give little sign of happiness, even of relief, at seeing him. And when Jacob dies, they fear that Joseph will take his revenge on them. "When Joseph's brethren saw that their father was dead, they said, 'Joseph will peradventure hate us, and will certainly requite us all the evil which we did unto him.'" So they send him a message saying that their dying father instructed him to pardon them. "And now, we pray thee, forgive the trespass of the servants of the God of thy father." It is surprising to find them identifying themselves in these terms, since to this point their piety has been expressed only as dread of divine retribution. And yet, no matter how sincere they are in speaking in this way, what they say is perfectly true. Just these men will lead the Hebrews into Egypt and bondage. Their families will multiply until they become a people. The life of the nation Israel will instruct and bless multitudes. The names of Joseph's brothers will be remembered on earth for as long as the God of Genesis is remembered. Jacob struggled to find words of blessing for most of them, yet, like everyone whose story is told here—like everyone, presumably—they are indispensable. Joseph's act of forgiveness in effect opens the way for them to assume their essential, though unexplained and unrecorded role in sacred history. In every instance where it arises, forgiveness is rewarded by consequences that could not have been foreseen or imagined. The application of this doctrine is straightforward.

So what constraints are there on Joseph when the lives of his brothers seem to be his to take if he chooses? If providence has a use for them, their survival could be said to be predetermined. But the scene in which Joseph again pardons his brothers fully and finally is beautiful because, Egyptianized as he is, never favored with the visionary

dreams like those that engaged and instructed his fore-
fathers, he has seen the actual workings of providence, another kind of vision. When his brothers raise the matter of
his possible vengeance against them, he says, "Fear not:
for am I in the place of God?" Yes, he is, in the sense
that his mercy toward them seconds what he sees as God's
will. And yes, in the sense that he sees beyond a human
conception of justice, which shapes his brothers' fearful
expectations, to the good issue of everything that has happened to him—good he reckons in terms of the lives he
has saved. "As for you, ye thought evil against me; but
God meant it unto good, to bring to pass, as it is this day,
to save much people alive." He promises to look after his
brothers and their "little ones," who are never forgotten
when people are thought of in their vulnerable humanity.

At the end of his life, Joseph is revealed as a true heir
of the covenant. He says to his brothers, "God will surely
visit you, and bring you out of this land unto the land
which he sware to Abraham, to Isaac, and to Jacob . . .
God will surely visit you, and ye shall carry up my bones
from hence." And, after generations, when the Israelites
made their exodus from Egypt, "Moses took the bones of
Joseph with him."

GENESIS

KING JAMES
VERSION

GENESIS 1

[1] In the beginning God created the heaven and the earth. [2] And the earth was without form, and void; and darkness was upon the face of the deep. And the Spirit of God moved upon the face of the waters. [3] And God said, Let there be light: and there was light. [4] And God saw the light, that it was good: and God divided the light from the darkness. [5] And God called the light Day, and the darkness he called Night. And the evening and the morning were the first day. [6] And God said, Let there be a firmament in the midst of the waters, and let it divide the waters from the waters. [7] And God made the firmament, and divided the waters which were under the firmament from the waters which were above the firmament: and it was so. [8] And God called the firmament Heaven. And the evening and the morning were the second day. [9] And God said, Let the waters under the heaven be gathered together unto one place, and let the dry land appear: and it was so. [10] And God called the dry land Earth; and the gathering together of the waters called he Seas: and God saw that it was good. [11] And God said, Let

the earth bring forth grass, the herb yielding seed, and the fruit tree yielding fruit after his kind, whose seed is in itself, upon the earth: and it was so. [12] And the earth brought forth grass, and herb yielding seed after his kind, and the tree yielding fruit, whose seed was in itself, after his kind: and God saw that it was good. [13] And the evening and the morning were the third day. [14] And God said, Let there be lights in the firmament of the heaven to divide the day from the night; and let them be for signs, and for seasons, and for days, and years: [15] And let them be for lights in the firmament of the heaven to give light upon the earth: and it was so. [16] And God made two great lights; the greater light to rule the day, and the lesser light to rule the night: he made the stars also. [17] And God set them in the firmament of the heaven to give light upon the earth, [18] And to rule over the day and over the night, and to divide the light from the darkness: and God saw that it was good. [19] And the evening and the morning were the fourth day. [20] And God said, Let the waters bring forth abundantly the moving creature that hath life, and fowl that may fly above the earth in the open firmament of heaven. [21] And God created great whales, and every living creature that moveth, which the waters brought forth abundantly, after their kind, and every winged fowl after his kind: and God saw that it was good. [22] And God blessed them, saying, Be fruitful, and multiply, and fill the waters in the seas, and let fowl multiply in the earth. [23] And the evening and the morning were the fifth day. [24] And God said, Let the earth bring forth the living creature after his kind, cattle, and creeping thing, and beast of the earth after his kind: and it was so. [25] And God made the beast of the earth after his kind, and cattle after their kind, and every thing that creepeth upon the earth after his kind: and God saw that it was good. [26] And God said, Let us make man in our image, after our likeness: and let them have dominion over the fish of the sea, and over the fowl of the air, and over the cattle, and over all the earth, and over every creeping thing that creepeth upon the earth. [27] So God created man in his own image, in the image of God created he him; male and female created he them. [28] And God blessed them, and God said unto them, Be fruitful, and multiply, and replenish the earth, and subdue it: and have dominion over the fish of the sea, and over the fowl of the air, and over every living thing that moveth upon the earth. [29] And God said, Behold, I have given you every herb bearing seed, which is upon the face of all the earth, and every tree, in the which is the fruit of a tree yielding seed; to you it shall be for meat. [30] And to every beast of the earth, and to every fowl of the air, and to every thing that creepeth upon the earth, wherein there is life, I have given every green herb for meat: and it was so. [31] And God saw every thing that he had made, and, behold, it was very good. And the evening and the morning were the sixth day.

GENESIS 2

[1] Thus the heavens and the earth were finished, and all the host of them. [2] And on the seventh day God ended his work which he had made; and he rested on the seventh day from all his work which he had made. [3] And God blessed the seventh day, and sanctified it: because that in it he had rested from all his work which God created and made. [4] These are the generations of the heavens and of the earth when they were created, in the day that the LORD God made the earth and the heavens, [5] And every plant of the field before it was in the earth, and every herb of the field

before it grew: for the LORD God had not caused it to rain upon the earth, and there was not a man to till the ground. [6] But there went up a mist from the earth, and watered the whole face of the ground. [7] And the LORD God formed man of the dust of the ground, and breathed into his nostrils the breath of life; and man became a living soul. [8] And the LORD God planted a garden eastward in Eden; and there he put the man whom he had formed. [9] And out of the ground made the LORD God to grow every tree that is pleasant to the sight, and good for food; the tree of life also in the midst of the garden, and the tree of knowledge of good and evil. [10] And a river went out of Eden to water the garden; and from thence it was parted, and became into four heads. [11] The name of the first is Pison: that is it which compasseth the whole land of Havilah, where there is gold; [12] And the gold of that land is good: there is bdellium and the onyx stone. [13] And the name of the second river is Gihon: the same is it that compasseth the whole land of Ethiopia. [14] And the name of the third river is Hiddekel: that is it which goeth toward the east of Assyria. And the fourth river is Euphrates. [15] And the LORD God took the man, and put him into the garden of Eden to dress it and to keep it. [16] And the LORD God commanded the man, saying, Of every tree of the garden thou mayest freely eat: [17] But of the tree of the knowledge of good and evil, thou shalt not eat of it: for in the day that thou eatest thereof thou shalt surely die. [18] And the LORD God said, It is not good that the man should be alone; I will make him an help meet for him. [19] And out of the ground the LORD God formed every beast of the field, and every fowl of the air; and brought them unto Adam to see what he would call them: and whatsoever Adam called every living creature, that was the name thereof. [20] And Adam gave names to all cattle, and to the fowl of the air, and to every beast of the field; but for Adam there was not found an help meet for him. [21] And the LORD God caused a deep sleep to fall upon Adam, and he slept: and he took one of his ribs, and closed up the flesh instead thereof; [22] And the rib, which the LORD God had taken from man, made he a woman, and brought her unto the man.[23] And Adam said, This is now bone of my bones, and flesh of my flesh: she shall be called Woman, because she was taken out of Man. [24] Therefore shall a man leave his father and his mother, and shall cleave unto his wife: and they shall be one flesh. [25] And they were both naked, the man and his wife, and were not ashamed.

GENESIS 3

[1] Now the serpent was more subtil than any beast of the field which the LORD God had made. And he said unto the woman, Yea, hath God said, Ye shall not eat of every tree of the garden? [2] And the woman said unto the serpent, We may eat of the fruit of the trees of the garden: [3] But of the fruit of the tree which is in the midst of the garden, God hath said, Ye shall not eat of it, neither shall ye touch it, lest ye die. [4] And the serpent said unto the woman, Ye shall not surely die: [5] For God doth know that in the day ye eat thereof, then your eyes shall be opened, and ye shall be as gods, knowing good and evil. [6] And when the woman saw that the tree was good for food, and that it was pleasant to the eyes, and a tree to be desired to make one wise, she took of the fruit thereof, and did eat, and gave also unto her husband with her; and he did eat. [7] And the eyes of them both were opened, and they knew that they were naked; and they sewed fig leaves together, and made themselves aprons.

[8] And they heard the voice of the LORD God walking in the garden in the cool of the day: and Adam and his wife hid themselves from the presence of the LORD God amongst the trees of the garden. [9] And the LORD God called unto Adam, and said unto him, Where art thou? [10] And he said, I heard thy voice in the garden, and I was afraid, because I was naked; and I hid myself. [11] And he said, Who told thee that thou wast naked? Hast thou eaten of the tree, whereof I commanded thee that thou shouldest not eat? [12] And the man said, The woman whom thou gavest to be with me, she gave me of the tree, and I did eat. [13] And the LORD God said unto the woman, What is this that thou hast done? And the woman said, The serpent beguiled me, and I did eat. [14] And the LORD God said unto the serpent, Because thou hast done this, thou art cursed above all cattle, and above every beast of the field; upon thy belly shalt thou go, and dust shalt thou eat all the days of thy life: [15] And I will put enmity between thee and the woman, and between thy seed and her seed; it shall bruise thy head, and thou shalt bruise his heel. [16] Unto the woman he said, I will greatly multiply thy sorrow and thy conception; in sorrow thou shalt bring forth children; and thy desire shall be to thy husband, and he shall rule over thee. [17] And unto Adam he said, Because thou hast hearkened unto the voice of thy wife, and hast eaten of the tree, of which I commanded thee, saying, Thou shalt not eat of it: cursed is the ground for thy sake; in sorrow shalt thou eat of it all the days of thy life; [18] Thorns also and thistles shall it bring forth to thee; and thou shalt eat the herb of the field; [19] In the sweat of thy face shalt thou eat bread, till thou return unto the ground; for out of it wast thou taken: for dust thou art, and unto dust shalt thou return. [20] And Adam called his wife's name Eve; because she was the mother of all living. [21] Unto Adam also and to

his wife did the LORD God make coats of skins, and clothed them. [22] And the LORD God said, Behold, the man is become as one of us, to know good and evil: and now, lest he put forth his hand, and take also of the tree of life, and eat, and live for ever: [23] Therefore the LORD God sent him forth from the garden of Eden, to till the ground from whence he was taken. [24] So he drove out the man; and he placed at the east of the garden of Eden Cherubims, and a flaming sword which turned every way, to keep the way of the tree of life.

GENESIS 4

[1] And Adam knew Eve his wife; and she conceived, and bare Cain, and said, I have gotten a man from the LORD. [2] And she again bare his brother Abel. And Abel was a keeper of sheep, but Cain was a tiller of the ground. [3] And in process of time it came to pass, that Cain brought of the fruit of the ground an offering unto the LORD.[4] And Abel, he also brought of the firstlings of his flock and of the fat thereof. And the LORD had respect unto Abel and to his offering: [5] But unto Cain and to his offering he had not respect. And Cain was very wroth, and his countenance fell. [6] And the LORD said unto Cain, Why art thou wroth? and why is thy countenance fallen? [7] If thou doest well, shalt thou not be accepted? and if thou doest not well, sin lieth at the door. And unto thee shall be his desire, and thou shalt rule over him. [8] And Cain talked with Abel his brother: and it came to pass, when they were in the field, that Cain rose up against Abel his brother, and slew him. [9] And the LORD said unto Cain, Where is Abel thy brother? And he said, I know not: Am I my brother's keeper? [10] And he said, What hast thou

done? the voice of thy brother's blood crieth unto me from the ground. [11] And now art thou cursed from the earth, which hath opened her mouth to receive thy brother's blood from thy hand; [12] When thou tillest the ground, it shall not henceforth yield unto thee her strength; a fugitive and a vagabond shalt thou be in the earth. [13] And Cain said unto the LORD, My punishment is greater than I can bear. [14] Behold, thou hast driven me out this day from the face of the earth; and from thy face shall I be hid; and I shall be a fugitive and a vagabond in the earth; and it shall come to pass, that every one that findeth me shall slay me. [15] And the LORD said unto him, Therefore whosoever slayeth Cain, vengeance shall be taken on him sevenfold. And the LORD set a mark upon Cain, lest any finding him should kill him. [16] And Cain went out from the presence of the LORD, and dwelt in the land of Nod, on the east of Eden. [17] And Cain knew his wife; and she conceived, and bare Enoch: and he builded a city, and called the name of the city, after the name of his son, Enoch. [18] And unto Enoch was born Irad: and Irad begat Mehujael: and Mehujael begat Methusael: and Methusael begat Lamech. [19] And Lamech took unto him two wives: the name of the one was Adah, and the name of the other Zillah. [20] And Adah bare Jabal: he was the father of such as dwell in tents, and of such as have cattle. [21] And his brother's name was Jubal: he was the father of all such as handle the harp and organ. [22] And Zillah, she also bare Tubal-cain, an instructer of every artificer in brass and iron: and the sister of Tubal-cain was Naamah. [23] And Lamech said unto his wives, Adah and Zillah, Hear my voice; ye wives of Lamech, hearken unto my speech: for I have slain a man to my wounding, and a young man to my hurt. [24] If Cain shall be avenged sevenfold, truly Lamech seventy and sevenfold. [25] And Adam knew his wife again; and she bare a son, and called his name Seth: For God, said she, hath appointed me another seed instead of Abel, whom Cain slew. [26] And to Seth, to him also there was born a son; and he called his name Enos: then began men to call upon the name of the LORD.

GENESIS 5

[1] This is the book of the generations of Adam. In the day that God created man, in the likeness of God made he him; [2] Male and female created he them; and blessed them, and called their name Adam, in the day when they were created. [3] And Adam lived an hundred and thirty years, and begat a son in his own likeness, after his image; and called his name Seth: [4] And the days of Adam after he had begotten Seth were eight hundred years: and he begat sons and daughters: [5] And all the days that Adam lived were nine hundred and thirty years: and he died. [6] And Seth lived an hundred and five years, and begat Enos: [7] And Seth lived after he begat Enos eight hundred and seven years, and begat sons and daughters: [8] And all the days of Seth were nine hundred and twelve years: and he died. [9] And Enos lived ninety years, and begat Cainan: [10] And Enos lived after he begat Cainan eight hundred and fifteen years, and begat sons and daughters: [11] And all the days of Enos were nine hundred and five years: and he died. [12] And Cainan lived seventy years, and begat Mahalaleel: [13] And Cainan lived after he begat Mahalaleel eight hundred and forty years, and begat sons and daughters: [14] And all the days of Cainan were nine hundred and ten years: and he died. [15] And Mahalaleel lived sixty and five years, and begat Jared: [16] And Mahalaleel lived after he begat Jared eight hundred and thirty

years, and begat sons and daughters: [17] And all the days of Mahalaleel were eight hundred ninety and five years: and he died. [18] And Jared lived an hundred sixty and two years, and he begat Enoch: [19] And Jared lived after he begat Enoch eight hundred years, and begat sons and daughters: [20] And all the days of Jared were nine hundred sixty and two years: and he died. [21] And Enoch lived sixty and five years, and begat Methuselah: [22] And Enoch walked with God after he begat Methuselah three hundred years, and begat sons and daughters: [23] And all the days of Enoch were three hundred sixty and five years: [24] And Enoch walked with God: and he was not; for God took him. [25] And Methuselah lived an hundred eighty and seven years, and begat Lamech: [26] And Methuselah lived after he begat Lamech seven hundred eighty and two years, and begat sons and daughters: [27] And all the days of Methuselah were nine hundred sixty and nine years: and he died. [28] And Lamech lived an hundred eighty and two years, and begat a son: [29] And he called his name Noah, saying, This same shall comfort us concerning our work and toil of our hands, because of the ground which the LORD hath cursed. [30] And Lamech lived after he begat Noah five hundred ninety and five years, and begat sons and daughters: [31] And all the days of Lamech were seven hundred seventy and seven years: and he died. [32] And Noah was five hundred years old: and Noah begat Shem, Ham, and Japheth.

GENESIS 6

[1] And it came to pass, when men began to multiply on the face of the earth, and daughters were born unto them, [2] That the sons of God saw the daughters of men that

they were fair; and they took them wives of all which they chose. [3] And the LORD said, My spirit shall not always strive with man, for that he also is flesh: yet his days shall be an hundred and twenty years. [4] There were giants in the earth in those days; and also after that, when the sons of God came in unto the daughters of men, and they bare children to them, the same became mighty men which were of old, men of renown. [5] And God saw that the wickedness of man was great in the earth, and that every imagination of the thoughts of his heart was only evil continually. [6] And it repented the LORD that he had made man on the earth, and it grieved him at his heart. [7] And the LORD said, I will destroy man whom I have created from the face of the earth; both man, and beast, and the creeping thing, and the fowls of the air; for it repenteth me that I have made them. [8] But Noah found grace in the eyes of the LORD. [9] These are the generations of Noah: Noah was a just man and perfect in his generations, and Noah walked with God. [10] And Noah begat three sons, Shem, Ham, and Japheth. [11] The earth also was corrupt before God, and the earth was filled with violence. [12] And God looked upon the earth, and, behold, it was corrupt; for all flesh had corrupted his way upon the earth. [13] And God said unto Noah, The end of all flesh is come before me; for the earth is filled with violence through them; and, behold, I will destroy them with the earth. [14] Make thee an ark of gopher wood; rooms shalt thou make in the ark, and shalt pitch it within and without with pitch. [15] And this is the fashion which thou shalt make it of: The length of the ark shall be three hundred cubits, the breadth of it fifty cubits, and the height of it thirty cubits. [16] A window shalt thou make to the ark, and in a cubit shalt thou finish it above; and the door of the ark shalt thou set in the side thereof; with lower, second, and third stories shalt thou make it. [17] And, behold, I, even I, do bring a flood of waters upon the earth, to destroy all flesh, wherein is the breath of life, from under heaven; and every thing that is in the earth shall die. [18] But with thee will I establish my covenant; and thou shalt come into the ark, thou, and thy sons, and thy wife, and thy sons' wives with thee. [19] And of every living thing of all flesh, two of every sort shalt thou bring into the ark, to keep them alive with thee; they shall be male and female. [20] Of fowls after their kind, and of cattle after their kind, of every creeping thing of the earth after his kind, two of every sort shall come unto thee, to keep them alive. [21] And take thou unto thee of all food that is eaten, and thou shalt gather it to thee; and it shall be for food for thee, and for them. [22] Thus did Noah; according to all that God commanded him, so did he.

GENESIS 7

[1] And the LORD said unto Noah, Come thou and all thy house into the ark; for thee have I seen righteous before me in this generation. [2] Of every clean beast thou shalt take to thee by sevens, the male and his female: and of beasts that are not clean by two, the male and his female. [3] Of fowls also of the air by sevens, the male and the female; to keep seed alive upon the face of all the earth. [4] For yet seven days, and I will cause it to rain upon the earth forty days and forty nights; and every living substance that I have made will I destroy from off the face of the earth. [5] And Noah did according unto all that the LORD commanded him. [6] And Noah was six hundred years old when the flood of waters was upon the earth. [7] And Noah went in, and his sons, and his wife, and his sons' wives with him, into the ark, because of the waters

of the flood. [8] Of clean beasts, and of beasts that are not clean, and of fowls, and of every thing that creepeth upon the earth, [9] There went in two and two unto Noah into the ark, the male and the female, as God had commanded Noah. [10] And it came to pass after seven days, that the waters of the flood were upon the earth. [11] In the six hundredth year of Noah's life, in the second month, the seventeenth day of the month, the same day were all the fountains of the great deep broken up, and the windows of heaven were opened. [12] And the rain was upon the earth forty days and forty nights. [13] In the selfsame day entered Noah, and Shem, and Ham, and Japheth, the sons of Noah, and Noah's wife, and the three wives of his sons with them, into the ark; [14] They, and every beast after his kind, and all the cattle after their kind, and every creeping thing that creepeth upon the earth after his kind, and every fowl after his kind, every bird of every sort. [15] And they went in unto Noah into the ark, two and two of all flesh, wherein is the breath of life. [16] And they that went in, went in male and female of all flesh, as God had commanded him: and the LORD shut him in. [17] And the flood was forty days upon the earth; and the waters increased, and bare up the ark, and it was lift up above the earth. [18] And the waters prevailed, and were increased greatly upon the earth; and the ark went upon the face of the waters. [19] And the waters prevailed exceedingly upon the earth; and all the high hills, that were under the whole heaven, were covered. [20] Fifteen cubits upward did the waters prevail; and the mountains were covered. [21] And all flesh died that moved upon the earth, both of fowl, and of cattle, and of beast, and of every creeping thing that creepeth upon the earth, and every man: [22] All in whose nostrils was the breath of life, of all that was in the dry land, died. [23] And every living substance was destroyed which was upon the face of the ground, both man, and cattle, and the creeping things, and the fowl of the heaven; and they were destroyed from the earth: and Noah only remained alive, and they that were with him in the ark. [24] And the waters prevailed upon the earth an hundred and fifty days.

GENESIS 8

[1] And God remembered Noah, and every living thing, and all the cattle that was with him in the ark: and God made a wind to pass over the earth, and the waters asswaged; [2] The fountains also of the deep and the windows of heaven were stopped, and the rain from heaven was restrained; [3] And the waters returned from off the earth continually: and after the end of the hundred and fifty days the waters were abated. [4] And the ark rested in the seventh month, on the seventeenth day of the month, upon the mountains of Ararat. [5] And the waters decreased continually until the tenth month: in the tenth month, on the first day of the month, were the tops of the mountains seen. [6] And it came to pass at the end of forty days, that Noah opened the window of the ark which he had made: [7] And he sent forth a raven, which went forth to and fro, until the waters were dried up from off the earth. [8] Also he sent forth a dove from him, to see if the waters were abated from off the face of the ground; [9] But the dove found no rest for the sole of her foot, and she returned unto him into the ark, for the waters were on the face of the whole earth: then he put forth his hand, and took her, and pulled her in unto him into the ark. [10] And he stayed yet other seven days; and again he sent forth the dove out of the ark; [11] And the dove came in to him in the evening; and, lo, in her mouth was an olive leaf pluckt off: so Noah knew that

the waters were abated from off the earth. [12] And he stayed yet other seven days; and sent forth the dove; which returned not again unto him any more. [13] And it came to pass in the six hundredth and first year, in the first month, the first day of the month, the waters were dried up from off the earth: and Noah removed the covering of the ark, and looked, and, behold, the face of the ground was dry. [14] And in the second month, on the seven and twentieth day of the month, was the earth dried. [15] And God spake unto Noah, saying, [16] Go forth of the ark, thou, and thy wife, and thy sons, and thy sons' wives with thee. [17] Bring forth with thee every living thing that is with thee, of all flesh, both of fowl, and of cattle, and of every creeping thing that creepeth upon the earth; that they may breed abundantly in the earth, and be fruitful, and multiply upon the earth. [18] And Noah went forth, and his sons, and his wife, and his sons' wives with him: [19] Every beast, every creeping thing, and every fowl, and whatsoever creepeth upon the earth, after their kinds, went forth out of the ark. [20] And Noah builded an altar unto the LORD; and took of every clean beast, and of every clean fowl, and offered burnt offerings on the altar. [21] And the LORD smelled a sweet savour; and the LORD said in his heart, I will not again curse the ground any more for man's sake; for the imagination of man's heart is evil from his youth; neither will I again smite any more every thing living, as I have done. [22] While the earth remaineth, seedtime and harvest, and cold and heat, and summer and winter, and day and night shall not cease.

GENESIS 9

[1] And God blessed Noah and his sons, and said unto them, Be fruitful, and multiply, and replenish the earth. [2] And

the fear of you and the dread of you shall be upon every beast of the earth, and upon every fowl of the air, upon all that moveth upon the earth, and upon all the fishes of the sea; into your hand are they delivered. [3] Every moving thing that liveth shall be meat for you; even as the green herb have I given you all things. [4] But flesh with the life thereof, which is the blood thereof, shall ye not eat. [5] And surely your blood of your lives will I require; at the hand of every beast will I require it, and at the hand of man; at the hand of every man's brother will I require the life of man. [6] Whoso sheddeth man's blood, by man shall his blood be shed: for in the image of God made he man. [7] And you, be ye fruitful, and multiply; bring forth abundantly in the earth, and multiply therein. [8] And God spake unto Noah, and to his sons with him, saying, [9] And I, behold, I establish my covenant with you, and with your seed after you; [10] And with every living creature that is with you, of the fowl, of the cattle, and of every beast of the earth with you; from all that go out of the ark, to every beast of the earth. [11] And I will establish my covenant with you; neither shall all flesh be cut off any more by the waters of a flood; neither shall there any more be a flood to destroy the earth. [12] And God said, This is the token of the covenant which I make between me and you and every living creature that is with you, for perpetual generations: [13] I do set my bow in the cloud, and it shall be for a token of a covenant between me and the earth. [14] And it shall come to pass, when I bring a cloud over the earth, that the bow shall be seen in the cloud: [15] And I will remember my covenant, which is between me and you and every living creature of all flesh; and the waters shall no more become a flood to destroy all flesh. [16] And the bow shall be in the cloud; and I will look upon it, that I may remember the everlasting covenant between God and every living creature of all flesh that is upon the earth. [17] And God said unto Noah, This is the token of the covenant, which I have established between me and all flesh that is upon the earth. [18] And the sons of Noah, that went forth of the ark, were Shem, and Ham, and Japheth: and Ham is the father of Canaan. [19] These are the three sons of Noah: and of them was the whole earth overspread. [20] And Noah began to be an husbandman, and he planted a vineyard: [21] And he drank of the wine, and was drunken; and he was uncovered within his tent. [22] And Ham, the father of Canaan, saw the nakedness of his father, and told his two brethren without. [23] And Shem and Japheth took a garment, and laid it upon both their shoulders, and went backward, and covered the nakedness of their father; and their faces were backward, and they saw not their father's nakedness. [24] And Noah awoke from his wine, and knew what his younger son had done unto him. [25] And he said, Cursed be Canaan; a servant of servants shall he be unto his brethren. [26] And he said, Blessed be the LORD God of Shem; and Canaan shall be his servant. [27] God shall enlarge Japheth, and he shall dwell in the tents of Shem; and Canaan shall be his servant. [28] And Noah lived after the flood three hundred and fifty years. [29] And all the days of Noah were nine hundred and fifty years: and he died.

GENESIS 10

[1] Now these are the generations of the sons of Noah, Shem, Ham, and Japheth: and unto them were sons born after the flood. [2] The sons of Japheth; Gomer, and Magog, and Madai, and Javan, and Tubal, and Meshech, and Tiras. [3] And

the sons of Gomer; Ashkenaz, and Riphath, and Togarmah. [4] And the sons of Javan; Elishah, and Tarshish, Kittim, and Dodanim. [5] By these were the isles of the Gentiles divided in their lands; every one after his tongue, after their families, in their nations. [6] And the sons of Ham; Cush, and Mizraim, and Phut, and Canaan. [7] And the sons of Cush; Seba, and Havilah, and Sabtah, and Raamah, and Sabtechah: and the sons of Raamah; Sheba, and Dedan. [8] And Cush begat Nimrod: he began to be a mighty one in the earth. [9] He was a mighty hunter before the LORD: wherefore it is said, Even as Nimrod the mighty hunter before the LORD. [10] And the beginning of his kingdom was Babel, and Erech, and Accad, and Calneh, in the land of Shinar. [11] Out of that land went forth Asshur, and builded Nineveh, and the city Rehoboth, and Calah, [12] And Resen between Nineveh and Calah: the same is a great city. [13] And Mizraim begat Ludim, and Anamim, and Lehabim, and Naphtuhim, [14] And Pathrusim, and Casluhim, (out of whom came Philistim,) and Caphtorim. [15] And Canaan begat Sidon his firstborn, and Heth, [16] And the Jebusite, and the Amorite, and the Girgasite, [17] And the Hivite, and the Arkite, and the Sinite, [18] And the Arvadite, and the Zemarite, and the Hamathite: and afterward were the families of the Canaanites spread abroad. [19] And the border of the Canaanites was from Sidon, as thou comest to Gerar, unto Gaza; as thou goest, unto Sodom, and Gomorrah, and Admah, and Zeboim, even unto Lasha. [20] These are the sons of Ham, after their families, after their tongues, in their countries, and in their nations. [21] Unto Shem also, the father of all the children of Eber, the brother of Japheth the elder, even to him were children born. [22] The children of Shem; Elam, and Asshur, and Arphaxad, and Lud, and Aram. [23] And the children of Aram; Uz, and Hul, and Gether, and Mash. [24] And Arphaxad begat Salah; and Salah begat Eber. [25] And unto Eber were born two sons: the name of one was Peleg; for in his days was the earth divided; and his brother's name was Joktan. [26] And Joktan begat Almodad, and Sheleph, and Hazarmaveth, and Jerah, [27] And Hadoram, and Uzal, and Diklah, [28] And Obal, and Abimael, and Sheba, [29] And Ophir, and Havilah, and Jobab: all these were the sons of Joktan. [30] And their dwelling was from Mesha, as thou goest unto Sephar a mount of the east. [31] These are the sons of Shem, after their families, after their tongues, in their lands, after their nations. [32] These are the families of the sons of Noah, after their generations, in their nations: and by these were the nations divided in the earth after the flood.

GENESIS 11

[1] And the whole earth was of one language, and of one speech. [2] And it came to pass, as they journeyed from the east, that they found a plain in the land of Shinar; and they dwelt there. [3] And they said one to another, Go to, let us make brick, and burn them throughly. And they had brick for stone, and slime had they for morter. [4] And they said, Go to, let us build us a city and a tower, whose top may reach unto heaven; and let us make us a name, lest we be scattered abroad upon the face of the whole earth. [5] And the LORD came down to see the city and the tower, which the children of men builded. [6] And the LORD said, Behold, the people is one, and they have all one language; and this they begin to do: and now nothing will be restrained from them, which

they have imagined to do. [7] Go to, let us go down, and there confound their language, that they may not understand one another's speech. [8] So the LORD scattered them abroad from thence upon the face of all the earth: and they left off to build the city. [9] Therefore is the name of it called Babel; because the LORD did there confound the language of all the earth: and from thence did the LORD scatter them abroad upon the face of all the earth. [10] These are the generations of Shem: Shem was an hundred years old, and begat Arphaxad two years after the flood: [11] And Shem lived after he begat Arphaxad five hundred years, and begat sons and daughters. [12] And Arphaxad lived five and thirty years, and begat Salah: [13] And Arphaxad lived after he begat Salah four hundred and three years, and begat sons and daughters. [14] And Salah lived thirty years, and begat Eber: [15] And Salah lived after he begat Eber four hundred and three years, and begat sons and daughters. [16] And Eber lived four and thirty years, and begat Peleg: [17] And Eber lived after he begat Peleg four hundred and thirty years, and begat sons and daughters. [18] And Peleg lived thirty years, and begat Reu: [19] And Peleg lived after he begat Reu two hundred and nine years, and begat sons and daughters. [20] And Reu lived two and thirty years, and begat Serug: [21] And Reu lived after he begat Serug two hundred and seven years, and begat sons and daughters. [22] And Serug lived thirty years, and begat Nahor: [23] And Serug lived after he begat Nahor two hundred years, and begat sons and daughters. [24] And Nahor lived nine and twenty years, and begat Terah: [25] And Nahor lived after he begat Terah an hundred and nineteen years, and begat sons and daughters. [26] And Terah lived seventy years, and begat Abram, Nahor, and Haran. [27] Now these are the generations of Terah: Terah begat Abram, Nahor, and Haran; and Haran begat Lot. [28] And Haran died before his father Terah in the land of his nativity, in Ur of the Chaldees. [29] And Abram and Nahor took them wives: the name of Abram's wife was Sarai; and the name of Nahor's wife, Milcah, the daughter of Haran, the father of Milcah, and the father of Iscah. [30] But Sarai was barren; she had no child. [31] And Terah took Abram his son, and Lot the son of Haran his son's son, and Sarai his daughter in law, his son Abram's wife; and they went forth with them from Ur of the Chaldees, to go into the land of Canaan; and they came unto Haran, and dwelt there. [32] And the days of Terah were two hundred and five years: and Terah died in Haran.

GENESIS 12

[1] Now the LORD had said unto Abram, Get thee out of thy country, and from thy kindred, and from thy father's house, unto a land that I will shew thee: [2] And I will make of thee a great nation, and I will bless thee, and make thy name great; and thou shalt be a blessing: [3] And I will bless them that bless thee, and curse him that curseth thee: and in thee shall all families of the earth be blessed. [4] So Abram departed, as the LORD had spoken unto him; and Lot went with him: and Abram was seventy and five years old when he departed out of Haran. [5] And Abram took Sarai his wife, and Lot his brother's son, and all their substance that they had gathered, and the souls that they had gotten in Haran; and they went forth to go into the land of Canaan; and into the land of Canaan they came. [6] And Abram passed through the land unto the place of Sichem, unto the plain of Moreh. And the

Canaanite was then in the land. [7] And the LORD appeared unto Abram, and said, Unto thy seed will I give this land: and there builded he an altar unto the LORD, who appeared unto him. [8] And he removed from thence unto a mountain on the east of Beth-el, and pitched his tent, having Beth-el on the west, and Hai on the east: and there he builded an altar unto the LORD, and called upon the name of the LORD. [9] And Abram journeyed, going on still toward the south. [10] And there was a famine in the land: and Abram went down into Egypt to sojourn there; for the famine was grievous in the land. [11] And it came to pass, when he was come near to enter into Egypt, that he said unto Sarai his wife, Behold now, I know that thou art a fair woman to look upon: [12] Therefore it shall come to pass, when the Egyptians shall see thee, that they shall say, This is his wife: and they will kill me, but they will save thee alive. [13] Say, I pray thee, thou art my sister: that it may be well with me for thy sake; and my soul shall live because of thee. [14] And it came to pass, that, when Abram was come into Egypt, the Egyptians beheld the woman that she was very fair. [15] The princes also of Pharaoh saw her, and commended her before Pharaoh: and the woman was taken into Pharaoh's house. [16] And he entreated Abram well for her sake: and he had sheep, and oxen, and he asses, and menservants, and maidservants, and she asses, and camels. [17] And the LORD plagued Pharaoh and his house with great plagues because of Sarai Abram's wife. [18] And Pharaoh called Abram, and said, What is this that thou hast done unto me? why didst thou not tell me that she was thy wife? [19] Why saidst thou, She is my sister? so I might have taken her to me to wife: now therefore behold thy wife, take her, and go thy way. [20] And Pharaoh commanded his men concerning him: and they sent him away, and his wife, and all that he had.

GENESIS 13

[1] And Abram went up out of Egypt, he, and his wife, and all that he had, and Lot with him, into the south. [2] And Abram was very rich in cattle, in silver, and in gold. [3] And he went on his journeys from the south even to Beth-el, unto the place where his tent had been at the beginning, between Beth-el and Hai; [4] Unto the place of the altar, which he had made there at the first: and there Abram called on the name of the LORD. [5] And Lot also, which went with Abram, had flocks, and herds, and tents. [6] And the land was not able to bear them, that they might dwell together: for their substance was great, so that they could not dwell together. [7] And there was a strife between the herdmen of Abram's cattle and the herdmen of Lot's cattle: and the Canaanite and the Perizzite dwelled then in the land. [8] And Abram said unto Lot, Let there be no strife, I pray thee, between me and thee, and between my herdmen and thy herdmen; for we be brethren. [9] Is not the whole land before thee? separate thyself, I pray thee, from me: if thou wilt take the left hand, then I will go to the right; or if thou depart to the right hand, then I will go to the left. [10] And Lot lifted up his eyes, and beheld all the plain of Jordan, that it was well watered every where, before the LORD destroyed Sodom and Gomorrah, even as the garden of the LORD, like the land of Egypt, as thou comest unto Zoar. [11] Then Lot chose him all the plain of Jordan; and Lot journeyed east: and they separated themselves the one from the other. [12] Abram dwelled in the land of Canaan, and Lot dwelled in the cities of the plain, and pitched his tent toward Sodom. [13] But the men of Sodom were wicked and sinners before the LORD exceedingly. [14] And the LORD said unto Abram, after that Lot was separated from him, Lift up now thine

eyes, and look from the place where thou art northward, and southward, and eastward, and westward: [15] For all the land which thou seest, to thee will I give it, and to thy seed for ever. [16] And I will make thy seed as the dust of the earth: so that if a man can number the dust of the earth, then shall thy seed also be numbered. [17] Arise, walk through the land in the length of it and in the breadth of it; for I will give it unto thee. [18] Then Abram removed his tent, and came and dwelt in the plain of Mamre, which is in Hebron, and built there an altar unto the LORD.

GENESIS 14

[1] And it came to pass in the days of Amraphel king of Shinar, Arioch king of Ellasar, Chedorlaomer king of Elam, and Tidal king of nations; [2] That these made war with Bera king of Sodom, and with Birsha king of Gomorrah, Shinab king of Admah, and Shemeber king of Zeboiim, and the king of Bela, which is Zoar. [3] All these were joined together in the vale of Siddim, which is the salt sea. [4] Twelve years they served Chedorlaomer, and in the thirteenth year they rebelled. [5] And in the fourteenth year came Chedorlaomer, and the kings that were with him, and smote the Rephaims in Ashteroth Karnaim, and the Zuzims in Ham, and the Emims in Shaveh Kiriathaim, [6] And the Horites in their mount Seir, unto El-paran, which is by the wilderness. [7] And they returned, and came to En-mishpat, which is Kadesh, and smote all the country of the Amalekites, and also the Amorites that dwelt in Hazezon-tamar. [8] And there went out the king of Sodom, and the king of Gomorrah, and the king of Admah, and the king of Zeboiim, and the king of Bela (the same is Zoar;) and they joined battle with them in the vale of Siddim; [9] With

Chedorlaomer the king of Elam, and with Tidal king of nations, and Amraphel king of Shinar, and Arioch king of Ellasar; four kings with five. [10] And the vale of Siddim was full of slimepits; and the kings of Sodom and Gomorrah fled, and fell there; and they that remained fled to the mountain. [11] And they took all the goods of Sodom and Gomorrah, and all their victuals, and went their way. [12] And they took Lot, Abram's brother's son, who dwelt in Sodom, and his goods, and departed. [13] And there came one that had escaped, and told Abram the Hebrew; for he dwelt in the plain of Mamre the Amorite, brother of Eschol, and brother of Aner: and these were confederate with Abram. [14] And when Abram heard that his brother was taken captive, he armed his trained servants, born in his own house, three hundred and eighteen, and pursued them unto Dan. [15] And he divided himself against them, he and his servants, by night, and smote them, and pursued them unto Hobah, which is on the left hand of Damascus. [16] And he brought back all the goods, and also brought again his brother Lot, and his goods, and the women also, and the people. [17] And the king of Sodom went out to meet him after his return from the slaughter of Chedorlaomer, and of the kings that were with him, at the valley of Shaveh, which is the king's dale. [18] And Melchizedek king of Salem brought forth bread and wine: and he was the priest of the most high God. [19] And he blessed him, and said, Blessed be Abram of the most high God, possessor of heaven and earth: [20] And blessed be the most high God, which hath delivered thine enemies into thy hand. And he gave him tithes of all. [21] And the king of Sodom said unto Abram, Give me the persons, and take the goods to thyself. [22] And Abram said to the king of Sodom, I have lift up mine hand unto the LORD, the most high God, the possessor of heaven and earth, [23] That I will not take from a thread even to a shoelatchet, and that I will not take any thing that is thine, lest thou shouldest say, I have made Abram rich: [24] Save only that which the young men have eaten, and the portion of the men which went with me, Aner, Eshcol, and Mamre; let them take their portion.

GENESIS 15

[1] After these things the word of the LORD came unto Abram in a vision, saying, Fear not, Abram: I am thy shield, and thy exceeding great reward. [2] And Abram said, Lord GOD, what wilt thou give me, seeing I go childless, and the steward of my house is this Eliezer of Damascus? [3] And Abram said, Behold, to me thou hast given no seed: and, lo, one born in my house is mine heir. [4] And, behold, the word of the LORD came unto him, saying, This shall not be thine heir; but he that shall come forth out of thine own bowels shall be thine heir. [5] And he brought him forth abroad, and said, Look now toward heaven, and tell the stars, if thou be able to number them: and he said unto him, So shall thy seed be. [6] And he believed in the LORD; and he counted it to him for righteousness. [7] And he said unto him, I am the LORD that brought thee out of Ur of the Chaldees, to give thee this land to inherit it. [8] And he said, Lord GOD, whereby shall I know that I shall inherit it? [9] And he said unto him, Take me an heifer of three years old, and a she goat of three years old, and a ram of three years old, and a turtledove, and a young pigeon. [10] And he took unto him all these, and divided them in the midst, and laid each piece one against another: but the birds divided he not. [11] And when the fowls came down upon the carcases, Abram drove them away. [12] And when the sun was going down, a deep sleep

fell upon Abram; and, lo, an horror of great darkness fell upon him. [13] And he said unto Abram, Know of a surety that thy seed shall be a stranger in a land that is not theirs, and shall serve them; and they shall afflict them four hundred years; [14] And also that nation, whom they shall serve, will I judge: and afterward shall they come out with great substance. [15] And thou shalt go to thy fathers in peace; thou shalt be buried in a good old age. [16] But in the fourth generation they shall come hither again: for the iniquity of the Amorites is not yet full. [17] And it came to pass, that, when the sun went down, and it was dark, behold a smoking furnace, and a burning lamp that passed between those pieces. [18] In the same day the LORD made a covenant with Abram, saying, Unto thy seed have I given this land, from the river of Egypt unto the great river, the river Euphrates: [19] The Kenites, and the Kenizzites, and the Kadmonites, [20] And the Hittites, and the Perizzites, and the Rephaims, [21] And the Amorites, and the Canaanites, and the Girgashites, and the Jebusites.

GENESIS 16

[1] Now Sarai Abram's wife bare him no children: and she had an handmaid, an Egyptian, whose name was Hagar. [2] And Sarai said unto Abram, Behold now, the LORD hath restrained me from bearing: I pray thee, go in unto my maid; it may be that I may obtain children by her. And Abram hearkened to the voice of Sarai. [3] And Sarai Abram's wife took Hagar her maid the Egyptian, after Abram had dwelt ten years in the land of Canaan, and gave her to her husband Abram to be his wife. [4] And he went in unto Hagar, and she conceived: and when she saw that she had conceived, her mistress was despised in her eyes. [5] And Sarai said unto Abram, My

wrong be upon thee: I have given my maid into thy bosom; and when she saw that she had conceived, I was despised in her eyes: the LORD judge between me and thee. [6] But Abram said unto Sarai, Behold, thy maid is in thy hand; do to her as it pleaseth thee. And when Sarai dealt hardly with her, she fled from her face. [7] And the angel of the LORD found her by a fountain of water in the wilderness, by the fountain in the way to Shur. [8] And he said, Hagar, Sarai's maid, whence camest thou? and whither wilt thou go? And she said, I flee from the face of my mistress Sarai. [9] And the angel of the LORD said unto her, Return to thy mistress, and submit thyself under her hands. [10] And the angel of the LORD said unto her, I will multiply thy seed exceedingly, that it shall not be numbered for multitude. [11] And the angel of the LORD said unto her, Behold, thou art with child, and shalt bear a son, and shalt call his name Ishmael; because the LORD hath heard thy affliction. [12] And he will be a wild man; his hand will be against every man, and every man's hand against him; and he shall dwell in the presence of all his brethren. [13] And she called the name of the LORD that spake unto her, Thou God seest me: for she said, Have I also here looked after him that seeth me? [14] Wherefore the well was called Beerlahai-roi; behold, it is between Kadesh and Bered. [15] And Hagar bare Abram a son: and Abram called his son's name, which Hagar bare, Ishmael. [16] And Abram was fourscore and six years old, when Hagar bare Ishmael to Abram.

GENESIS 17

[1] And when Abram was ninety years old and nine, the LORD appeared to Abram, and said unto him, I am the Almighty God; walk before me, and be thou perfect. [2] And

I will make my covenant between me and thee, and will multiply thee exceedingly. [3] And Abram fell on his face: and God talked with him, saying, [4] As for me, behold, my covenant is with thee, and thou shalt be a father of many nations. [5] Neither shall thy name any more be called Abram, but thy name shall be Abraham; for a father of many nations have I made thee. [6] And I will make thee exceeding fruitful, and I will make nations of thee, and kings shall come out of thee. [7] And I will establish my covenant between me and thee and thy seed after thee in their generations for an everlasting covenant, to be a God unto thee, and to thy seed after thee. [8] And I will give unto thee, and to thy seed after thee, the land wherein thou art a stranger, all the land of Canaan, for an everlasting possession; and I will be their God. [9] And God said unto Abraham, Thou shalt keep my covenant therefore, thou, and thy seed after thee in their generations. [10] This is my covenant, which ye shall keep, between me and you and thy seed after thee; Every man child among you shall be circumcised. [11] And ye shall circumcise the flesh of your foreskin; and it shall be a token of the covenant betwixt me and you. [12] And he that is eight days old shall be circumcised among you, every man child in your generations, he that is born in the house, or bought with money of any stranger, which is not of thy seed. [13] He that is born in thy house, and he that is bought with thy money, must needs be circumcised: and my covenant shall be in your flesh for an everlasting covenant. [14] And the uncircumcised man child whose flesh of his foreskin is not circumcised, that soul shall be cut off from his people; he hath broken my covenant. [15] And God said unto Abraham, As for Sarai thy wife, thou shalt not call her name Sarai, but Sarah shall her name be. [16] And I will bless her, and give thee a son also of her: yea, I will bless her, and she shall be a mother of nations;

kings of people shall be of her. [17] Then Abraham fell upon his face, and laughed, and said in his heart, Shall a child be born unto him that is an hundred years old? and shall Sarah, that is ninety years old, bear? [18] And Abraham said unto God, O that Ishmael might live before thee! [19] And God said, Sarah thy wife shall bear thee a son indeed; and thou shalt call his name Isaac: and I will establish my covenant with him for an everlasting covenant, and with his seed after him. [20] And as for Ishmael, I have heard thee: Behold, I have blessed him, and will make him fruitful, and will multiply him exceedingly; twelve princes shall he beget, and I will make him a great nation. [21] But my covenant will I establish with Isaac, which Sarah shall bear unto thee at this set time in the next year. [22] And he left off talking with him, and God went up from Abraham. [23] And Abraham took Ishmael his son, and all that were born in his house, and all that were bought with his money, every male among the men of Abraham's house; and circumcised the flesh of their foreskin in the selfsame day, as God had said unto him. [24] And Abraham was ninety years old and nine, when he was circumcised in the flesh of his foreskin. [25] And Ishmael his son was thirteen years old, when he was circumcised in the flesh of his foreskin. [26] In the selfsame day was Abraham circumcised, and Ishmael his son. [27] And all the men of his house, born in the house, and bought with money of the stranger, were circumcised with him.

GENESIS 18

[1] And the LORD appeared unto him in the plains of Mamre: and he sat in the tent door in the heat of the day; [2] And he lift up his eyes and looked, and, lo, three men stood

by him: and when he saw them, he ran to meet them from the tent door, and bowed himself toward the ground, [3] And said, My Lord, if now I have found favour in thy sight, pass not away, I pray thee, from thy servant: [4] Let a little water, I pray you, be fetched, and wash your feet, and rest yourselves under the tree: [5] And I will fetch a morsel of bread, and comfort ye your hearts; after that ye shall pass on: for therefore are ye come to your servant. And they said, So do, as thou hast said. [6] And Abraham hastened into the tent unto Sarah, and said, Make ready quickly three measures of fine meal, knead it, and make cakes upon the hearth. [7] And Abraham ran unto the herd, and fetcht a calf tender and good, and gave it unto a young man; and he hasted to dress it. [8] And he took butter, and milk, and the calf which he had dressed, and set it before them; and he stood by them under the tree, and they did eat. [9] And they said unto him, Where is Sarah thy wife? And he said, Behold, in the tent. [10] And he said, I will certainly return unto thee according to the time of life; and, lo, Sarah thy wife shall have a son. And Sarah heard it in the tent door, which was behind him. [11] Now Abraham and Sarah were old and well stricken in age; and it ceased to be with Sarah after the manner of women. [12] Therefore Sarah laughed within herself, saying, After I am waxed old shall I have pleasure, my lord being old also? [13] And the LORD said unto Abraham, Wherefore did Sarah laugh, saying, Shall I of a surety bear a child, which am old? [14] Is any thing too hard for the LORD? At the time appointed I will return unto thee, according to the time of life, and Sarah shall have a son. [15] Then Sarah denied, saying, I laughed not; for she was afraid. And he said, Nay; but thou didst laugh. [16] And the men rose up from thence, and looked toward Sodom: and Abraham went with them to bring them on the way. [17] And the LORD said,

Shall I hide from Abraham that thing which I do; [18] Seeing that Abraham shall surely become a great and mighty nation, and all the nations of the earth shall be blessed in him? [19] For I know him, that he will command his children and his household after him, and they shall keep the way of the LORD, to do justice and judgment; that the LORD may bring upon Abraham that which he hath spoken of him. [20] And the LORD said, Because the cry of Sodom and Gomorrah is great, and because their sin is very grievous; [21] I will go down now, and see whether they have done altogether according to the cry of it, which is come unto me; and if not, I will know. [22] And the men turned their faces from thence, and went toward Sodom: but Abraham stood yet before the LORD. [23] And Abraham drew near, and said, Wilt thou also destroy the righteous with the wicked? [24] Peradventure there be fifty righteous within the city: wilt thou also destroy and not spare the place for the fifty righteous that are therein? [25] That be far from thee to do after this manner, to slay the righteous with the wicked: and that the righteous should be as the wicked, that be far from thee: Shall not the Judge of all the earth do right? [26] And the LORD said, If I find in Sodom fifty righteous within the city, then I will spare all the place for their sakes. [27] And Abraham answered and said, Behold now, I have taken upon me to speak unto the Lord, which am but dust and ashes: [28] Peradventure there shall lack five of the fifty righteous: wilt thou destroy all the city for lack of five? And he said, If I find there forty and five, I will not destroy it. [29] And he spake unto him yet again, and said, Peradventure there shall be forty found there. And he said, I will not do it for forty's sake. [30] And he said unto him, Oh let not the Lord be angry, and I will speak: Peradventure there shall thirty be found there. And he said, I will not do it, if I find thirty there. [31] And he said,

Behold now, I have taken upon me to speak unto the Lord:
Peradventure there shall be twenty found there. And he said,
I will not destroy it for twenty's sake. [32] And he said, Oh
let not the Lord be angry, and I will speak yet but this once:
Peradventure ten shall be found there. And he said, I will not
destroy it for ten's sake. [33] And the LORD went his way, as
soon as he had left communing with Abraham: and Abraham
returned unto his place.

GENESIS 19

[1] And there came two angels to Sodom at even; and Lot sat
in the gate of Sodom: and Lot seeing them rose up to meet
them; and he bowed himself with his face toward the ground;
[2] And he said, Behold now, my lords, turn in, I pray you,
into your servant's house, and tarry all night, and wash your
feet, and ye shall rise up early, and go on your ways. And
they said, Nay; but we will abide in the street all night. [3]
And he pressed upon them greatly; and they turned in unto
him, and entered into his house; and he made them a feast,
and did bake unleavened bread, and they did eat. [4] But
before they lay down, the men of the city, even the men of
Sodom, compassed the house round, both old and young, all
the people from every quarter: [5] And they called unto Lot,
and said unto him, Where are the men which came in to thee
this night? bring them out unto us, that we may know them.
[6] And Lot went out at the door unto them, and shut the
door after him, [7] And said, I pray you, brethren, do not
so wickedly. [8] Behold now, I have two daughters which
have not known man; let me, I pray you, bring them out unto
you, and do ye to them as is good in your eyes: only unto
these men do nothing; for therefore came they under the

shadow of my roof. [9] And they said, Stand back. And they said again, This one fellow came in to sojourn, and he will needs be a judge: now will we deal worse with thee, than with them. And they pressed sore upon the man, even Lot, and came near to break the door. [10] But the men put forth their hand, and pulled Lot into the house to them, and shut to the door. [11] And they smote the men that were at the door of the house with blindness, both small and great: so that they wearied themselves to find the door. [12] And the men said unto Lot, Hast thou here any besides? son in law, and thy sons, and thy daughters, and whatsoever thou hast in the city, bring them out of this place: [13] For we will destroy this place, because the cry of them is waxen great before the face of the LORD; and the LORD hath sent us to destroy it. [14] And Lot went out, and spake unto his sons in law, which married his daughters, and said, Up, get you out of this place; for the LORD will destroy this city. But he seemed as one that mocked unto his sons in law. [15] And when the morning arose, then the angels hastened Lot, saying, Arise, take thy wife, and thy two daughters, which are here; lest thou be consumed in the iniquity of the city. [16] And while he lingered, the men laid hold upon his hand, and upon the hand of his wife, and upon the hand of his two daughters; the LORD being merciful unto him: and they brought him forth, and set him without the city. [17] And it came to pass, when they had brought them forth abroad, that he said, Escape for thy life; look not behind thee, neither stay thou in all the plain; escape to the mountain, lest thou be consumed. [18] And Lot said unto them, Oh, not so, my Lord: [19] Behold now, thy servant hath found grace in thy sight, and thou hast magnified thy mercy, which thou hast shewed unto me in saving my life; and I cannot escape to the mountain, lest some evil take me, and I die: [20] Behold now, this city is near to flee unto, and it is a little one: Oh, let me escape thither, (is it not a little one?) and my soul shall live. [21] And he said unto him, See, I have accepted thee concerning this thing also, that I will not overthrow this city, for the which thou hast spoken. [22] Haste thee, escape thither; for I cannot do any thing till thou be come thither. Therefore the name of the city was called Zoar. [23] The sun was risen upon the earth when Lot entered into Zoar. [24] Then the LORD rained upon Sodom and upon Gomorrah brimstone and fire from the LORD out of heaven; [25] And he overthrew those cities, and all the plain, and all the inhabitants of the cities, and that which grew upon the ground. [26] But his wife looked back from behind him, and she became a pillar of salt. [27] And Abraham gat up early in the morning to the place where he stood before the LORD: [28] And he looked toward Sodom and Gomorrah, and toward all the land of the plain, and beheld, and, lo, the smoke of the country went up as the smoke of a furnace. [29] And it came to pass, when God destroyed the cities of the plain, that God remembered Abraham, and sent Lot out of the midst of the overthrow, when he overthrew the cities in the which Lot dwelt. [30] And Lot went up out of Zoar, and dwelt in the mountain, and his two daughters with him; for he feared to dwell in Zoar: and he dwelt in a cave, he and his two daughters. [31] And the firstborn said unto the younger, Our father is old, and there is not a man in the earth to come in unto us after the manner of all the earth: [32] Come, let us make our father drink wine, and we will lie with him, that we may preserve seed of our father. [33] And they made their father drink wine that night: and the firstborn went in, and lay with her father; and he perceived not when she lay down, nor when she arose. [34] And it came to pass on the morrow, that the firstborn said unto the younger, Behold, I lay yesternight with my father: let us make him drink wine this night also; and go thou in, and lie with him, that we may preserve seed of our father. [35] And they made their father drink wine that night also: and the younger arose, and lay with him; and he perceived not when she lay down, nor when she arose. [36] Thus were both the daughters of Lot with child by their father. [37] And the firstborn bare a son, and called his name Moab: the same is the father of the Moabites unto this day. [38] And the younger, she also bare a son, and called his name Benammi: the same is the father of the children of Ammon unto this day.

GENESIS 20

[1] And Abraham journeyed from thence toward the south country, and dwelled between Kadesh and Shur, and sojourned in Gerar. [2] And Abraham said of Sarah his wife, She is my sister: and Abimelech king of Gerar sent, and took Sarah. [3] But God came to Abimelech in a dream by night, and said to him, Behold, thou art but a dead man, for the woman which thou hast taken; for she is a man's wife. [4] But Abimelech had not come near her: and he said, Lord, wilt thou slay also a righteous nation? [5] Said he not unto me, She is my sister? and she, even she herself said, He is my brother: in the integrity of my heart and innocency of my hands have I done this. [6] And God said unto him in a dream, Yea, I know that thou didst this in the integrity of thy heart; for I also withheld thee from sinning against me: therefore suffered I thee not to touch her. [7] Now therefore restore the man his wife; for he is a prophet, and he shall pray for thee, and thou shalt live: and if thou restore her not, know thou that thou shalt surely die, thou, and all that are thine. [8] Therefore Abimelech rose early in the morning, and called

all his servants, and told all these things in their ears: and the men were sore afraid. [9] Then Abimelech called Abraham, and said unto him, What hast thou done unto us? and what have I offended thee, that thou hast brought on me and on my kingdom a great sin? thou hast done deeds unto me that ought not to be done. [10] And Abimelech said unto Abraham, What sawest thou, that thou hast done this thing? [11] And Abraham said, Because I thought, Surely the fear of God is not in this place; and they will slay me for my wife's sake. [12] And yet indeed she is my sister; she is the daughter of my father, but not the daughter of my mother; and she became my wife. [13] And it came to pass, when God caused me to wander from my father's house, that I said unto her, This is thy kindness which thou shalt shew unto me; at every place whither we shall come, say of me, He is my brother. [14] And Abimelech took sheep, and oxen, and menservants, and womenservants, and gave them unto Abraham, and restored him Sarah his wife. [15] And Abimelech said, Behold, my land is before thee: dwell where it pleaseth thee. [16] And unto Sarah he said, Behold, I have given thy brother a thousand pieces of silver: behold, he is to thee a covering of the eyes, unto all that are with thee, and with all other: thus she was reproved. [17] So Abraham prayed unto God: and God healed Abimelech, and his wife, and his maidservants; and they bare children. [18] For the LORD had fast closed up all the wombs of the house of Abimelech, because of Sarah Abraham's wife.

GENESIS 21

[1] And the LORD visited Sarah as he had said, and the LORD did unto Sarah as he had spoken. [2] For Sarah conceived,

and bare Abraham a son in his old age, at the set time of which God had spoken to him. [3] And Abraham called the name of his son that was born unto him, whom Sarah bare to him, Isaac. [4] And Abraham circumcised his son Isaac being eight days old, as God had commanded him. [5] And Abraham was an hundred years old, when his son Isaac was born unto him. [6] And Sarah said, God hath made me to laugh, so that all that hear will laugh with me. [7] And she said, Who would have said unto Abraham, that Sarah should have given children suck? for I have born him a son in his old age. [8] And the child grew, and was weaned: and Abraham made a great feast the same day that Isaac was weaned. [9] And Sarah saw the son of Hagar the Egyptian, which she had born unto Abraham, mocking. [10] Wherefore she said unto Abraham, Cast out this bondwoman and her son: for the son of this bondwoman shall not be heir with my son, even with Isaac. [11] And the thing was very grievous in Abraham's sight because of his son. [12] And God said unto Abraham, Let it not be grievous in thy sight because of the lad, and because of thy bondwoman; in all that Sarah hath said unto thee, hearken unto her voice; for in Isaac shall thy seed be called. [13] And also of the son of the bondwoman will I make a nation, because he is thy seed. [14] And Abraham rose up early in the morning, and took bread, and a bottle of water, and gave it unto Hagar, putting it on her shoulder, and the child, and sent her away: and she departed, and wandered in the wilderness of Beer-sheba. [15] And the water was spent in the bottle, and she cast the child under one of the shrubs. [16] And she went, and sat her down over against him a good way off, as it were a bow shot: for she said, Let me not see the death of the child. And she sat over against him, and lift up her voice, and wept. [17] And God heard the voice of the lad; and the angel of God called to Hagar out of heaven, and said unto her, What aileth thee, Hagar? fear not; for God hath heard the voice of the lad where he is. [18] Arise, lift up the lad, and hold him in thine hand; for I will make him a great nation. [19] And God opened her eyes, and she saw a well of water; and she went, and filled the bottle with water, and gave the lad drink. [20] And God was with the lad; and he grew, and dwelt in the wilderness, and became an archer. [21] And he dwelt in the wilderness of Paran: and his mother took him a wife out of the land of Egypt. [22] And it came to pass at that time, that Abimelech and Phichol the chief captain of his host spake unto Abraham, saying, God is with thee in all that thou doest: [23] Now therefore swear unto me here by God that thou wilt not deal falsely with me, nor with my son, nor with my son's son: but according to the kindness that I have done unto thee, thou shalt do unto me, and to the land wherein thou hast sojourned. [24] And Abraham said, I will swear. [25] And Abraham reproved Abimelech because of a well of water, which Abimelech's servants had violently taken away. [26] And Abimelech said, I wot not who hath done this thing: neither didst thou tell me, neither yet heard I of it, but to day. [27] And Abraham took sheep and oxen, and gave them unto Abimelech; and both of them made a covenant. [28] And Abraham set seven ewe lambs of the flock by themselves. [29] And Abimelech said unto Abraham, What mean these seven ewe lambs which thou hast set by themselves? [30] And he said, For these seven ewe lambs shalt thou take of my hand, that they may be a witness unto me, that I have digged this well. [31] Wherefore he called that place Beer-sheba; because there they sware both of them. [32] Thus they made a covenant at Beer-sheba: then Abimelech rose up, and Phichol the chief captain of his host, and they returned into the land of the Philistines. [33] And Abraham planted a grove in Beer-sheba, and called there on the name of the LORD, the everlasting God. [34] And Abraham sojourned in the Philistines' land many days.

GENESIS 22

[1] And it came to pass after these things, that God did tempt Abraham, and said unto him, Abraham: and he said, Behold, here I am. [2] And he said, Take now thy son, thine only son Isaac, whom thou lovest, and get thee into the land of Moriah; and offer him there for a burnt offering upon one of the mountains which I will tell thee of. [3] And Abraham rose up early in the morning, and saddled his ass, and took two of his young men with him, and Isaac his son, and clave the wood for the burnt offering, and rose up, and went unto the place of which God had told him. [4] Then on the third day Abraham lifted up his eyes, and saw the place afar off. [5] And Abraham said unto his young men, Abide ye here with the ass; and I and the lad will go yonder and worship, and come again to you, [6] And Abraham took the wood of the burnt offering, and laid it upon Isaac his son; and he took the fire in his hand, and a knife; and they went both of them together. [7] And Isaac spake unto Abraham his father, and said, My father: and he said, Here am I, my son. And he said, Behold the fire and the wood: but where is the lamb for a burnt offering? [8] And Abraham said, My son, God will provide himself a lamb for a burnt offering: so they went both of them together. [9] And they came to the place which God had told him of; and Abraham built an altar there, and laid the wood in order, and bound Isaac his son, and laid him on the altar upon the wood. [10] And Abraham stretched forth his hand, and took the knife to slay his son. [11] And the

angel of the LORD called unto him out of heaven, and said, Abraham, Abraham: and he said, Here am I. [12] And he said, Lay not thine hand upon the lad, neither do thou any thing unto him: for now I know that thou fearest God, seeing thou hast not withheld thy son, thine only son from me. [13] And Abraham lifted up his eyes, and looked, and behold behind him a ram caught in a thicket by his horns: and Abraham went and took the ram, and offered him up for a burnt offering in the stead of his son. [14] And Abraham called the name of that place Jehovah-jireh: as it is said to this day, In the mount of the LORD it shall be seen. [15] And the angel of the LORD called unto Abraham out of heaven the second time, [16] And said, By myself have I sworn, saith the LORD, for because thou hast done this thing, and hast not withheld thy son, thine only son: [17] That in blessing I will bless thee, and in multiplying I will multiply thy seed as the stars of the heaven, and as the sand which is upon the sea shore; and thy seed shall possess the gate of his enemies; [18] And in thy seed shall all the nations of the earth be blessed; because thou hast obeyed my voice. [19] So Abraham returned unto his young men, and they rose up and went together to Beer-sheba; and Abraham dwelt at Beer-sheba. [20] And it came to pass after these things, that it was told Abraham, saying, Behold, Milcah, she hath also born children unto thy brother Nahor; [21] Huz his firstborn, and Buz his brother, and Kemuel the father of Aram, [22] And Chesed, and Hazo, and Pildash, and Jidlaph, and Bethuel. [23] And Bethuel begat Rebekah: these eight Milcah did bear to Nahor, Abraham's brother. [24] And his concubine, whose name was Reumah, she bare also Tebah, and Gaham, and Thahash, and Maachah.

GENESIS 23

[1] And Sarah was an hundred and seven and twenty years old: these were the years of the life of Sarah. [2] And Sarah died in Kirjath-arba; the same is Hebron in the land of Canaan: and Abraham came to mourn for Sarah, and to weep for her. [3] And Abraham stood up from before his dead, and spake unto the sons of Heth, saying, [4] I am a stranger and a sojourner with you: give me a possession of a buryingplace with you, that I may bury my dead out of my sight. [5] And the children of Heth answered Abraham, saying unto him, [6] Hear us, my lord: thou art a mighty prince among us: in the choice of our sepulchres bury thy dead; none of us shall withhold from thee his sepulchre, but that thou mayest bury thy dead. [7] And Abraham stood up, and bowed himself to the people of the land, even to the children of Heth. [8] And he communed with them, saying, If it be your mind that I should bury my dead out of my sight; hear me, and intreat for me to Ephron the son of Zohar, [9] That he may give me the cave of Machpelah, which he hath, which is in the end of his field; for as much money as it is worth he shall give it me for a possession of a buryingplace amongst you. [10] And Ephron dwelt among the children of Heth: and Ephron the Hittite answered Abraham in the audience of the children of Heth, even of all that went in at the gate of his city, saying, [11] Nay, my lord, hear me: the field give I thee, and the cave that is therein, I give it thee; in the presence of the sons of my people give I it thee: bury thy dead. [12] And Abraham bowed down himself before the people of the land. [13] And he spake unto Ephron in the audience of the people of the land, saying, But if thou wilt give it, I pray thee, hear me: I will give thee money for the field; take it of me, and I will bury my dead there. [14] And Ephron answered Abraham,

saying unto him, [15] My lord, hearken unto me: the land is worth four hundred shekels of silver; what is that betwixt me and thee? bury therefore thy dead. [16] And Abraham hearkened unto Ephron; and Abraham weighed to Ephron the silver, which he had named in the audience of the sons of Heth, four hundred shekels of silver, current money with the merchant. [17] And the field of Ephron, which was in Machpelah, which was before Mamre, the field, and the cave which was therein, and all the trees that were in the field, that were in all the borders round about, were made sure [18] Unto Abraham for a possession in the presence of the children of Heth, before all that went in at the gate of his city. [19] And after this, Abraham buried Sarah his wife in the cave of the field of Machpelah before Mamre: the same is Hebron in the land of Canaan. [20] And the field, and the cave that is therein, were made sure unto Abraham for a possession of a buryingplace by the sons of Heth.

GENESIS 24

[1] And Abraham was old, and well stricken in age: and the LORD had blessed Abraham in all things. [2] And Abraham said unto his eldest servant of his house, that ruled over all that he had, Put, I pray thee, thy hand under my thigh: [3] And I will make thee swear by the LORD, the God of heaven, and the God of the earth, that thou shalt not take a wife unto my son of the daughters of the Canaanites, among whom I dwell: [4] But thou shalt go unto my country, and to my kindred, and take a wife unto my son Isaac. [5] And the servant said unto him, Peradventure the woman will not be willing to follow me unto this land: must I needs bring thy son again unto the land from whence thou camest? [6] And Abraham

said unto him, Beware thou that thou bring not my son thither again. [7] The LORD God of heaven, which took me from my father's house, and from the land of my kindred, and which spake unto me, and that sware unto me, saying, Unto thy seed will I give this land; he shall send his angel before thee, and thou shalt take a wife unto my son from thence. [8] And if the woman will not be willing to follow thee, then thou shalt be clear from this my oath: only bring not my son thither again. [9] And the servant put his hand under the thigh of Abraham his master, and sware to him concerning that matter. [10] And the servant took ten camels of the camels of his master, and departed; for all the goods of his master were in his hand: and he arose, and went to Mesopotamia, unto the city of Nahor. [11] And he made his camels to kneel down without the city by a well of water at the time of the evening, even the time that women go out to draw water. [12] And he said, O LORD God of my master Abraham, I pray thee, send me good speed this day, and shew kindness unto my master Abraham. [13] Behold, I stand here by the well of water; and the daughters of the men of the city come out to draw water: [14] And let it come to pass, that the damsel to whom I shall say, Let down thy pitcher, I pray thee, that I may drink; and she shall say, Drink, and I will give thy camels drink also: let the same be she that thou hast appointed for thy servant Isaac; and thereby shall I know that thou hast shewed kindness unto my master. [15] And it came to pass, before he had done speaking, that, behold, Rebekah came out, who was born to Bethuel, son of Milcah, the wife of Nahor, Abraham's brother, with her pitcher upon her shoulder. [16] And the damsel was very fair to look upon, a virgin, neither had any man known her: and she went down to the well, and filled her pitcher, and came up. [17] And the servant ran to meet her, and said, Let me, I pray thee, drink a little water of thy pitcher. [18] And she said, Drink, my lord: and she hasted, and let down her pitcher upon her hand, and gave him drink. [19] And when she had done giving him drink, she said, I will draw water for thy camels also, until they have done drinking. [20] And she hasted, and emptied her pitcher into the trough, and ran again unto the well to draw water, and drew for all his camels. [21] And the man wondering at her held his peace, to wit whether the LORD had made his journey prosperous or not. [22] And it came to pass, as the camels had done drinking, that the man took a golden earring of half a shekel weight, and two bracelets for her hands of ten shekels weight of gold; [23] And said, Whose daughter art thou? tell me, I pray thee: is there room in thy father's house for us to lodge in? [24] And she said unto him, I am the daughter of Bethuel the son of Milcah, which she bare unto Nahor. [25] She said moreover unto him, We have both straw and provender enough, and room to lodge in. [26] And the man bowed down his head, and worshipped the LORD. [27] And he said, Blessed be the LORD God of my master Abraham, who hath not left destitute my master of his mercy and his truth: I being in the way, the LORD led me to the house of my master's brethren. [28] And the damsel ran, and told them of her mother's house these things. [29] And Rebekah had a brother, and his name was Laban: and Laban ran out unto the man, unto the well. [30] And it came to pass, when he saw the earring and bracelets upon his sister's hands, and when he heard the words of Rebekah his sister, saying, Thus spake the man unto me; that he came unto the man; and, behold, he stood by the camels at the well. [31] And he said, Come in, thou blessed of the LORD; wherefore standest thou without? for I have prepared the house, and room for the camels. [32] And the man came into the house: and he ungirded his camels, and gave straw and provender for the camels, and water to wash his feet, and the men's feet that were with him. [33] And there was set meat before him to eat: but he said, I will not eat, until I have told mine errand. And he said, Speak on. [34] And he said, I am Abraham's servant. [35] And the LORD hath blessed my master greatly; and he is become great: and he hath given him flocks, and herds, and silver, and gold, and menservants, and maidservants, and camels, and asses. [36] And Sarah my master's wife bare a son to my master when she was old: and unto him hath he given all that he hath. [37] And my master made me swear, saying, Thou shalt not take a wife to my son of the daughters of the Canaanites, in whose land I dwell: [38] But thou shalt go unto my father's house, and to my kindred, and take a wife unto my son. [39] And I said unto my master, Peradventure the woman will not follow me. [40] And he said unto me, The LORD, before whom I walk, will send his angel with thee, and prosper thy way; and thou shalt take a wife for my son of my kindred, and of my father's house: [41] Then shalt thou be clear from this my oath, when thou comest to my kindred; and if they give not thee one, thou shalt be clear from my oath. [42] And I came this day unto the well, and said, O LORD God of my master Abraham, if now thou do prosper my way which I go; [43] Behold, I stand by the well of water; and it shall come to pass, that when the virgin cometh forth to draw water, and I say to her, Give me, I pray thee, a little water of thy pitcher to drink; [44] And she say to me, Both drink thou, and I will also draw for thy camels: let the same be the woman whom the LORD hath appointed out for my master's son. [45] And before I had done speaking in mine heart, behold, Rebekah came forth with her pitcher on her shoulder; and she went down unto the well, and drew water: and I said unto her, Let me drink, I pray thee. [46] And she made haste, and let down her pitcher from her shoulder, and said, Drink, and I will give thy camels drink also: so I drank, and she made the camels drink also. [47] And I asked her, and said, Whose daughter art thou? And she said, The daughter of Bethuel, Nahor's son, whom Milcah bare unto him: and I put the earring upon her face, and the bracelets upon her hands. [48] And I bowed down my head, and worshipped the LORD, and blessed the LORD God of my master Abraham, which had led me in the right way to take my master's brother's daughter unto his son. [49] And now if ye will deal kindly and truly with my master, tell me: and if not, tell me; that I may turn to the right hand, or to the left. [50] Then Laban and Bethuel answered and said, The thing proceedeth from the LORD: we cannot speak unto thee bad or good. [51] Behold, Rebekah is before thee, take her, and go, and let her be thy master's son's wife, as the LORD hath spoken. [52] And it came to pass, that, when Abraham's servant heard their words, he worshipped the LORD, bowing himself to the earth. [53] And the servant brought forth jewels of silver, and jewels of gold, and raiment, and gave them to Rebekah: he gave also to her brother and to her mother precious things. [54] And they did eat and drink, he and the men that were with him, and tarried all night; and they rose up in the morning, and he said, Send me away unto my master. [55] And her brother and her mother said, Let the damsel abide with us a few days, at the least ten; after that she shall go. [56] And he said unto them, Hinder me not, seeing the LORD hath prospered my way; send me away that I may go to my master. [57] And they said, We will call the damsel, and enquire at her mouth. [58] And they called Rebekah, and said unto her, Wilt thou go with this man? And she said, I will go. [59] And they sent away Rebekah their sister, and her nurse, and Abraham's servant, and his men. [60] And they blessed Rebekah, and said unto her, Thou art our sister, be thou the mother of thousands of millions, and let thy seed possess the gate of those which hate them. [61] And Rebekah arose, and her damsels, and they rode upon the camels, and followed the man: and the servant took Rebekah, and went his way. [62] And Isaac came from the way of the well Lahai-roi; for he dwelt in the south country. [63] And Isaac went out to meditate in the field at the eventide: and he lifted up his eyes, and saw, and, behold, the camels were coming. [64] And Rebekah lifted up her eyes, and when she saw Isaac, she lighted off the camel. [65] For she had said unto the servant, What man is this that walketh in the field to meet us? And the servant had said, It is my master: therefore she took a vail, and covered herself. [66] And the servant told Isaac all things that he had done. [67] And Isaac brought her into his mother Sarah's tent, and took Rebekah, and she became his wife; and he loved her: and Isaac was comforted after his mother's death.

GENESIS 25

[1] Then again Abraham took a wife, and her name was Keturah. [2] And she bare him Zimran, and Jokshan, and Medan, and Midian, and Ishbak, and Shuah. [3] And Jokshan begat Sheba, and Dedan. And the sons of Dedan were Asshurim, and Letushim, and Leummim. [4] And the sons of Midian; Ephah, and Epher, and Hanoch, and Abidah, and Eldaah. All these were the children of Keturah. [5] And Abraham gave all that he had unto Isaac. [6] But unto the sons of the concubines, which Abraham had, Abraham gave gifts, and sent them away from Isaac his son, while he yet lived, eastward, unto the east country. [7] And these are the days of the years of Abraham's life which he lived, an hundred

threescore and fifteen years. [8] Then Abraham gave up the ghost, and died in a good old age, an old man, and full of years; and was gathered to his people. [9] And his sons Isaac and Ishmael buried him in the cave of Machpelah, in the field of Ephron the son of Zohar the Hittite, which is before Mamre; [10] The field which Abraham purchased of the sons of Heth: there was Abraham buried, and Sarah his wife. [11] And it came to pass after the death of Abraham, that God blessed his son Isaac; and Isaac dwelt by the well Lahai-roi. [12] Now these are the generations of Ishmael, Abraham's son, whom Hagar the Egyptian, Sarah's handmaid, bare unto Abraham: [13] And these are the names of the sons of Ishmael, by their names, according to their generations: the firstborn of Ishmael, Nebajoth; and Kedar, and Adbeel, and Mibsam, [14] And Mishma, and Dumah, and Massa, [15] Hadar, and Tema, Jetur, Naphish, and Kedemah: [16] These are the sons of Ishmael, and these are their names, by their towns, and by their castles; twelve princes according to their nations. [17] And these are the years of the life of Ishmael, an hundred and thirty and seven years: and he gave up the ghost and died; and was gathered unto his people. [18] And they dwelt from Havilah unto Shur, that is before Egypt, as thou goest toward Assyria: and he died in the presence of all his brethren. [19] And these are the generations of Isaac, Abraham's son: Abraham begat Isaac: [20] And Isaac was forty years old when he took Rebekah to wife, the daughter of Bethuel the Syrian of Padan-aram, the sister to Laban the Syrian. [21] And Isaac intreated the LORD for his wife, because she was barren: and the LORD was intreated of him, and Rebekah his wife conceived. [22] And the children struggled together within her; and she said, If it be so, why am I thus? And she went to enquire of the LORD. [23] And the LORD said unto her, Two nations are in thy womb, and two manner of people shall be separated from thy bowels; and the one people shall be stronger than the other people; and the elder shall serve the younger. [24] And when her days to be delivered were fulfilled, behold, there were twins in her womb. [25] And the first came out red, all over like an hairy garment; and they called his name Esau. [26] And after that came his brother out, and his hand took hold on Esau's heel; and his name was called Jacob: and Isaac was three-score years old when she bare them. [27] And the boys grew: and Esau was a cunning hunter, a man of the field; and Jacob was a plain man, dwelling in tents. [28] And Isaac loved Esau, because he did eat of his venison: but Rebekah loved Jacob. [29] And Jacob sod pottage: and Esau came from the field, and he was faint: [30] And Esau said to Jacob, Feed me, I pray thee, with that same red pottage; for I am faint: therefore was his name called Edom. [31] And Jacob said, Sell me this day thy birthright. [32] And Esau said, Behold, I am at the point to die: and what profit shall this birthright do to me? [33] And Jacob said, Swear to me this day; and he sware unto him: and he sold his birthright unto Jacob. [34] Then Jacob gave Esau bread and pottage of lentiles; and he did eat and drink, and rose up, and went his way: thus Esau despised his birthright.

GENESIS 26

[1] And there was a famine in the land, beside the first famine that was in the days of Abraham. And Isaac went unto Abimelech king of the Philistines unto Gerar. [2] And the LORD appeared unto him, and said, Go not down into Egypt; dwell in the land which I shall tell thee of: [3] Sojourn in this land, and I will be with thee, and will bless thee; for unto

thee, and unto thy seed, I will give all these countries, and I will perform the oath which I sware unto Abraham thy father; [4] And I will make thy seed to multiply as the stars of heaven, and will give unto thy seed all these countries; and in thy seed shall all the nations of the earth be blessed; [5] Because that Abraham obeyed my voice, and kept my charge, my commandments, my statutes, and my laws. [6] And Isaac dwelt in Gerar: [7] And the men of the place asked him of his wife; and he said, She is my sister: for he feared to say, She is my wife; lest, said he, the men of the place should kill me for Rebekah; because she was fair to look upon. [8] And it came to pass, when he had been there a long time, that Abimelech king of the Philistines looked out at a window, and saw, and, behold, Isaac was sporting with Rebekah his wife. [9] And Abimelech called Isaac, and said, Behold, of a surety she is thy wife: and how saidst thou, She is my sister? And Isaac said unto him, Because I said, Lest I die for her. [10] And Abimelech said, What is this thou hast done unto us? one of the people might lightly have lien with thy wife, and thou shouldest have brought guiltiness upon us. [11] And Abimelech charged all his people, saying, He that toucheth this man or his wife shall surely be put to death. [12] Then Isaac sowed in that land, and received in the same year an hundredfold: and the LORD blessed him. [13] And the man waxed great, and went forward, and grew until he became very great: [14] For he had possession of flocks, and possessions of herds, and great store of servants: and the Philistines envied him. [15] For all the wells which his father's servants had digged in the days of Abraham his father, the Philistines had stopped them, and filled them with earth. [16] And Abimelech said unto Isaac, Go from us; for thou art much mightier than we. [17] And Isaac departed thence, and pitched his tent in the valley of Gerar, and dwelt there. [18] And Isaac digged again the wells of water, which they had digged in the days of Abraham his father; for the Philistines had stopped them after the death of Abraham: and he called their names after the names by which his father had called them. [19] And Isaac's servants digged in the valley, and found there a well of springing water. [20] And the herdmen of Gerar did strive with Isaac's herdmen, saying, The water is ours: and he called the name of the well Esek; because they strove with him. [21] And they digged another well, and strove for that also: and he called the name of it Sitnah. [22] And he removed from thence, and digged another well; and for that they strove not: and he called the name of it Rehoboth; and he said, For now the LORD hath made room for us, and we shall be fruitful in the land. [23] And he went up from thence to Beer-sheba. [24] And the LORD appeared unto him the same night, and said, I am the God of Abraham thy father: fear not, for I am with thee, and will bless thee, and multiply thy seed for my servant Abraham's sake. [25] And he builded an altar there, and called upon the name of the LORD, and pitched his tent there: and there Isaac's servants digged a well. [26] Then Abimelech went to him from Gerar, and Ahuzzath one of his friends, and Phichol the chief captain of his army. [27] And Isaac said unto them, Wherefore come ye to me, seeing ye hate me, and have sent me away from you? [28] And they said, We saw certainly that the LORD was with thee: and we said, Let there be now an oath betwixt us, even betwixt us and thee, and let us make a covenant with thee; [29] That thou wilt do us no hurt, as we have not touched thee, and as we have done unto thee nothing but good, and have sent thee away in peace: thou art now the blessed of the LORD. [30] And he made them a feast, and they did eat and drink. [31] And they rose up betimes in the morning, and sware one to another: and Isaac sent them away, and they departed from him in peace. [32] And it came to pass the same day, that Isaac's servants came, and told him concerning the well which they had digged, and said unto him, We have found water. [33] And he called it Shebah: therefore the name of the city is Beer-sheba unto this day. [34] And Esau was forty years old when he took to wife Judith the daughter of Beeri the Hittite, and Bashemath the daughter of Elon the Hittite: [35] Which were a grief of mind unto Isaac and to Rebekah.

GENESIS 27

[1] And it came to pass, that when Isaac was old, and his eyes were dim, so that he could not see, he called Esau his eldest son, and said unto him, My son: and he said unto him, Behold, here am I. [2] And he said, Behold now, I am old, I know not the day of my death: [3] Now therefore take, I pray thee, thy weapons, thy quiver and thy bow, and go out to the field, and take me some venison; [4] And make me savoury meat, such as I love, and bring it to me, that I may eat; that my soul may bless thee before I die. [5] And Rebekah heard when Isaac spake to Esau his son. And Esau went to the field to hunt for venison, and to bring it. [6] And Rebekah spake unto Jacob her son, saying, Behold, I heard thy father speak unto Esau thy brother, saying, [7] Bring me venison, and make me savoury meat, that I may eat, and bless thee before the LORD before my death. [8] Now therefore, my son, obey my voice according to that which I command thee. [9] Go now to the flock, and fetch me from thence two good kids of the goats; and I will make them savoury meat for thy father, such as he loveth: [10] And thou shalt bring

it to thy father, that he may eat, and that he may bless thee before his death. [11] And Jacob said to Rebekah his mother, Behold, Esau my brother is a hairy man, and I am a smooth man: [12] My father peradventure will feel me, and I shall seem to him as a deceiver; and I shall bring a curse upon me, and not a blessing. [13] And his mother said unto him, Upon me be thy curse, my son: only obey my voice, and go fetch me them. [14] And he went, and fetched, and brought them to his mother: and his mother made savoury meat, such as his father loved. [15] And Rebekah took goodly raiment of her eldest son Esau, which were with her in the house, and put them upon Jacob her younger son: [16] And she put the skins of the kids of the goats upon his hands, and upon the smooth of his neck: [17] And she gave the savoury meat and the bread, which she had prepared, into the hand of her son Jacob. [18] And he came unto his father, and said, My father: and he said, Here am I; who art thou, my son? [19] And Jacob said unto his father, I am Esau thy firstborn; I have done according as thou badest me: arise, I pray thee, sit and eat of my venison, that thy soul may bless me. [20] And Isaac said unto his son, How is it that thou hast found it so quickly, my son? And he said, Because the LORD thy God brought it to me. [21] And Isaac said unto Jacob, Come near, I pray thee, that I may feel thee, my son, whether thou be my very son Esau or not. [22] And Jacob went near unto Isaac his father; and he felt him, and said, The voice is Jacob's voice, but the hands are the hands of Esau. [23] And he discerned him not, because his hands were hairy, as his brother Esau's hands: so he blessed him. [24] And he said, Art thou my very son Esau? And he said, I am. [25] And he said, Bring it near to me, and I will eat of my son's venison, that my soul may bless thee. And he brought it near to him, and he did eat: and he brought him wine, and he drank. [26] And his father Isaac said unto him, Come near now, and kiss me, my son. [27] And he came near, and kissed him: and he smelled the smell of his raiment, and blessed him, and said, See, the smell of my son is as the smell of a field which the LORD hath blessed: [28] Therefore God give thee of the dew of heaven, and the fatness of the earth, and plenty of corn and wine: [29] Let people serve thee, and nations bow down to thee: be lord over thy brethren, and let thy mother's sons bow down to thee: cursed be every one that curseth thee, and blessed be he that blesseth thee. [30] And it came to pass, as soon as Isaac had made an end of blessing Jacob, and Jacob was yet scarce gone out from the presence of Isaac his father, that Esau his brother came in from his hunting. [31] And he also had made savoury meat, and brought it unto his father, and said unto his father, Let my father arise, and eat of his son's venison, that thy soul may bless me. [32] And Isaac his father said unto him, Who art thou? And he said, I am thy son, thy firstborn Esau. [33] And Isaac trembled very exceedingly, and said, Who? where is he that hath taken venison, and brought it me, and I have eaten of all before thou camest, and have blessed him? yea, and he shall be blessed. [34] And when Esau heard the words of his father, he cried with a great and exceeding bitter cry, and said unto his father, Bless me, even me also, O my father. [35] And he said, Thy brother came with subtilty, and hath taken away thy blessing. [36] And he said, Is not he rightly named Jacob? for he hath supplanted me these two times: he took away my birthright; and, behold, now he hath taken away my blessing. And he said, Hast thou not reserved a blessing for me? [37] And Isaac answered and said unto Esau, Behold, I have made him thy lord, and all his brethren have I given to him for servants; and with corn and wine have I sustained him: and what shall I do now unto thee, my son? [38] And Esau

said unto his father, Hast thou but one blessing, my father?
bless me, even me also, O my father. And Esau lifted up his
voice, and wept. [39] And Isaac his father answered and said
unto him, Behold, thy dwelling shall be the fatness of the
earth, and of the dew of heaven from above; [40] And by thy
sword shalt thou live, and shalt serve thy brother; and it shall
come to pass when thou shalt have the dominion, that thou
shalt break his yoke from off thy neck. [41] And Esau hated
Jacob because of the blessing wherewith his father blessed
him: and Esau said in his heart, The days of mourning for
my father are at hand; then will I slay my brother Jacob. [42]
And these words of Esau her elder son were told to Rebekah:
and she sent and called Jacob her younger son, and said unto
him, Behold, thy brother Esau, as touching thee, doth comfort himself, purposing to kill thee. [43] Now therefore, my
son, obey my voice; and arise, flee thou to Laban my brother
to Haran; [44] And tarry with him a few days, until thy
brother's fury turn away; [45] Until thy brother's anger turn
away from thee, and he forget that which thou hast done to
him: then I will send, and fetch thee from thence: why should
I be deprived also of you both in one day? [46] And Rebekah
said to Isaac, I am weary of my life because of the daughters
of Heth: if Jacob take a wife of the daughters of Heth, such
as these which are of the daughters of the land, what good
shall my life do me?

GENESIS 28

[1] And Isaac called Jacob, and blessed him, and charged him,
and said unto him, Thou shalt not take a wife of the daughters
of Canaan. [2] Arise, go to Padan-aram, to the house of
Bethuel thy mother's father; and take thee a wife from thence

of the daughters of Laban thy mother's brother. [3] And
God Almighty bless thee, and make thee fruitful, and multiply thee, that thou mayest be a multitude of people; [4]
And give thee the blessing of Abraham, to thee, and to thy
seed with thee; that thou mayest inherit the land wherein
thou art a stranger, which God gave unto Abraham. [5] And
Isaac sent away Jacob: and he went to Padan-aram unto
Laban, son of Bethuel the Syrian, the brother of Rebekah,
Jacob's and Esau's mother. [6] When Esau saw that Isaac
had blessed Jacob, and sent him away to Padan-aram, to
take him a wife from thence; and that as he blessed him he
gave him a charge, saying, Thou shalt not take a wife of the
daughters of Canaan; [7] And that Jacob obeyed his father
and his mother, and was gone to Padan-aram; [8] And Esau
seeing that the daughters of Canaan pleased not Isaac his
father; [9] Then went Esau unto Ishmael, and took unto the
wives which he had Mahalath the daughter of Ishmael Abraham's son, the sister of Nebajoth, to be his wife. [10] And
Jacob went out from Beer-sheba, and went toward Haran.
[11] And he lighted upon a certain place, and tarried there
all night, because the sun was set; and he took of the stones
of that place, and put them for his pillows, and lay down in
that place to sleep. [12] And he dreamed, and behold a ladder set up on the earth, and the top of it reached to heaven:
and behold the angels of God ascending and descending on
it. [13] And, behold, the LORD stood above it, and said, I
am the LORD God of Abraham thy father, and the God of
Isaac: the land whereon thou liest, to thee will I give it, and to
thy seed; [14] And thy seed shall be as the dust of the earth,
and thou shalt spread abroad to the west, and to the east,
and to the north, and to the south: and in thee and in thy
seed shall all the families of the earth be blessed. [15] And,
behold, I am with thee, and will keep thee in all places whither

thou goest, and will bring thee again into this land; for I will not leave thee, until I have done that which I have spoken to thee of. [16] And Jacob awaked out of his sleep, and he said, Surely the LORD is in this place; and I knew it not. [17] And he was afraid, and said, How dreadful is this place! this is none other but the house of God, and this is the gate of heaven. [18] And Jacob rose up early in the morning, and took the stone that he had put for his pillows, and set it up for a pillar, and poured oil upon the top of it. [19] And he called the name of that place Beth-el: but the name of that city was called Luz at the first. [20] And Jacob vowed a vow, saying, If God will be with me, and will keep me in this way that I go, and will give me bread to eat, and raiment to put on, [21] So that I come again to my father's house in peace; then shall the LORD be my God: [22] And this stone, which I have set for a pillar, shall be God's house: and of all that thou shalt give me I will surely give the tenth unto thee.

GENESIS 29

[1] Then Jacob went on his journey, and came into the land of the people of the east. [2] And he looked, and behold a well in the field, and, lo, there were three flocks of sheep lying by it; for out of that well they watered the flocks: and a great stone was upon the well's mouth. [3] And thither were all the flocks gathered: and they rolled the stone from the well's mouth, and watered the sheep, and put the stone again upon the well's mouth in his place. [4] And Jacob said unto them, My brethren, whence be ye? And they said, Of Haran are we. [5] And he said unto them, Know ye Laban the son of Nahor? And they said, We know him. [6] And he

said unto them, Is he well? And they said, He is well: and, behold, Rachel his daughter cometh with the sheep. [7] And he said, Lo, it is yet high day, neither is it time that the cattle should be gathered together: water ye the sheep, and go and feed them. [8] And they said, We cannot, until all the flocks be gathered together, and till they roll the stone from the well's mouth; then we water the sheep. [9] And while he yet spake with them, Rachel came with her father's sheep: for she kept them. [10] And it came to pass, when Jacob saw Rachel the daughter of Laban his mother's brother, and the sheep of Laban his mother's brother, that Jacob went near, and rolled the stone from the well's mouth, and watered the flock of Laban his mother's brother. [11] And Jacob kissed Rachel, and lifted up his voice, and wept. [12] And Jacob told Rachel that he was her father's brother, and that he was Rebekah's son: and she ran and told her father. [13] And it came to pass, when Laban heard the tidings of Jacob his sister's son, that he ran to meet him, and embraced him, and kissed him, and brought him to his house. And he told Laban all these things. [14] And Laban said to him, Surely thou art my bone and my flesh. And he abode with him the space of a month. [15] And Laban said unto Jacob, Because thou art my brother, shouldest thou therefore serve me for nought? tell me, what shall thy wages be? [16] And Laban had two daughters: the name of the elder was Leah, and the name of the younger was Rachel. [17] Leah was tender eyed; but Rachel was beautiful and well favoured. [18] And Jacob loved Rachel; and said, I will serve thee seven years for Rachel thy younger daughter. [19] And Laban said, It is better that I give her to thee, than that I should give her to another man: abide with me. [20] And Jacob served seven years for Rachel; and they seemed unto him but a few days, for the love he had to her. [21] And Jacob said unto Laban, Give me my wife, for my days are fulfilled, that I may go in unto her. [22] And Laban gathered together all the men of the place, and made a feast. [23] And it came to pass in the evening, that he took Leah his daughter, and brought her to him; and he went in unto her. [24] And Laban gave unto his daughter Leah Zilpah his maid for an handmaid. [25] And it came to pass, that in the morning, behold, it was Leah: and he said to Laban, What is this thou hast done unto me? did not I serve with thee for Rachel? wherefore then hast thou beguiled me? [26] And Laban said, It must not be so done in our country, to give the younger before the firstborn. [27] Fulfil her week, and we will give thee this also for the service which thou shalt serve with me yet seven other years. [28] And Jacob did so, and fulfilled her week: and he gave him Rachel his daughter to wife also. [29] And Laban gave to Rachel his daughter Bilhah his handmaid to be her maid. [30] And he went in also unto Rachel, and he loved also Rachel more than Leah, and served with him yet seven other years. [31] And when the LORD saw that Leah was hated, he opened her womb: but Rachel was barren. [32] And Leah conceived, and bare a son, and she called his name Reuben: for she said, Surely the LORD hath looked upon my affliction; now therefore my husband will love me. [33] And she conceived again, and bare a son; and said, Because the LORD hath heard that I was hated, he hath therefore given me this son also: and she called his name Simeon. [34] And she conceived again, and bare a son; and said, Now this time will my husband be joined unto me, because I have born him three sons: therefore was his name called Levi. [35] And she conceived again, and bare a son: and she said, Now will I praise the LORD: therefore she called his name Judah; and left bearing.

GENESIS 30

[1] And when Rachel saw that she bare Jacob no children, Rachel envied her sister; and said unto Jacob, Give me children, or else I die. [2] And Jacob's anger was kindled against Rachel: and he said, Am I in God's stead, who hath withheld from thee the fruit of the womb? [3] And she said, Behold my maid Bilhah, go in unto her; and she shall bear upon my knees that I may also have children by her. [4] And she gave him Bilhah her handmaid to wife: and Jacob went in unto her. [5] And Bilhah conceived, and bare Jacob a son. [6] And Rachel said, God hath judged me, and hath also heard my voice, and hath given me a son: therefore called she his name Dan. [7] And Bilhah Rachel's maid conceived again, and bare Jacob a second son. [8] And Rachel said, With great wrestlings have I wrestled with my sister, and I have prevailed: and she called his name Naphtali. [9] When Leah saw that she had left bearing, she took Zilpah her maid, and gave her Jacob to wife. [10] And Zilpah Leah's maid bare Jacob a son. [11] And Leah said, A troop cometh: and she called his name Gad. [12] And Zilpah Leah's maid bare Jacob a second son. [13] And Leah said, Happy am I, for the daughters will call me blessed: and she called his name Asher. [14] And Reuben went in the days of wheat harvest, and found mandrakes in the field, and brought them unto his mother Leah. Then Rachel said to Leah, Give me, I pray thee, of thy son's mandrakes. [15] And she said unto her, Is it a small matter that thou hast taken my husband? and wouldest thou take away my son's mandrakes also? And Rachel said, Therefore he shall lie with thee to night for thy son's mandrakes. [16] And Jacob came out of the field in the evening, and Leah went out to meet him, and said, Thou must come in unto me; for surely I have hired thee with my

son's mandrakes. And he lay with her that night. [17] And God hearkened unto Leah, and she conceived, and bare Jacob the fifth son. [18] And Leah said, God hath given me my hire, because I have given my maiden to my husband: and she called his name Issachar. [19] And Leah conceived again, and bare Jacob the sixth son. [20] And Leah said, God hath endued me with a good dowry; now will my husband dwell with me, because I have born him six sons: and she called his name Zebulun. [21] And afterwards she bare a daughter, and called her name Dinah. [22] And God remembered Rachel, and God hearkened to her, and opened her womb. [23] And she conceived, and bare a son; and said, God hath taken away my reproach: [24] And she called his name Joseph; and said, The LORD shall add to me another son. [25] And it came to pass, when Rachel had born Joseph, that Jacob said unto Laban, Send me away, that I may go unto mine own place, and to my country. [26] Give me my wives and my children, for whom I have served thee, and let me go: for thou knowest my service which I have done thee. [27] And Laban said unto him, I pray thee, if I have found favour in thine eyes, tarry: for I have learned by experience that the LORD hath blessed me for thy sake. [28] And he said, Appoint me thy wages, and I will give it. [29] And he said unto him, Thou knowest how I have served thee, and how thy cattle was with me. [30] For it was little which thou hadst before I came, and it is now increased unto a multitude; and the LORD hath blessed thee since my coming: and now when shall I provide for mine own house also? [31] And he said, What shall I give thee? And Jacob said, Thou shalt not give me any thing: if thou wilt do this thing for me, I will again feed and keep thy flock: [32] I will pass through all thy flock to day, removing from thence all the speckled and spotted cattle, and all the brown cattle among the sheep, and the spotted and speckled among the goats: and of such shall be my hire. [33] So shall my righteousness answer for me in time to come, when it shall come for my hire before thy face: every one that is not speckled and spotted among the goats, and brown among the sheep, that shall be counted stolen with me. [34] And Laban said, Behold, I would it might be according to thy word. [35] And he removed that day the he goats that were ringstraked and spotted, and all the she goats that were speckled and spotted, and every one that had some white in it, and all the brown among the sheep, and gave them into the hand of his sons. [36] And he set three days' journey betwixt himself and Jacob: and Jacob fed the rest of Laban's flocks. [37] And Jacob took him rods of green poplar, and of the hazel and chesnut tree; and pilled white strakes in them, and made the white appear which was in the rods. [38] And he set the rods which he had pilled before the flocks in the gutters in the watering troughs when the flocks came to drink, that they should conceive when they came to drink. [39] And the flocks conceived before the rods, and brought forth cattle ringstraked, speckled, and spotted. [40] And Jacob did separate the lambs, and set the faces of the flocks toward the ringstraked, and all the brown in the flock of Laban; and he put his own flocks by themselves, and put them not unto Laban's cattle. [41] And it came to pass, whensoever the stronger cattle did conceive, that Jacob laid the rods before the eyes of the cattle in the gutters, that they might conceive among the rods. [42] But when the cattle were feeble, he put them not in: so the feebler were Laban's, and the stronger Jacob's. [43] And the man increased exceedingly, and had much cattle, and maidservants, and menservants, and camels, and asses.

GENESIS 31

[1] And he heard the words of Laban's sons, saying, Jacob hath taken away all that was our father's; and of that which was our father's hath he gotten all this glory. [2] And Jacob beheld the countenance of Laban, and, behold, it was not toward him as before. [3] And the LORD said unto Jacob, Return unto the land of thy fathers, and to thy kindred; and I will be with thee. [4] And Jacob sent and called Rachel and Leah to the field unto his flock, [5] And said unto them, I see your father's countenance, that it is not toward me as before; but the God of my father hath been with me. [6] And ye know that with all my power I have served your father. [7] And your father hath deceived me, and changed my wages ten times; but God suffered him not to hurt me. [8] If he said thus, The speckled shall be thy wages; then all the cattle bare speckled: and if he said thus, The ringstraked shall be thy hire; then bare all the cattle ringstraked. [9] Thus God hath taken away the cattle of your father, and given them to me. [10] And it came to pass at the time that the cattle conceived, that I lifted up mine eyes, and saw in a dream, and, behold, the rams which leaped upon the cattle were ringstraked, speckled, and grisled. [11] And the angel of God spake unto me in a dream, saying, Jacob: And I said, Here am I. [12] And he said, Lift up now thine eyes, and see, all the rams which leap upon the cattle are ringstraked, speckled, and grisled: for I have seen all that Laban doeth unto thee. [13] I am the God of Beth-el, where thou anointedst the pillar, and where thou vowedst a vow unto me: now arise, get thee out from this land, and return unto the land of thy kindred. [14] And Rachel and Leah answered and said unto him, Is there yet any portion or inheritance for us in our father's house? [15] Are we not counted of him strangers?

for he hath sold us, and hath quite devoured also our money. [16] For all the riches which God hath taken from our father, that is ours, and our children's: now then, whatsoever God hath said unto thee, do. [17] Then Jacob rose up, and set his sons and his wives upon camels; [18] And he carried away all his cattle, and all his goods which he had gotten, the cattle of his getting, which he had gotten in Padan-aram, for to go to Isaac his father in the land of Canaan. [19] And Laban went to shear his sheep: and Rachel had stolen the images that were her father's. [20] And Jacob stole away unawares to Laban the Syrian, in that he told him not that he fled. [21] So he fled with all that he had; and he rose up, and passed over the river, and set his face toward the mount Gilead. [22] And it was told Laban on the third day that Jacob was fled. [23] And he took his brethren with him, and pursued after him seven days' journey; and they overtook him in the mount Gilead. [24] And God came to Laban the Syrian in a dream by night, and said unto him, Take heed that thou speak not to Jacob either good or bad. [25] Then Laban overtook Jacob. Now Jacob had pitched his tent in the mount: and Laban with his brethren pitched in the mount of Gilead. [26] And Laban said to Jacob, What hast thou done, that thou hast stolen away unawares to me, and carried away my daughters, as captives taken with the sword? [27] Wherefore didst thou flee away secretly, and steal away from me; and didst not tell me, that I might have sent thee away with mirth, and with songs, with tabret, and with harp? [28] And hast not suffered me to kiss my sons and my daughters? thou hast now done foolishly in so doing. [29] It is in the power of my hand to do you hurt: but the God of your father spake unto me yesternight, saying, Take thou heed that thou speak not to Jacob either good or bad. [30] And now, though thou wouldest needs be gone, because thou sore longedst after thy father's house, yet wherefore hast thou stolen my gods? [31] And Jacob answered and said to Laban, Because I was afraid: for I said, Peradventure thou wouldest take by force thy daughters from me. [32] With whomsoever thou findest thy gods, let him not live: before our brethren discern thou what is thine with me, and take it to thee. For Jacob knew not that Rachel had stolen them. [33] And Laban went into Jacob's tent, and into Leah's tent, and into the two maidservants' tents; but he found them not. Then went he out of Leah's tent, and entered into Rachel's tent. [34] Now Rachel had taken the images, and put them in the camel's furniture, and sat upon them. And Laban searched all the tent, but found them not. [35] And she said to her father, Let it not displease my lord that I cannot rise up before thee; for the custom of women is upon me. And he searched, but found not the images. [36] And Jacob was wroth, and chode with Laban: and Jacob answered and said to Laban, What is my trespass? what is my sin, that thou hast so hotly pursued after me? [37] Whereas thou hast searched all my stuff, what hast thou found of all thy household stuff? set it here before my brethren and thy brethren, that they may judge betwixt us both. [38] This twenty years have I been with thee; thy ewes and thy she goats have not cast their young, and the rams of thy flock have I not eaten. [39] That which was torn of beasts I brought not unto thee; I bare the loss of it; of my hand didst thou require it, whether stolen by day, or stolen by night. [40] Thus I was; in the day the drought consumed me, and the frost by night; and my sleep departed from mine eyes. [41] Thus have I been twenty years in thy house; I served thee fourteen years for thy two daughters, and six years for thy cattle: and thou hast changed my wages ten times. [42] Except the God of my father, the God of Abraham, and the fear of Isaac, had been with me, surely thou hadst sent me away now empty. God hath seen mine affliction and the labour of my hands, and rebuked thee yesternight. [43] And Laban answered and said unto Jacob, These daughters are my daughters, and these children are my children, and these cattle are my cattle, and all that thou seest is mine: and what can I do this day unto these my daughters, or unto their children which they have born? [44] Now therefore come thou, let us make a covenant, I and thou; and let it be for a witness between me and thee. [45] And Jacob took a stone, and set it up for a pillar. [46] And Jacob said unto his brethren, Gather stones; and they took stones, and made an heap: and they did eat there upon the heap. [47] And Laban called it Jegar-sahadutha: but Jacob called it Galeed. [48] And Laban said, This heap is a witness between me and thee this day. Therefore was the name of it called Galeed; [49] And Mizpah; for he said, The LORD watch between me and thee, when we are absent one from another. [50] If thou shalt afflict my daughters, or if thou shalt take other wives beside my daughters, no man is with us; see, God is witness betwixt me and thee. [51] And Laban said to Jacob, Behold this heap, and behold this pillar, which I have cast betwixt me and thee; [52] This heap be witness, and this pillar be witness, that I will not pass over this heap to thee, and that thou shalt not pass over this heap and this pillar unto me, for harm. [53] The God of Abraham, and the God of Nahor, the God of their father, judge betwixt us. And Jacob sware by the fear of his father Isaac. [54] Then Jacob offered sacrifice upon the mount, and called his brethren to eat bread: and they did eat bread, and tarried all night in the mount. [55] And early in the morning Laban rose up, and kissed his sons and his daughters, and blessed them: and Laban departed, and returned unto his place.

GENESIS 32

[1] And Jacob went on his way, and the angels of God met him. [2] And when Jacob saw them, he said, This is God's host: and he called the name of that place Mahanaim. [3] And Jacob sent messengers before him to Esau his brother unto the land of Seir, the country of Edom. [4] And he commanded them, saying, Thus shall ye speak unto my lord Esau; Thy servant Jacob saith thus, I have sojourned with Laban, and stayed there until now: [5] And I have oxen, and asses, flocks, and menservants, and womenservants: and I have sent to tell my lord, that I may find grace in thy sight. [6] And the messengers returned to Jacob, saying, We came to thy brother Esau, and also he cometh to meet thee, and four hundred men with him. [7] Then Jacob was greatly afraid and distressed: and he divided the people that was with him, and the flocks, and herds, and the camels, into two bands; [8] And said, If Esau come to the one company, and smite it, then the other company which is left shall escape. [9] And Jacob said, O God of my father Abraham, and God of my father Isaac, the LORD which saidst unto me, Return unto thy country, and to thy kindred, and I will deal well with thee: [10] I am not worthy of the least of all the mercies, and of all the truth, which thou hast shewed unto thy servant; for with my staff I passed over this Jordan; and now I am become two bands. [11] Deliver me, I pray thee, from the hand of my brother, from the hand of Esau: for I fear him, lest he will come and smite me, and the mother with the children. [12] And thou saidst, I will surely do thee good, and make thy seed as the sand of the sea, which cannot be numbered for multitude. [13] And he lodged there that same night; and took of that which came to his hand a present for Esau his brother; [14] Two hundred she goats, and twenty he goats,

two hundred ewes, and twenty rams, [15] Thirty milch camels with their colts, forty kine, and ten bulls, twenty she asses, and ten foals. [16] And he delivered them into the hand of his servants, every drove by themselves; and said unto his servants, Pass over before me, and put a space betwixt drove and drove. [17] And he commanded the foremost, saying, When Esau my brother meeteth thee, and asketh thee, saying, Whose art thou? and whither goest thou? and whose are these before thee? [18] Then thou shalt say, They be thy servant Jacob's; it is a present sent unto my lord Esau: and, behold, also he is behind us. [19] And so commanded he the second, and the third, and all that followed the droves, saying, On this manner shall ye speak unto Esau, when ye find him. [20] And say ye moreover, Behold, thy servant Jacob is behind us. For he said, I will appease him with the present that goeth before me, and afterward I will see his face; peradventure he will accept of me. [21] So went the present over before him: and himself lodged that night in the company. [22] And he rose up that night, and took his two wives, and his two womenservants, and his eleven sons, and passed over the ford Jabbok. [23] And he took them, and sent them over the brook, and sent over that he had. [24] And Jacob was left alone; and there wrestled a man with him until the breaking of the day. [25] And when he saw that he prevailed not against him, he touched the hollow of his thigh; and the hollow of Jacob's thigh was out of joint, as he wrestled with him. [26] And he said, Let me go, for the day breaketh. And he said, I will not let thee go, except thou bless me. [27] And he said unto him, What is thy name? And he said, Jacob. [28] And he said, Thy name shall be called no more Jacob, but Israel: for as a prince hast thou power with God and with men, and hast prevailed. [29] And Jacob asked him, and said, Tell me, I pray thee, thy name. And he said, Wherefore is it that thou dost ask after my name? And he blessed him there. [30] And Jacob called the name of the place Peniel: for I have seen God face to face, and my life is preserved. [31] And as he passed over Penuel the sun rose upon him, and he halted upon his thigh. [32] Therefore the children of Israel eat not of the sinew which shrank, which is upon the hollow of the thigh, unto this day: because he touched the hollow of Jacob's thigh in the sinew that shrank.

GENESIS 33

[1] And Jacob lifted up his eyes, and looked, and, behold, Esau came, and with him four hundred men. And he divided the children unto Leah, and unto Rachel, and unto the two handmaids. [2] And he put the handmaids and their children foremost, and Leah and her children after, and Rachel and Joseph hindermost. [3] And he passed over before them, and bowed himself to the ground seven times, until he came near to his brother. [4] And Esau ran to meet him, and embraced him, and fell on his neck, and kissed him: and they wept. [5] And he lifted up his eyes, and saw the women and the children; and said, Who are those with thee? And he said, The children which God hath graciously given thy servant. [6] Then the handmaidens came near, they and their children, and they bowed themselves. [7] And Leah also with her children came near, and bowed themselves: and after came Joseph near and Rachel, and they bowed themselves. [8] And he said, What meanest thou by all this drove which I met? And he said, These are to find grace in the sight of my lord. [9] And Esau said, I have enough, my brother; keep that thou hast unto thyself. [10] And Jacob said, Nay, I pray thee, if now I have found grace in thy sight,

then receive my present at my hand: for therefore I have seen thy face, as though I had seen the face of God, and thou wast pleased with me. [11] Take, I pray thee, my blessing that is brought to thee; because God hath dealt graciously with me, and because I have enough. And he urged him, and he took it. [12] And he said, Let us take our journey, and let us go, and I will go before thee. [13] And he said unto him, My lord knoweth that the children are tender, and the flocks and herds with young are with me: and if men should over-drive them one day, all the flock will die. [14] Let my lord, I pray thee, pass over before his servant: and I will lead on softly, according as the cattle that goeth before me and the children be able to endure, until I come unto my lord unto Seir. [15] And Esau said, Let me now leave with thee some of the folk that are with me. And he said, What needeth it? let me find grace in the sight of my lord. [16] So Esau returned that day on his way unto Seir. [17] And Jacob journeyed to Succoth, and built him an house, and made booths for his cattle: therefore the name of the place is called Succoth. [18] And Jacob came to Shalem, a city of Shechem, which is in the land of Canaan, when he came from Padan-aram; and pitched his tent before the city. [19] And he bought a parcel of a field, where he had spread his tent, at the hand of the children of Hamor, Shechem's father, for an hundred pieces of money. [20] And he erected there an altar, and called it El-elohe-Israel.

GENESIS 34

[1] And Dinah the daughter of Leah, which she bare unto Jacob, went out to see the daughters of the land. [2] And when Shechem the son of Hamor the Hivite, prince of the

country, saw her, he took her, and lay with her, and defiled her. [3] And his soul clave unto Dinah the daughter of Jacob, and he loved the damsel, and spake kindly unto the damsel. [4] And Shechem spake unto his father Hamor, saying, Get me this damsel to wife. [5] And Jacob heard that he had defiled Dinah his daughter: now his sons were with his cattle in the field: and Jacob held his peace until they were come. [6] And Hamor the father of Shechem went out unto Jacob to commune with him. [7] And the sons of Jacob came out of the field when they heard it: and the men were grieved, and they were very wroth, because he had wrought folly in Israel in lying with Jacob's daughter; which thing ought not to be done. [8] And Hamor communed with them, saying, The soul of my son Shechem longeth for your daughter: I pray you give her him to wife. [9] And make ye marriages with us, and give your daughters unto us, and take our daughters unto you. [10] And ye shall dwell with us: and the land shall be before you; dwell and trade ye therein, and get you possessions therein. [11] And Shechem said unto her father and unto her brethren, Let me find grace in your eyes, and what ye shall say unto me I will give. [12] Ask me never so much dowry and gift, and I will give according as ye shall say unto me: but give me the damsel to wife. [13] And the sons of Jacob answered Shechem and Hamor his father deceitfully, and said, because he had defiled Dinah their sister: [14] And they said unto them, We cannot do this thing, to give our sister to one that is uncircumcised; for that were a reproach unto us: [15] But in this will we consent unto you: If ye will be as we be, that every male of you be circumcised; [16] Then will we give our daughters unto you, and we will take your daughters to us, and we will dwell with you, and we will become one people. [17] But if ye will not hearken unto us, to be circumcised; then will we take our daughter, and we will be gone. [18] And their words pleased Hamor, and Shechem Hamor's son. [19] And the young man deferred not to do the thing, because he had delight in Jacob's daughter: and he was more honourable than all the house of his father. [20] And Hamor and Shechem his son came unto the gate of their city, and communed with the men of their city, saying, [21] These men are peaceable with us; therefore let them dwell in the land, and trade therein; for the land, behold, it is large enough for them; let us take their daughters to us for wives, and let us give them our daughters. [22] Only herein will the men consent unto us for to dwell with us, to be one people, if every male among us be circumcised, as they are circumcised. [23] Shall not their cattle and their substance and every beast of theirs be ours? only let us consent unto them, and they will dwell with us. [24] And unto Hamor and unto Shechem his son hearkened all that went out of the gate of his city; and every male was circumcised, all that went out of the gate of his city. [25] And it came to pass on the third day, when they were sore, that two of the sons of Jacob, Simeon and Levi, Dinah's brethren, took each man his sword, and came upon the city boldly, and slew all the males. [26] And they slew Hamor and Shechem his son with the edge of the sword, and took Dinah out of Shechem's house, and went out. [27] The sons of Jacob came upon the slain, and spoiled the city, because they had defiled their sister. [28] They took their sheep, and their oxen, and their asses, and that which was in the city, and that which was in the field, [29] And all their wealth, and all their little ones, and their wives took they captive, and spoiled even all that was in the house. [30] And Jacob said to Simeon and Levi, Ye have troubled me to make me to stink among the inhabitants of the land, among the Canaanites and the Perizzites: and I being few in number, they shall gather themselves together against me, and slay me; and I shall be destroyed, I and my house. [31] And they said, Should he deal with our sister as with an harlot?

GENESIS 35

[1] And God said unto Jacob, Arise, go up to Beth-el, and dwell there: and make there an altar unto God, that appeared unto thee when thou fleddest from the face of Esau thy brother. [2] Then Jacob said unto his household, and to all that were with him, Put away the strange gods that are among you, and be clean, and change your garments: [3] And let us arise, and go up to Beth-el; and I will make there an altar unto God, who answered me in the day of my distress, and was with me in the way which I went. [4] And they gave unto Jacob all the strange gods which were in their hand, and all their earrings which were in their ears; and Jacob hid them under the oak which was by Shechem. [5] And they journeyed: and the terror of God was upon the cities that were round about them, and they did not pursue after the sons of Jacob. [6] So Jacob came to Luz, which is in the land of Canaan, that is, Beth-el, he and all the people that were with him. [7] And he built there an altar, and called the place El-beth-el: because there God appeared unto him, when he fled from the face of his brother. [8] But Deborah Rebekah's nurse died, and she was buried beneath Beth-el under an oak: and the name of it was called Allon-bachuth. [9] And God appeared unto Jacob again, when he came out of Padan-aram, and blessed him. [10] And God said unto him, Thy name is Jacob: thy name shall not be called any more Jacob, but Israel shall be thy name: and he called his name Israel. [11] And God said unto him, I am God Almighty: be fruitful and multiply; a nation and a company of nations shall be of thee, and kings shall

come out of thy loins; [12] And the land which I gave Abraham and Isaac, to thee I will give it, and to thy seed after thee will I give the land. [13] And God went up from him in the place where he talked with him. [14] And Jacob set up a pillar in the place where he talked with him, even a pillar of stone: and he poured a drink offering thereon, and he poured oil thereon. [15] And Jacob called the name of the place where God spake with him, Beth-el. [16] And they journeyed from Beth-el; and there was but a little way to come to Ephrath: and Rachel travailed, and she had hard labour. [17] And it came to pass, when she was in hard labour, that the midwife said unto her, Fear not; thou shalt have this son also. [18] And it came to pass, as her soul was in departing, (for she died) that she called his name Ben-oni: but his father called him Benjamin. [19] And Rachel died, and was buried in the way to Ephrath, which is Beth-lehem. [20] And Jacob set a pillar upon her grave: that is the pillar of Rachel's grave unto this day. [21] And Israel journeyed, and spread his tent beyond the tower of Edar. [22] And it came to pass, when Israel dwelt in that land, that Reuben went and lay with Bilhah his father's concubine: and Israel heard it. Now the sons of Jacob were twelve: [23] The sons of Leah; Reuben, Jacob's firstborn, and Simeon, and Levi, and Judah, and Issachar, and Zebulun: [24] The sons of Rachel; Joseph, and Benjamin: [25] And the sons of Bilhah, Rachel's handmaid; Dan, and Naphtali: [26] And the sons of Zilpah, Leah's handmaid; Gad, and Asher: these are the sons of Jacob, which were born to him in Padan-aram. [27] And Jacob came unto Isaac his father unto Mamre, unto the city of Arbah, which is Hebron, where Abraham and Isaac sojourned. [28] And the days of Isaac were an hundred and fourscore years. [29] And Isaac gave up the ghost, and died, and was gathered unto his people, being old and full of days: and his sons Esau and Jacob buried him.

GENESIS 36

[1] Now these are the generations of Esau, who is Edom. [2] Esau took his wives of the daughters of Canaan; Adah the daughter of Elon the Hittite, and Aholibamah the daughter of Anah the daughter of Zibeon the Hivite; [3] And Bashemath Ishmael's daughter, sister of Nebajoth. [4] And Adah bare to Esau Eliphaz; and Bashemath bare Reuel; [5] And Aholibamah bare Jeush, and Jaalam, and Korah: these are the sons of Esau, which were born unto him in the land of Canaan. [6] And Esau took his wives, and his sons, and his daughters, and all the persons of his house, and his cattle, and all his beasts, and all his substance, which he had got in the land of Canaan; and went into the country from the face of his brother Jacob. [7] For their riches were more than that they might dwell together; and the land wherein they were strangers could not bear them because of their cattle. [8] Thus dwelt Esau in mount Seir: Esau is Edom. [9] And these are the generations of Esau the father of the Edomites in mount Seir: [10] These are the names of Esau's sons; Eliphaz the son of Adah the wife of Esau, Reuel the son of Bashemath the wife of Esau. [11] And the sons of Eliphaz were Teman, Omar, Zepho, and Gatam, and Kenaz. [12] And Timna was concubine to Eliphaz Esau's son; and she bare to Eliphaz Amalek: these were the sons of Adah Esau's wife. [13] And these are the sons of Reuel; Nahath, and Zerah, Shammah, and Mizzah: these were the sons of Bashemath Esau's wife. [14] And these were the sons of Aholibamah, the daughter of Anah the daughter of Zibeon, Esau's wife: and she bare to Esau Jeush, and Jaalam, and Korah. [15] These were dukes of the sons of Esau: the sons of Eliphaz the firstborn son of Esau; duke Teman, duke Omar, duke Zepho, duke Kenaz, [16] Duke Korah, duke Gatam, and duke Amalek: these are

the dukes that came of Eliphaz in the land of Edom; these were the sons of Adah. [17] And these are the sons of Reuel Esau's son; duke Nahath, duke Zerah, duke Shammah, duke Mizzah: these are the dukes that came of Reuel in the land of Edom; these are the sons of Bashemath Esau's wife. [18] And these are the sons of Aholibamah Esau's wife; duke Jeush, duke Jaalam, duke Korah: these were the dukes that came of Aholibamah the daughter of Anah, Esau's wife. [19] These are the sons of Esau, who is Edom, and these are their dukes. [20] These are the sons of Seir the Horite, who inhabited the land; Lotan, and Shobal, and Zibeon, and Anah, [21] And Dishon, and Ezer, and Dishan: these are the dukes of the Horites, the children of Seir in the land of Edom. [22] And the children of Lotan were Hori and Hemam; and Lotan's sister was Timna. [23] And the children of Shobal were these; Alvan, and Manahath, and Ebal, Shepho, and Onam. [24] And these are the children of Zibeon; both Ajah, and Anah: this was that Anah that found the mules in the wilderness, as he fed the asses of Zibeon his father. [25] And the children of Anah were these; Dishon, and Aholibamah the daughter of Anah. [26] And these are the children of Dishon; Hemdan, and Eshban, and Ithran, and Cheran. [27] The children of Ezer are these; Bilhan, and Zaavan, and Akan. [28] The children of Dishan are these: Uz, and Aran. [29] These are the dukes that came of the Horites; duke Lotan, duke Shobal, duke Zibeon, duke Anah, [30] Duke Dishon, duke Ezer, duke Dishan: these are the dukes that came of Hori, among their dukes in the land of Seir. [31] And these are the kings that reigned in the land of Edom, before there reigned any king over the children of Israel. [32] And Bela the son of Beor reigned in Edom: and the name of his city was Dinhabah. [33] And Bela died, and Jobab the son of Zerah of Bozrah reigned in his stead. [34] And Jobab died, and Husham of the land of Temani reigned in his stead. [35] And Husham died, and Hadad the son of Bedad, who smote Midian in the field of Moab, reigned in his stead: and the name of his city was Avith. [36] And Hadad died, and Samlah of Masrekah reigned in his stead. [37] And Samlah died, and Saul of Rehoboth by the river reigned in his stead. [38] And Saul died, and Baal-hanan the son of Achbor reigned in his stead. [39] And Baal-hanan the son of Achbor died, and Hadar reigned in his stead: and the name of his city was Pau; and his wife's name was Mehetabel, the daughter of Matred, the daughter of Mezahab. [40] And these are the names of the dukes that came of Esau, according to their families, after their places, by their names; duke Timnah, duke Alvah, duke Jetheth, [41] Duke Aholibamah, duke Elah, duke Pinon, [42] Duke Kenaz, duke Teman, duke Mibzar, [43] Duke Magdiel, duke Iram: these be the dukes of Edom, according to their habitations in the land of their possession: he is Esau the father of the Edomites.

GENESIS 37

[1] And Jacob dwelt in the land wherein his father was a stranger, in the land of Canaan. [2] These are the generations of Jacob. Joseph, being seventeen years old, was feeding the flock with his brethren; and the lad was with the sons of Bilhah, and with the sons of Zilpah, his father's wives: and Joseph brought unto his father their evil report. [3] Now Israel loved Joseph more than all his children, because he was the son of his old age: and he made him a coat of many colours. [4] And when his brethren saw that their father loved him more than all his brethren, they hated him, and could not speak peaceably unto him. [5] And Joseph dreamed a

dream, and he told it his brethren: and they hated him yet the more. [6] And he said unto them, Hear, I pray you, this dream which I have dreamed: [7] For, behold, we were binding sheaves in the field, and, lo, my sheaf arose, and also stood upright; and, behold, your sheaves stood round about, and made obeisance to my sheaf. [8] And his brethren said to him, Shalt thou indeed reign over us? or shalt thou indeed have dominion over us? And they hated him yet the more for his dreams, and for his words. [9] And he dreamed yet another dream, and told it his brethren, and said, Behold, I have dreamed a dream more; and, behold, the sun and the moon and the eleven stars made obeisance to me. [10] And he told it to his father, and to his brethren: and his father rebuked him, and said unto him, What is this dream that thou hast dreamed? Shall I and thy mother and thy brethren indeed come to bow down ourselves to thee to the earth? [11] And his brethren envied him; but his father observed the saying. [12] And his brethren went to feed their father's flock in Shechem. [13] And Israel said unto Joseph, Do not thy brethren feed the flock in Shechem? come, and I will send thee unto them. And he said to him, Here am I. [14] And he said to him, Go, I pray thee, see whether it be well with thy brethren, and well with the flocks; and bring me word again. So he sent him out of the vale of Hebron, and he came to Shechem. [15] And a certain man found him, and, behold, he was wandering in the field: and the man asked him, saying, What seekest thou? [16] And he said, I seek my brethren: tell me, I pray thee, where they feed their flocks. [17] And the man said, They are departed hence; for I heard them say, Let us go to Dothan. And Joseph went after his brethren, and found them in Dothan. [18] And when they saw him afar off, even before he came near unto them, they conspired against him to slay him. [19] And they said one to another, Behold, this dreamer cometh. [20] Come now therefore, and let us slay him, and cast him into some pit, and we will say, Some evil beast hath devoured him: and we shall see what will become of his dreams. [21] And Reuben heard it, and he delivered him out of their hands; and said, Let us not kill him. [22] And Reuben said unto them, Shed no blood, but cast him into this pit that is in the wilderness, and lay no hand upon him; that he might rid him out of their hands, to deliver him to his father again. [23] And it came to pass, when Joseph was come unto his brethren, that they stript Joseph out of his coat, his coat of many colours that was on him; [24] And they took him, and cast him into a pit: and the pit was empty, there was no water in it. [25] And they sat down to eat bread: and they lifted up their eyes and looked, and, behold, a company of Ishmeelites came from Gilead with their camels bearing spicery and balm and myrrh, going to carry it down to Egypt. [26] And Judah said unto his brethren, What profit is it if we slay our brother, and conceal his blood? [27] Come, and let us sell him to the Ishmeelites, and let not our hand be upon him; for he is our brother and our flesh. And his brethren were content. [28] Then there passed by Midianites merchantmen; and they drew and lifted up Joseph out of the pit, and sold Joseph to the Ishmeelites for twenty pieces of silver: and they brought Joseph into Egypt. [29] And Reuben returned unto the pit; and, behold, Joseph was not in the pit; and he rent his clothes. [30] And he returned unto his brethren, and said, The child is not; and I, whither shall I go? [31] And they took Joseph's coat, and killed a kid of the goats, and dipped the coat in the blood; [32] And they sent the coat of many colours, and they brought it to their father; and said, This have we found: know now whether it be thy son's coat or no. [33] And he knew it, and said, It is my son's coat; an evil beast hath devoured him; Joseph is without doubt rent in pieces. [34] And Jacob rent his clothes, and put sackcloth upon his loins, and mourned for his son many days. [35] And all his sons and all his daughters rose up to comfort him; but he refused to be comforted; and he said, For I will go down into the grave unto my son mourning. Thus his father wept for him. [36] And the Midianites sold him into Egypt unto Potiphar, an officer of Pharaoh's, and captain of the guard.

GENESIS 38

[1] And it came to pass at that time, that Judah went down from his brethren, and turned in to a certain Adullamite, whose name was Hirah. [2] And Judah saw there a daughter of a certain Canaanite, whose name was Shuah; and he took her, and went in unto her. [3] And she conceived, and bare a son; and he called his name Er. [4] And she conceived again, and bare a son; and she called his name Onan. [5] And she yet again conceived, and bare a son; and called his name Shelah: and he was at Chezib, when she bare him. [6] And Judah took a wife for Er his firstborn, whose name was Tamar. [7] And Er, Judah's firstborn, was wicked in the sight of the LORD; and the LORD slew him. [8] And Judah said unto Onan, Go in unto thy brother's wife, and marry her, and raise up seed to thy brother. [9] And Onan knew that the seed should not be his; and it came to pass, when he went in unto his brother's wife, that he spilled it on the ground, lest that he should give seed to his brother. [10] And the thing which he did displeased the LORD: wherefore he slew him also. [11] Then said Judah to Tamar his daughter in law, Remain a widow at thy father's house, till Shelah my son be grown: for he said, Lest peradventure he die also, as

his brethren did. And Tamar went and dwelt in her father's house. [12] And in process of time the daughter of Shuah Judah's wife died; and Judah was comforted, and went up unto his sheepshearers to Timnath, he and his friend Hirah the Adullamite. [13] And it was told Tamar, saying, Behold thy father in law goeth up to Timnath to shear his sheep. [14] And she put her widow's garments off from her, and covered her with a vail, and wrapped herself, and sat in an open place, which is by the way to Timnath; for she saw that Shelah was grown, and she was not given unto him to wife. [15] When Judah saw her, he thought her to be an harlot; because she had covered her face. [16] And he turned unto her by the way, and said, Go to, I pray thee, let me come in unto thee; (for he knew not that she was his daughter in law.) And she said, What wilt thou give me, that thou mayest come in unto me? [17] And he said, I will send thee a kid from the flock. And she said, Wilt thou give me a pledge, till thou send it? [18] And he said, What pledge shall I give thee? And she said, Thy signet, and thy bracelets, and thy staff that is in thine hand. And he gave it her, and came in unto her, and she conceived by him. [19] And she arose, and went away, and laid by her vail from her, and put on the garments of her widowhood. [20] And Judah sent the kid by the hand of his friend the Adullamite, to receive his pledge from the woman's hand: but he found her not. [21] Then he asked the men of that place, saying, Where is the harlot, that was openly by the way side? And they said, There was no harlot in this place. [22] And he returned to Judah, and said, I cannot find her; and also the men of the place said, that there was no harlot in this place. [23] And Judah said, Let her take it to her, lest we be shamed: behold, I sent this kid, and thou hast not found her. [24] And it came to pass about three months after, that it was told Judah, saying, Tamar thy daughter in law hath played the harlot; and also, behold, she is with child by whoredom. And Judah said, Bring her forth, and let her be burnt. [25] When she was brought forth, she sent to her father in law, saying, By the man, whose these are, am I with child: and she said, Discern, I pray thee, whose are these, the signet, and bracelets, and staff. [26] And Judah acknowledged them, and said, She hath been more righteous than I; because that I gave her not to Shelah my son. And he knew her again no more. [27] And it came to pass in the time of her travail, that, behold, twins were in her womb. [28] And it came to pass, when she travailed, that the one put out his hand: and the midwife took and bound upon his hand a scarlet thread, saying, This came out first, [29] And it came to pass, as he drew back his hand, that, behold, his brother came out: and she said, How hast thou broken forth? this breach be upon thee: therefore his name was called Pharez. [30] And afterward came out his brother, that had the scarlet thread upon his hand: and his name was called Zarah.

GENESIS 39

[1] And Joseph was brought down to Egypt; and Potiphar, an officer of Pharaoh, captain of the guard, an Egyptian, bought him of the hands of the Ishmeelites, which had brought him down thither. [2] And the LORD was with Joseph, and he was a prosperous man; and he was in the house of his master the Egyptian. [3] And his master saw that the LORD was with him, and that the LORD made all that he did to prosper in his hand. [4] And Joseph found grace in his sight, and he served him: and he made him overseer over his house, and all that he had he put into his hand. [5] And it came to pass from the time that he had made him overseer in his house,

and over all that he had, that the LORD blessed the Egyptian's house for Joseph's sake; and the blessing of the LORD was upon all that he had in the house, and in the field. [6] And he left all that he had in Joseph's hand; and he knew not ought he had, save the bread which he did eat. And Joseph was a goodly person, and well favoured. [7] And it came to pass after these things, that his master's wife cast her eyes upon Joseph; and she said, Lie with me. [8] But he refused, and said unto his master's wife, Behold, my master wotteth not what is with me in the house, and he hath committed all that he hath to my hand; [9] There is none greater in this house than I; neither hath he kept back any thing from me but thee, because thou art his wife: how then can I do this great wickedness, and sin against God? [10] And it came to pass, as she spake to Joseph day by day, that he hearkened not unto her, to lie by her, or to be with her. [11] And it came to pass about this time, that Joseph went into the house to do his business; and there was none of the men of the house there within. [12] And she caught him by his garment, saying, Lie with me: and he left his garment in her hand, and fled, and got him out. [13] And it came to pass, when she saw that he had left his garment in her hand, and was fled forth, [14] That she called unto the men of her house, and spake unto them, saying, See, he hath brought in an Hebrew unto us to mock us; he came in unto me to lie with me, and I cried with a loud voice: [15] And it came to pass, when he heard that I lifted up my voice and cried, that he left his garment with me, and fled, and got him out. [16] And she laid up his garment by her, until his lord came home. [17] And she spake unto him according to these words, saying, The Hebrew servant, which thou hast brought unto us, came in unto me to mock me: [18] And it came to pass, as I lifted up my voice and cried, that he left his garment with me, and fled out. [19] And it came to pass, when his master heard the words of his wife, which she spake unto him, saying, After this manner did thy servant to me; that his wrath was kindled. [20] And Joseph's master took him, and put him into the prison, a place where the king's prisoners were bound: and he was there in the prison. [21] But the LORD was with Joseph, and shewed him mercy, and gave him favour in the sight of the keeper of the prison. [22] And the keeper of the prison committed to Joseph's hand all the prisoners that were in the prison; and whatsoever they did there, he was the doer of it. [23] The keeper of the prison looked not to any thing that was under his hand; because the LORD was with him, and that which he did, the LORD made it to prosper.

GENESIS 40

[1] And it came to pass after these things, that the butler of the king of Egypt and his baker had offended their lord the king of Egypt. [2] And Pharaoh was wroth against two of his officers, against the chief of the butlers, and against the chief of the bakers. [3] And he put them in ward in the house of the captain of the guard, into the prison, the place where Joseph was bound. [4] And the captain of the guard charged Joseph with them, and he served them: and they continued a season in ward. [5] And they dreamed a dream both of them, each man his dream in one night, each man according to the interpretation of his dream, the butler and the baker of the king of Egypt, which were bound in the prison. [6] And Joseph came in unto them in the morning, and looked upon them, and, behold, they were sad. [7] And he asked Pharaoh's officers that were with him in the ward of his lord's house, saying, Wherefore look ye so sadly to day? [8] And

they said unto him, We have dreamed a dream, and there is no interpreter of it. And Joseph said unto them, Do not interpretations belong to God? tell me them, I pray you. [9] And the chief butler told his dream to Joseph, and said to him, In my dream, behold, a vine was before me; [10] And in the vine were three branches: and it was as though it budded, and her blossoms shot forth; and the clusters thereof brought forth ripe grapes: [11] And Pharaoh's cup was in my hand: and I took the grapes, and pressed them into Pharaoh's cup, and I gave the cup into Pharaoh's hand. [12] And Joseph said unto him, This is the interpretation of it: The three branches are three days: [13] Yet within three days shall Pharaoh lift up thine head, and restore thee unto thy place: and thou shalt deliver Pharaoh's cup into his hand, after the former manner when thou wast his butler. [14] But think on me when it shall be well with thee, and shew kindness, I pray thee, unto me, and make mention of me unto Pharaoh, and bring me out of this house: [15] For indeed I was stolen away out of the land of the Hebrews: and here also have I done nothing that they should put me into the dungeon. [16] When the chief baker saw that the interpretation was good, he said unto Joseph, I also was in my dream, and, behold, I had three white baskets on my head: [17] And in the uppermost basket there was of all manner of bakemeats for Pharaoh; and the birds did eat them out of the basket upon my head. [18] And Joseph answered and said, This is the interpretation thereof: The three baskets are three days: [19] Yet within three days shall Pharaoh lift up thy head from off thee, and shall hang thee on a tree; and the birds shall eat thy flesh from off thee. [20] And it came to pass the third day, which was Pharaoh's birthday, that he made a feast unto all his servants: and he lifted up the head of the chief butler and of the chief baker among his servants. [21] And he restored the chief butler unto his butlership again; and he gave the cup into Pharaoh's hand: [22] But he hanged the chief baker: as Joseph had interpreted to them. [23] Yet did not the chief butler remember Joseph, but forgat him.

GENESIS 41

[1] And it came to pass at the end of two full years, that Pharaoh dreamed: and, behold, he stood by the river. [2] And, behold, there came up out of the river seven well favoured kine and fatfleshed; and they fed in a meadow. [3] And, behold, seven other kine came up after them out of the river, ill favoured and leanfleshed; and stood by the other kine upon the brink of the river. [4] And the ill favoured and lean-fleshed kine did eat up the seven well favoured and fat kine. So Pharaoh awoke. [5] And he slept and dreamed the second time: and, behold, seven ears of corn came up upon one stalk, rank and good. [6] And, behold, seven thin ears and blasted with the east wind sprung up after them. [7] And the seven thin ears devoured the seven rank and full ears. And Pharaoh awoke, and, behold, it was a dream. [8] And it came to pass in the morning that his spirit was troubled; and he sent and called for all the magicians of Egypt, and all the wise men thereof: and Pharaoh told them his dream; but there was none that could interpret them unto Pharaoh. [9] Then spake the chief butler unto Pharaoh, saying, I do remember my faults this day: [10] Pharaoh was wroth with his servants, and put me in ward in the captain of the guard's house, both me and the chief baker: [11] And we dreamed a dream in one night, I and he; we dreamed each man according to the interpretation of his dream. [12] And there was there with us a young man, an Hebrew, servant to the

captain of the guard; and we told him, and he interpreted to us our dreams; to each man according to his dream he did interpret. [13] And it came to pass, as he interpreted to us, so it was; me he restored unto mine office, and him he hanged. [14] Then Pharaoh sent and called Joseph, and they brought him hastily out of the dungeon: and he shaved himself, and changed his raiment, and came in unto Pharaoh. [15] And Pharaoh said unto Joseph, I have dreamed a dream, and there is none that can interpret it: and I have heard say of thee, that thou canst understand a dream to interpret it. [16] And Joseph answered Pharaoh, saying, It is not in me: God shall give Pharaoh an answer of peace. [17] And Pharaoh said unto Joseph, In my dream, behold, I stood upon the bank of the river: [18] And, behold, there came up out of the river seven kine, fatfleshed and well favoured; and they fed in a meadow: [19] And, behold, seven other kine came up after them, poor and very ill favoured and leanfleshed, such as I never saw in all the land of Egypt for badness: [20] And the lean and the ill favoured kine did eat up the first seven fat kine: [21] And when they had eaten them up, it could not be known that they had eaten them; but they were still ill favoured, as at the beginning. So I awoke. [22] And I saw in my dream, and, behold, seven ears came up in one stalk, full and good: [23] And, behold, seven ears, withered, thin, and blasted with the east wind, sprung up after them: [24] And the thin ears devoured the seven good ears: and I told this unto the magicians; but there was none that could declare it to me. [25] And Joseph said unto Pharaoh, The dream of Pharaoh is one: God hath shewed Pharaoh what he is about to do. [26] The seven good kine are seven years; and the seven good ears are seven years: the dream is one. [27] And the seven thin and ill favoured kine that came up after them are seven years; and the seven empty ears blasted with the east wind shall be seven years of famine. [28] This is the thing which I have spoken unto Pharaoh: What God is about to do he sheweth unto Pharaoh. [29] Behold, there come seven years of great plenty throughout all the land of Egypt: [30] And there shall arise after them seven years of famine; and all the plenty shall be forgotten in the land of Egypt; and the famine shall consume the land; [31] And the plenty shall not be known in the land by reason of that famine following; for it shall be very grievous. [32] And for that the dream was doubled unto Pharaoh twice; it is because the thing is established by God, and God will shortly bring it to pass. [33] Now therefore let Pharaoh look out a man discreet and wise, and set him over the land of Egypt. [34] Let Pharaoh do this, and let him appoint officers over the land, and take up the fifth part of the land of Egypt in the seven plenteous years. [35] And let them gather all the food of those good years that come, and lay up corn under the hand of Pharaoh, and let them keep food in the cities. [36] And that food shall be for store to the land against the seven years of famine, which shall be in the land of Egypt; that the land perish not through the famine. [37] And the thing was good in the eyes of Pharaoh, and in the eyes of all his servants. [38] And Pharaoh said unto his servants, Can we find such a one as this is, a man in whom the Spirit of God is? [39] And Pharaoh said unto Joseph, Forasmuch as God hath shewed thee all this, there is none so discreet and wise as thou art: [40] Thou shalt be over my house, and according unto thy word shall all my people be ruled: only in the throne will I be greater than thou. [41] And Pharaoh said unto Joseph, See, I have set thee over all the land of Egypt. [42] And Pharaoh took off his ring from his hand, and put it upon Joseph's hand, and arrayed him in vestures of fine linen, and put a gold chain about his neck; [43] And he made him to ride in the second chariot which he had; and they cried before him, Bow the knee: and he made him ruler over all the land of Egypt. [44] And Pharaoh said unto Joseph, I am Pharaoh, and without thee shall no man lift up his hand or foot in all the land of Egypt. [45] And Pharaoh called Joseph's name Zaphnath-paaneah; and he gave him to wife Asenath the daughter of Poti-pherah priest of On. And Joseph went out over all the land of Egypt. [46] And Joseph was thirty years old when he stood before Pharaoh king of Egypt. And Joseph went out from the presence of Pharaoh, and went throughout all the land of Egypt. [47] And in the seven plenteous years the earth brought forth by handfuls. [48] And he gathered up all the food of the seven years, which were in the land of Egypt, and laid up the food in the cities: the food of the field, which was round about every city, laid he up in the same. [49] And Joseph gathered corn as the sand of the sea, very much, until he left numbering; for it was without number. [50] And unto Joseph were born two sons before the years of famine came, which Asenath the daughter of Poti-pherah priest of On bare unto him. [51] And Joseph called the name of the firstborn Manasseh: For God, said he, hath made me forget all my toil, and all my father's house. [52] And the name of the second called he Ephraim: For God hath caused me to be fruitful in the land of my affliction. [53] And the seven years of plente-ousness, that was in the land of Egypt, were ended. [54] And the seven years of dearth began to come, according as Joseph had said: and the dearth was in all lands; but in all the land of Egypt there was bread. [55] And when all the land of Egypt was famished, the people cried to Pharaoh for bread: and Pharaoh said unto all the Egyptians, Go unto Joseph; what he saith to you, do. [56] And the famine was over all the face of the earth: and Joseph opened all the storehouses, and sold unto the Egyptians; and the famine waxed sore in the land of

Egypt. [57] And all countries came into Egypt to Joseph for
to buy corn; because that the famine was so sore in all lands.

GENESIS 42

[1] Now when Jacob saw that there was corn in Egypt, Jacob said unto his sons, Why do ye look one upon another?
[2] And he said, Behold, I have heard that there is corn in
Egypt: get you down thither, and buy for us from thence;
that we may live, and not die. [3] And Joseph's ten brethren
went down to buy corn in Egypt. [4] But Benjamin, Joseph's
brother, Jacob sent not with his brethren; for he said, Lest
peradventure mischief befall him. [5] And the sons of Israel
came to buy corn among those that came: for the famine was
in the land of Canaan. [6] And Joseph was the governor over
the land, and he it was that sold to all the people of the land:
and Joseph's brethren came, and bowed down themselves
before him with their faces to the earth. [7] And Joseph saw
his brethren, and he knew them, but made himself strange
unto them, and spake roughly unto them; and he said unto
them, Whence come ye? And they said, From the land of
Canaan to buy food. [8] And Joseph knew his brethren, but
they knew not him. [9] And Joseph remembered the dreams
which he dreamed of them, and said unto them, Ye are spies;
to see the nakedness of the land ye are come. [10] And they
said unto him, Nay, my lord, but to buy food are thy servants
come. [11] We are all one man's sons; we are true men, thy
servants are no spies. [12] And he said unto them, Nay, but
to see the nakedness of the land ye are come. [13] And they
said, Thy servants are twelve brethren, the sons of one man
in the land of Canaan; and, behold, the youngest is this day
with our father, and one is not. [14] And Joseph said unto

them, That is it that I spake unto you, saying, Ye are spies: [15] Hereby ye shall be proved: By the life of Pharaoh ye shall not go forth hence, except your youngest brother come hither. [16] Send one of you, and let him fetch your brother, and ye shall be kept in prison, that your words may be proved, whether there be any truth in you: or else by the life of Pharaoh surely ye are spies. [17] And he put them all together into ward three days. [18] And Joseph said unto them the third day, This do, and live; for I fear God: [19] If ye be true men, let one of your brethren be bound in the house of your prison: go ye, carry corn for the famine of your houses: [20] But bring your youngest brother unto me; so shall your words be verified, and ye shall not die. And they did so. [21] And they said one to another, We are verily guilty concerning our brother, in that we saw the anguish of his soul, when he besought us, and we would not hear; therefore is this distress come upon us. [22] And Reuben answered them, saying, Spake I not unto you, saying, Do not sin against the child; and ye would not hear? therefore, behold, also his blood is required. [23] And they knew not that Joseph understood them; for he spake unto them by an interpreter. [24] And he turned himself about from them, and wept; and returned to them again, and communed with them, and took from them Simeon, and bound him before their eyes. [25] Then Joseph commanded to fill their sacks with corn, and to restore every man's money into his sack, and to give them provision for the way: and thus did he unto them. [26] And they laded their asses with the corn, and departed thence. [27] And as one of them opened his sack to give his ass provender in the inn, he espied his money; for, behold, it was in his sack's mouth. [28] And he said unto his brethren, My money is restored; and, lo, it is even in my sack: and their heart failed them, and they were afraid, saying one to another, What is this that God hath done unto us? [29] And they came unto Jacob their father unto the land of Canaan, and told him all that befell unto them; saying, [30] The man, who is the lord of the land, spake roughly to us, and took us for spies of the country. [31] And we said unto him, We are true men; we are no spies: [32] We be twelve brethren, sons of our father; one is not, and the youngest is this day with our father in the land of Canaan. [33] And the man, the lord of the country, said unto us, Hereby shall I know that ye are true men; leave one of your brethren here with me, and take food for the famine of your households, and be gone: [34] And bring your youngest brother unto me: then shall I know that ye are no spies, but that ye are true men: so will I deliver you your brother, and ye shall traffick in the land. [35] And it came to pass as they emptied their sacks, that, behold, every man's bundle of money was in his sack: and when both they and their father saw the bundles of money, they were afraid. [36] And Jacob their father said unto them, Me have ye bereaved of my children: Joseph is not, and Simeon is not, and ye will take Benjamin away: all these things are against me. [37] And Reuben spake unto his father, saying, Slay my two sons, if I bring him not to thee: deliver him into my hand, and I will bring him to thee again. [38] And he said, My son shall not go down with you; for his brother is dead, and he is left alone: if mischief befall him by the way in the which ye go, then shall ye bring down my gray hairs with sorrow to the grave.

GENESIS 43

[1] And the famine was sore in the land. [2] And it came to pass, when they had eaten up the corn which they had

brought out of Egypt, their father said unto them, Go again, buy us a little food. [3] And Judah spake unto him, saying, The man did solemnly protest unto us, saying, Ye shall not see my face, except your brother be with you. [4] If thou wilt send our brother with us, we will go down and buy thee food: [5] But if thou wilt not send him, we will not go down: for the man said unto us, Ye shall not see my face, except your brother be with you. [6] And Israel said, Wherefore dealt ye so ill with me, as to tell the man whether ye had yet a brother? [7] And they said, The man asked us straitly of our state, and of our kindred, saying, Is your father yet alive? have ye another brother? and we told him according to the tenor of these words: could we certainly know that he would say, Bring your brother down? [8] And Judah said unto Israel his father, Send the lad with me, and we will arise and go; that we may live, and not die, both we, and thou, and also our little ones. [9] I will be surety for him; of my hand shalt thou require him: if I bring him not unto thee, and set him before thee, then let me bear the blame for ever: [10] For except we had lingered, surely now we had returned this second time. [11] And their father Israel said unto them, If it must be so now, do this; take of the best fruits in the land in your vessels, and carry down the man a present, a little balm, and a little honey, spices, and myrrh, nuts, and almonds: [12] And take double money in your hand; and the money that was brought again in the mouth of your sacks, carry it again in your hand; peradventure it was an oversight: [13] Take also your brother, and arise, go again unto the man: [14] And God Almighty give you mercy before the man, that he may send away your other brother, and Benjamin. If I be bereaved of my children, I am bereaved. [15] And the men took that present, and they took double money in their hand, and Benjamin; and rose up, and went down to Egypt, and stood before Joseph. [16] And when

Joseph saw Benjamin with them, he said to the ruler of his house, Bring these men home, and slay, and make ready; for these men shall dine with me at noon. [17] And the man did as Joseph bade; and the man brought the men into Joseph's house. [18] And the men were afraid, because they were brought into Joseph's house; and they said, Because of the money that was returned in our sacks at the first time are we brought in; that he may seek occasion against us, and fall upon us, and take us for bondmen, and our asses. [19] And they came near to the steward of Joseph's house, and they communed with him at the door of the house, [20] And said, O sir, we came indeed down at the first time to buy food: [21] And it came to pass, when we came to the inn, that we opened our sacks, and, behold, every man's money was in the mouth of his sack, our money in full weight: and we have brought it again in our hand. [22] And other money have we brought down in our hands to buy food: we cannot tell who put our money in our sacks. [23] And he said, Peace be to you, fear not: your God, and the God of your father, hath given you treasure in your sacks: I had your money. And he brought Simeon out unto them. [24] And the man brought the men into Joseph's house, and gave them water, and they washed their feet; and he gave their asses provender. [25] And they made ready the present against Joseph came at noon: for they heard that they should eat bread there. [26] And when Joseph came home, they brought him the present which was in their hand into the house, and bowed themselves to him to the earth. [27] And he asked them of their welfare, and said, Is your father well, the old man of whom ye spake? Is he yet alive? [28] And they answered, Thy servant our father is in good health, he is yet alive. And they bowed down their heads, and made obeisance. [29] And he lifted up his eyes, and saw his brother Benjamin, his mother's son, and said, Is this your younger brother, of whom ye spake unto me? And he said, God be gracious unto thee, my son. [30] And Joseph made haste; for his bowels did yearn upon his brother: and he sought where to weep; and he entered into his chamber, and wept there. [31] And he washed his face, and went out, and refrained himself, and said, Set on bread. [32] And they set on for him by himself, and for them by themselves, and for the Egyptians, which did eat with him, by themselves: because the Egyptians might not eat bread with the Hebrews; for that is an abomination unto the Egyptians. [33] And they sat before him, the firstborn according to his birthright, and the youngest according to his youth: and the men marvelled one at another. [34] And he took and sent messes unto them from before him: but Benjamin's mess was five times so much as any of theirs. And they drank, and were merry with him.

GENESIS 44

[1] And he commanded the steward of his house, saying, Fill the men's sacks with food, as much as they can carry, and put every man's money in his sack's mouth. [2] And put my cup, the silver cup, in the sack's mouth of the youngest, and his corn money. And he did according to the word that Joseph had spoken. [3] As soon as the morning was light, the men were sent away, they and their asses. [4] And when they were gone out of the city, and not yet far off, Joseph said unto his steward, Up, follow after the men; and when thou dost overtake them, say unto them, Wherefore have ye rewarded evil for good? [5] Is not this it in which my lord drinketh, and whereby indeed he divineth? ye have done evil

in so doing. [6] And he overtook them, and he spake unto them these same words. [7] And they said unto him, Wherefore saith my lord these words? God forbid that thy servants should do according to this thing: [8] Behold, the money, which we found in our sacks' mouths, we brought again unto thee out of the land of Canaan: how then should we steal out of thy lord's house silver or gold? [9] With whomsoever of thy servants it be found, both let him die, and we also will be my lord's bondmen. [10] And he said, Now also let it be according unto your words; he with whom it is found shall be my servant; and ye shall be blameless. [11] Then they speedily took down every man his sack to the ground, and opened every man his sack. [12] And he searched, and began at the eldest, and left at the youngest: and the cup was found in Benjamin's sack. [13] Then they rent their clothes, and laded every man his ass, and returned to the city. [14] And Judah and his brethren came to Joseph's house; for he was yet there: and they fell before him on the ground. [15] And Joseph said unto them, What deed is this that ye have done? wot ye not that such a man as I can certainly divine? [16] And Judah said, What shall we say unto my lord? what shall we speak? or how shall we clear ourselves? God hath found out the iniquity of thy servants: behold, we are my lord's servants, both we, and he also with whom the cup is found. [17] And he said, God forbid that I should do so: but the man in whose hand the cup is found, he shall be my servant; and as for you, get you up in peace unto your father. [18] Then Judah came near unto him, and said, Oh my lord, let thy servant, I pray thee, speak a word in my lord's ears, and let not thine anger burn against thy servant: for thou art even as Pharaoh. [19] My lord asked his servants, saying, Have ye a father, or a brother? [20] And we said unto my lord, We have a father, an old man, and a child of his old age, a little one; and his brother is dead, and he alone is left of his mother, and his father loveth him. [21] And thou saidst unto thy servants, Bring him down unto me, that I may set mine eyes upon him. [22] And we said unto my lord, The lad cannot leave his father: for if he should leave his father, his father would die. [23] And thou saidst unto thy servants, Except your youngest brother come down with you, ye shall see my face no more. [24] And it came to pass when we came up unto thy servant my father, we told him the words of my lord. [25] And our father said, Go again, and buy us a little food. [26] And we said, We cannot go down: if our youngest brother be with us, then will we go down: for we may not see the man's face, except our youngest brother be with us. [27] And thy servant my father said unto us, Ye know that my wife bare me two sons: [28] And the one went out from me, and I said, Surely he is torn in pieces; and I saw him not since: [29] And if ye take this also from me, and mischief befall him, ye shall bring down my gray hairs with sorrow to the grave. [30] Now therefore when I come to thy servant my father, and the lad be not with us; seeing that his life is bound up in the lad's life; [31] It shall come to pass, when he seeth that the lad is not with us, that he will die: and thy servants shall bring down the gray hairs of thy servant our father with sorrow to the grave. [32] For thy servant became surety for the lad unto my father, saying, If I bring him not unto thee, then I shall bear the blame to my father for ever. [33] Now therefore, I pray thee, let thy servant abide instead of the lad a bondman to my lord; and let the lad go up with his brethren. [34] For how shall I go up to my father, and the lad be not with me? lest peradventure I see the evil that shall come on my father.

GENESIS 45

[1] Then Joseph could not refrain himself before all them that stood by him; and he cried, Cause every man to go out from me. And there stood no man with him, while Joseph made himself known unto his brethren. [2] And he wept aloud: and the Egyptians and the house of Pharaoh heard. [3] And Joseph said unto his brethren, I am Joseph; doth my father yet live? And his brethren could not answer him; for they were troubled at his presence. [4] And Joseph said unto his brethren, Come near to me, I pray you. And they came near. And he said, I am Joseph your brother, whom ye sold into Egypt. [5] Now therefore be not grieved, nor angry with yourselves, that ye sold me hither: for God did send me before you to preserve life. [6] For these two years hath the famine been in the land: and yet there are five years, in the which there shall neither be earing nor harvest. [7] And God sent me before you to preserve you a posterity in the earth, and to save your lives by a great deliverance. [8] So now it was not you that sent me hither, but God: and he hath made me a father to Pharaoh, and lord of all his house, and a ruler throughout all the land of Egypt. [9] Haste ye, and go up to my father, and say unto him, Thus saith thy son Joseph, God hath made me lord of all Egypt: come down unto me, tarry not: [10] And thou shalt dwell in the land of Goshen, and thou shalt be near unto me, thou, and thy children, and thy children's children, and thy flocks, and thy herds, and all that thou hast: [11] And there will I nourish thee; for yet there are five years of famine; lest thou, and thy household, and all that thou hast, come to poverty. [12] And, behold, your eyes see, and the eyes of my brother Benjamin, that it is my mouth that speaketh unto you. [13] And ye shall tell my father of all

my glory in Egypt, and of all that ye have seen; and ye shall haste and bring down my father hither. [14] And he fell upon his brother Benjamin's neck, and wept; and Benjamin wept upon his neck. [15] Moreover he kissed all his brethren, and wept upon them: and after that his brethren talked with him. [16] And the fame thereof was heard in Pharaoh's house, saying, Joseph's brethren are come: and it pleased Pharaoh well, and his servants. [17] And Pharaoh said unto Joseph, Say unto thy brethren, This do ye; lade your beasts, and go, get you unto the land of Canaan; [18] And take your father and your households, and come unto me: and I will give you the good of the land of Egypt, and ye shall eat the fat of the land. [19] Now thou art commanded, this do ye; take you wagons out of the land of Egypt for your little ones, and for your wives, and bring your father, and come. [20] Also regard not your stuff; for the good of all the land of Egypt is yours. [21] And the children of Israel did so: and Joseph gave them wagons, according to the commandment of Pharaoh, and gave them provision for the way. [22] To all of them he gave each man changes of raiment; but to Benjamin he gave three hundred pieces of silver, and five changes of raiment. [23] And to his father he sent after this manner; ten asses laden with the good things of Egypt, and ten she asses laden with corn and bread and meat for his father by the way. [24] So he sent his brethren away, and they departed: and he said unto them, See that ye fall not out by the way. [25] And they went up out of Egypt, and came into the land of Canaan unto Jacob their father, [26] And told him, saying, Joseph is yet alive, and he is governor over all the land of Egypt. And Jacob's heart fainted, for he believed them not. [27] And they told him all the words of Joseph, which he had said unto them: and when he saw the wagons which Joseph had sent to carry him, the spirit of Jacob their father revived:

[28] And Israel said, It is enough; Joseph my son is yet alive: I will go and see him before I die.

GENESIS 46

[1] And Israel took his journey with all that he had, and came to Beer-sheba, and offered sacrifices unto the God of his father Isaac. [2] And God spake unto Israel in the visions of the night, and said, Jacob, Jacob. And he said, Here am I. [3] And he said, I am God, the God of thy father: fear not to go down into Egypt; for I will there make of thee a great nation: [4] I will go down with thee into Egypt; and I will also surely bring thee up again: and Joseph shall put his hand upon thine eyes. [5] And Jacob rose up from Beer-sheba: and the sons of Israel carried Jacob their father, and their little ones, and their wives, in the wagons which Pharaoh had sent to carry him. [6] And they took their cattle, and their goods, which they had gotten in the land of Canaan, and came into Egypt, Jacob, and all his seed with him: [7] His sons, and his sons' sons with him, his daughters, and his sons' daughters, and all his seed brought he with him into Egypt. [8] And these are the names of the children of Israel, which came into Egypt, Jacob and his sons: Reuben, Jacob's firstborn. [9] And the sons of Reuben; Hanoch, and Phallu, and Hezron, and Carmi. [10] And the sons of Simeon; Jemuel, and Jamin, and Ohad, and Jachin, and Zohar, and Shaul the son of a Canaanitish woman. [11] And the sons of Levi; Gershon, Kohath, and Merari. [12] And the sons of Judah; Er, and Onan, and Shelah, and Pharez, and Zarah: but Er and Onan died in the land of Canaan. And the sons of Pharez were Hezron and Hamul. [13] And the sons of Issachar; Tola, and Phuvah, and Job, and Shimron. [14] And the sons of Zebulun;

Sered, and Elon, and Jahleel. [15] These be the sons of Leah, which she bare unto Jacob in Padan-aram, with his daughter Dinah: all the souls of his sons and his daughters were thirty and three. [16] And the sons of Gad; Ziphion, and Haggi, Shuni, and Ezbon, Eri, and Arodi, and Areli. [17] And the sons of Asher; Jimnah, and Ishuah, and Isui, and Beriah, and Serah their sister: and the sons of Beriah; Heber, and Malchiel. [18] These are the sons of Zilpah, whom Laban gave to Leah his daughter, and these she bare unto Jacob, even sixteen souls. [19] The sons of Rachel Jacob's wife; Joseph, and Benjamin. [20] And unto Joseph in the land of Egypt were born Manasseh and Ephraim, which Asenath the daughter of Poti-pherah priest of On bare unto him. [21] And the sons of Benjamin were Belah, and Becher, and Ashbel, Gera, and Naaman, Ehi, and Rosh, Muppim, and Huppim, and Ard. [22] These are the sons of Rachel, which were born to Jacob: all the souls were fourteen. [23] And the sons of Dan; Hushim. [24] And the sons of Naphtali; Jahzeel, and Guni, and Jezer, and Shillem. [25] These are the sons of Bilhah, which Laban gave unto Rachel his daughter, and she bare these unto Jacob: all the souls were seven. [26] All the souls that came with Jacob into Egypt, which came out of his loins, besides Jacob's sons' wives, all the souls were threescore and six; [27] And the sons of Joseph, which were born him in Egypt, were two souls: all the souls of the house of Jacob, which came into Egypt, were threescore and ten. [28] And he sent Judah before him unto Joseph, to direct his face unto Goshen; and they came into the land of Goshen. [29] And Joseph made ready his chariot, and went up to meet Israel his father, to Goshen, and presented himself unto him; and he fell on his neck, and wept on his neck a good while. [30] And Israel said unto Joseph, Now let me die, since I have seen thy face, because thou art yet alive. [31] And Joseph said unto his brethren, and unto his father's house, I will go up, and shew Pharaoh, and say unto him, My brethren, and my father's house, which were in the land of Canaan, are come unto me; [32] And the men are shepherds, for their trade hath been to feed cattle; and they have brought their flocks, and their herds, and all that they have. [33] And it shall come to pass, when Pharaoh shall call you, and shall say, What is your occupation? [34] That ye shall say, Thy servants' trade hath been about cattle from our youth even until now, both we, and also our fathers: that ye may dwell in the land of Goshen; for every shepherd is an abomination unto the Egyptians.

GENESIS 47

[1] Then Joseph came and told Pharaoh, and said, My father and my brethren, and their flocks, and their herds, and all that they have, are come out of the land of Canaan; and, behold, they are in the land of Goshen. [2] And he took some of his brethren, even five men, and presented them unto Pharaoh. [3] And Pharaoh said unto his brethren, What is your occupation? And they said unto Pharaoh, Thy servants are shepherds, both we, and also our fathers. [4] They said moreover unto Pharaoh, For to sojourn in the land are we come; for thy servants have no pasture for their flocks; for the famine is sore in the land of Canaan: now therefore, we pray thee, let thy servants dwell in the land of Goshen. [5] And Pharaoh spake unto Joseph, saying, Thy father and thy brethren are come unto thee: [6] The land of Egypt is before thee; in the best of the land make thy father and brethren to dwell; in the land of Goshen let them dwell: and if thou knowest any men of activity among them, then make them

rulers over my cattle. [7] And Joseph brought in Jacob his father, and set him before Pharaoh: and Jacob blessed Pharaoh. [8] And Pharaoh said unto Jacob, How old art thou? [9] And Jacob said unto Pharaoh, The days of the years of my pilgrimage are an hundred and thirty years: few and evil have the days of the years of my life been, and have not attained unto the days of the years of the life of my fathers in the days of their pilgrimage. [10] And Jacob blessed Pharaoh, and went out from before Pharaoh. [11] And Joseph placed his father and his brethren, and gave them a possession in the land of Egypt, in the best of the land, in the land of Rameses, as Pharaoh had commanded. [12] And Joseph nourished his father, and his brethren, and all his father's household, with bread, according to their families. [13] And there was no bread in all the land; for the famine was very sore, so that the land of Egypt and all the land of Canaan fainted by reason of the famine. [14] And Joseph gathered up all the money that was found in the land of Egypt, and in the land of Canaan, for the corn which they bought: and Joseph brought the money into Pharaoh's house. [15] And when money failed in the land of Egypt, and in the land of Canaan, all the Egyptians came unto Joseph, and said, Give us bread: for why should we die in thy presence? for the money faileth. [16] And Joseph said, Give your cattle; and I will give you for your cattle, if money fail. [17] And they brought their cattle unto Joseph: and Joseph gave them bread in exchange for horses, and for the flocks, and for the cattle of the herds, and for the asses: and he fed them with bread for all their cattle for that year. [18] When that year was ended, they came unto him the second year, and said unto him, We will not hide it from my lord, how that our money is spent; my lord also hath our herds of cattle; there is not ought left in the sight of my lord, but our bodies, and our lands: [19] Wherefore shall we die before thine eyes, both we and our land? buy us and our land for bread, and we and our land will be servants unto Pharaoh: and give us seed, that we may live, and not die, that the land be not desolate. [20] And Joseph bought all the land of Egypt for Pharaoh; for the Egyptians sold every man his field, because the famine prevailed over them: so the land became Pharaoh's. [21] And as for the people, he removed them to cities from one end of the borders of Egypt even to the other end thereof. [22] Only the land of the priests bought he not; for the priests had a portion assigned them of Pharaoh, and did eat their portion which Pharaoh gave them: wherefore they sold not their lands. [23] Then Joseph said unto the people, Behold, I have bought you this day and your land for Pharaoh: lo, here is seed for you, and ye shall sow the land. [24] And it shall come to pass in the increase, that ye shall give the fifth part unto Pharaoh, and four parts shall be your own, for seed of the field, and for your food, and for them of your households, and for food for your little ones. [25] And they said, Thou hast saved our lives: let us find grace in the sight of my lord, and we will be Pharaoh's servants. [26] And Joseph made it a law over the land of Egypt unto this day, that Pharaoh should have the fifth part; except the land of the priests only, which became not Pharaoh's. [27] And Israel dwelt in the land of Egypt, in the country of Goshen; and they had possessions therein, and grew, and multiplied exceedingly. [28] And Jacob lived in the land of Egypt seventeen years: so the whole age of Jacob was an hundred forty and seven years. [29] And the time drew nigh that Israel must die: and he called his son Joseph, and said unto him, If now I have found grace in thy sight, put, I pray thee, thy hand under my thigh, and deal kindly and truly with me; bury me not, I pray thee, in Egypt: [30] But I will lie with my fathers, and thou shalt carry me out

of Egypt, and bury me in their buryingplace. And he said, I
will do as thou hast said. [31] And he said, Swear unto me.
And he sware unto him. And Israel bowed himself upon the
bed's head.

GENESIS 48

[1] And it came to pass after these things, that one told Joseph, Behold, thy father is sick: and he took with him his
two sons, Manasseh and Ephraim. [2] And one told Jacob,
and said, Behold, thy son Joseph cometh unto thee: and Israel
strengthened himself, and sat upon the bed. [3] And Jacob
said unto Joseph, God Almighty appeared unto me at Luz in
the land of Canaan, and blessed me, [4] And said unto me,
Behold, I will make thee fruitful, and multiply thee, and I will
make of thee a multitude of people; and will give this land
to thy seed after thee for an everlasting possession. [5] And
now thy two sons, Ephraim and Manasseh, which were born
unto thee in the land of Egypt before I came unto thee into
Egypt, are mine; as Reuben and Simeon, they shall be mine.
[6] And thy issue, which thou begettest after them, shall be
thine, and shall be called after the name of their brethren
in their inheritance. [7] And as for me, when I came from
Padan, Rachel died by me in the land of Canaan in the way,
when yet there was but a little way to come unto Ephrath:
and I buried her there in the way of Ephrath; the same is
Beth-lehem. [8] And Israel beheld Joseph's sons, and said,
Who are these? [9] And Joseph said unto his father, They
are my sons, whom God hath given me in this place. And he
said, Bring them, I pray thee, unto me, and I will bless them.
[10] Now the eyes of Israel were dim for age, so that he could
not see. And he brought them near unto him; and he kissed

them, and embraced them. [11] And Israel said unto Joseph, I had not thought to see thy face: and, lo, God hath shewed me also thy seed. [12] And Joseph brought them out from between his knees, and he bowed himself with his face to the earth. [13] And Joseph took them both, Ephraim in his right hand toward Israel's left hand, and Manasseh in his left hand toward Israel's right hand, and brought them near unto him. [14] And Israel stretched out his right hand, and laid it upon Ephraim's head, who was the younger, and his left hand upon Manasseh's head, guiding his hands wittingly; for Manasseh was the firstborn. [15] And he blessed Joseph, and said, God, before whom my fathers Abraham and Isaac did walk, the God which fed me all my life long unto this day, [16] The Angel which redeemed me from all evil, bless the lads; and let my name be named on them, and the name of my fathers Abraham and Isaac; and let them grow into a multitude in the midst of the earth. [17] And when Joseph saw that his father laid his right hand upon the head of Ephraim, it displeased him: and he held up his father's hand, to remove it from Ephraim's head unto Manasseh's head. [18] And Joseph said unto his father, Not so, my father: for this is the firstborn; put thy right hand upon his head. [19] And his father refused, and said, I know it, my son, I know it: he also shall become a people, and he also shall be great: but truly his younger brother shall be greater than he, and his seed shall become a multitude of nations. [20] And he blessed them that day, saying, In thee shall Israel bless, saying, God make thee as Ephraim and as Manasseh: and he set Ephraim before Manasseh. [21] And Israel said unto Joseph, Behold, I die: but God shall be with you, and bring you again unto the land of your fathers. [22] Moreover I have given to thee one portion above thy brethren, which I took out of the hand of the Amorite with my sword and with my bow.

GENESIS 49

[1] And Jacob called unto his sons, and said, Gather yourselves together, that I may tell you that which shall befall you in the last days. [2] Gather yourselves together, and hear, ye sons of Jacob; and hearken unto Israel your father. [3] Reuben, thou art my firstborn, my might, and the beginning of my strength, the excellency of dignity, and the excellency of power: [4] Unstable as water, thou shalt not excel; because thou wentest up to thy father's bed; then defiledst thou it: he went up to my couch. [5] Simeon and Levi are brethren; instruments of cruelty are in their habitations. [6] O my soul, come not thou into their secret; unto their assembly, mine honour, be not thou united: for in their anger they slew a man, and in their selfwill they digged down a wall. [7] Cursed be their anger, for it was fierce; and their wrath, for it was cruel: I will divide them in Jacob, and scatter them in Israel. [8] Judah, thou art he whom thy brethren shall praise: thy hand shall be in the neck of thine enemies; thy father's children shall bow down before thee. [9] Judah is a lion's whelp: from the prey, my son, thou art gone up: he stooped down, he couched as a lion, and as an old lion; who shall rouse him up? [10] The sceptre shall not depart from Judah, nor a lawgiver from between his feet, until Shiloh come; and unto him shall the gathering of the people be. [11] Binding his foal unto the vine, and his ass's colt unto the choice vine; he washed his garments in wine, and his clothes in the blood of grapes: [12] His eyes shall be red with wine, and his teeth white with milk. [13] Zebulun shall dwell at the haven of the sea; and he shall be for an haven of ships; and his border shall be unto Zidon. [14] Issachar is a strong ass couching down between two burdens: [15] And he saw that rest was good, and the land that it was pleasant; and bowed

his shoulder to bear, and became a servant unto tribute. [16] Dan shall judge his people, as one of the tribes of Israel. [17] Dan shall be a serpent by the way, an adder in the path, that biteth the horse heels, so that his rider shall fall backward. [18] I have waited for thy salvation, O LORD. [19] Gad, a troop shall overcome him: but he shall overcome at the last. [20] Out of Asher his bread shall be fat, and he shall yield royal dainties. [21] Naphtali is a hind let loose: he giveth goodly words. [22] Joseph is a fruitful bough, even a fruitful bough by a well; whose branches run over the wall: [23] The archers have sorely grieved him, and shot at him, and hated him: [24] But his bow abode in strength, and the arms of his hands were made strong by the hands of the mighty God of Jacob; (from thence is the shepherd, the stone of Israel:) [25] Even by the God of thy father, who shall help thee; and by the Almighty, who shall bless thee with blessings of heaven above, blessings of the deep that lieth under, blessings of the breasts, and of the womb: [26] The blessings of thy father have prevailed above the blessings of my progenitors unto the utmost bound of the everlasting hills: they shall be on the head of Joseph, and on the crown of the head of him that was separate from his brethren. [27] Benjamin shall ravin as a wolf: in the morning he shall devour the prey, and at night he shall divide the spoil. [28] All these are the twelve tribes of Israel: and this is it that their father spake unto them, and blessed them; every one according to his blessing he blessed them. [29] And he charged them, and said unto them, I am to be gathered unto my people: bury me with my fathers in the cave that is in the field of Ephron the Hittite, [30] In the cave that is in the field of Machpelah, which is before Mamre, in the land of Canaan, which Abraham bought with the field of Ephron the Hittite for a possession of a buryingplace. [31] There they buried Abraham and Sarah his wife; there they

buried Isaac and Rebekah his wife; and there I buried Leah.
[32] The purchase of the field and of the cave that is therein
was from the children of Heth. [33] And when Jacob had
made an end of commanding his sons, he gathered up his
feet into the bed, and yielded up the ghost, and was gathered
unto his people.

GENESIS 50

[1] And Joseph fell upon his father's face, and wept upon
him, and kissed him. [2] And Joseph commanded his servants the physicians to embalm his father: and the physicians
embalmed Israel. [3] And forty days were fulfilled for him;
for so are fulfilled the days of those which are embalmed: and
the Egyptians mourned for him threescore and ten days. [4]
And when the days of his mourning were past, Joseph spake
unto the house of Pharaoh, saying, If now I have found grace
in your eyes, speak, I pray you, in the ears of Pharaoh, saying,
[5] My father made me swear, saying, Lo, I die: in my grave
which I have digged for me in the land of Canaan, there shalt
thou bury me. Now therefore let me go up, I pray thee, and
bury my father, and I will come again. [6] And Pharaoh said,
Go up, and bury thy father, according as he made thee swear.
[7] And Joseph went up to bury his father: and with him
went up all the servants of Pharaoh, the elders of his house,
and all the elders of the land of Egypt, [8] And all the house
of Joseph, and his brethren, and his father's house: only their
little ones, and their flocks, and their herds, they left in the
land of Goshen. [9] And there went up with him both chari-
ots and horsemen: and it was a very great company. [10] And
they came to the threshingfloor of Atad, which is beyond
Jordan, and there they mourned with a great and very sore

lamentation: and he made a mourning for his father seven days. [11] And when the inhabitants of the land, the Canaanites, saw the mourning in the floor of Atad, they said, This is a grievous mourning to the Egyptians: wherefore the name of it was called Abel-mizraim, which is beyond Jordan. [12] And his sons did unto him according as he commanded them: [13] For his sons carried him into the land of Canaan, and buried him in the cave of the field of Machpelah, which Abraham bought with the field for a possession of a burying-place of Ephron the Hittite, before Mamre. [14] And Joseph returned into Egypt, he, and his brethren, and all that went up with him to bury his father, after he had buried his father. [15] And when Joseph's brethren saw that their father was dead, they said, Joseph will peradventure hate us, and will certainly requite us all the evil which we did unto him. [16] And they sent a messenger unto Joseph, saying, Thy father did command before he died, saying, [17] So shall ye say unto Joseph, Forgive, I pray thee now, the trespass of thy brethren, and their sin; for they did unto thee evil: and now, we pray thee, forgive the trespass of the servants of the God of thy father. And Joseph wept when they spake unto him. [18] And his brethren also went and fell down before his face; and they said, Behold, we be thy servants. [19] And Joseph said unto them, Fear not: for am I in the place of God? [20] But as for you, ye thought evil against me; but God meant it unto good, to bring to pass, as it is this day, to save much people alive. [21] Now therefore fear ye not: I will nourish you, and your little ones. And he comforted them, and spake kindly unto them. [22] And Joseph dwelt in Egypt, he, and his father's house: and Joseph lived an hundred and ten years. [23] And Joseph saw Ephraim's children of the third generation: the children also of Machir the son Manasseh were brought up upon Joseph's knees. [24] And

Joseph said unto his brethren, I die: and God will surely visit you, and bring you out of this land unto the land which he sware to Abraham, to Isaac, and to Jacob. [25] And Joseph took an oath of the children of Israel, saying, God will surely visit you, and ye shall carry up my bones from hence. [26] So Joseph died, being an hundred and ten years old: and they embalmed him, and he was put in a coffin in Egypt.